GHAFFAR KHAN

For Edward & Julia

In gratitude
affection &
esteem

Raj

Aug 2004.

GHAFFAR KHAN

Nonviolent Badshah of the Pakhtuns

RAJMOHAN GANDHI

PENGUIN

VIKING

VIKING

Penguin Books India (P) Ltd, 11 Community Centre, Panchsheel Park, New Delhi 110 017, India

Penguin Books Ltd, 80 Strand, London WC2R 0RL, UK

Penguin Group (USA) Inc., 375 Hudson Street, New York, NY 10014, USA

Penguin Books Australia Ltd, 250 Camberwell Road, Camberwell, Victoria 3124, Australia

Penguin Books Canada Ltd, 10 Alcorn Avenue, Suite 300, Toronto, Ontario M4V 3B2, Canada

Penguin Group (NZ), cnr Airborne and Rosedale Roads, Albany, Auckland 1310, New Zealand

Penguin Books (South Africa) (Pty) Ltd, 24 Sturdee Avenue, Rosebank 2196, South Africa

First published in Viking by Penguin Books India 2004

Copyright © Rajmohan Gandhi 2004

10 9 8 7 6 5 4 3 2 1

Typeset in Perpetua by Mantra Virtual Services, New Delhi

Printed at Chaman Offset Printers, New Delhi

Contents

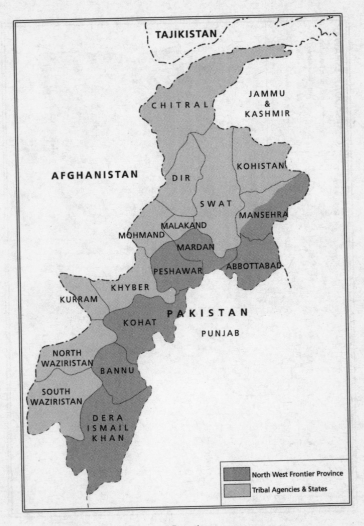

Map 1.
The North-West Frontier's 'settled' and 'tribal' territories

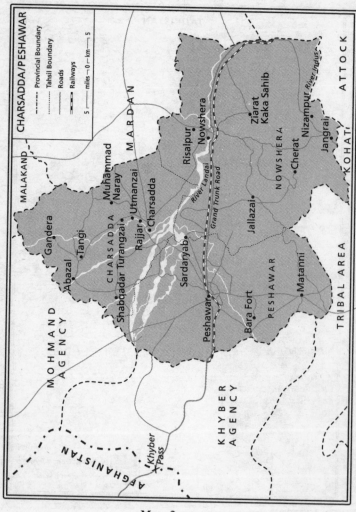

Map 2.

Between the Khyber and the Indus, Ghaffar Khan's homeland

Preface

When in the mid-1980s I was studying Muslims prominent in the subcontinent's recent history for my *Understanding the Muslim Mind*, an obvious subject was the towering figure of Khan Abdul Ghaffar Khan. I had first met him in 1945 or 1946, when I was a boy of about ten and he was visiting Delhi and staying, along with his older brother Dr Khan Sahib, in my father's Connaught Circus flat. The events of August 1947 soon made him an outsider, but I was able to meet him again, during his visits to India, in 1969 and 1987. However, as far as *Understanding the Muslim Mind* was concerned, I was not taking up any living person, which in the mid-1980s Badshah Khan very much was, despite being in the mid-nineties himself.

Now, after all these years, I feel thankful to be able to offer this portrait. A goad towards it was applied to me on 9 September 2001 when my wife and I were visiting Badshah Khan's family in the countryside of the Peshawar/Charsadda valley. Asfandyar Khan, eldest son of Badshah Khan's second son Wali Khan and a political player himself in the Frontier and in Pakistan as a whole, said that he missed a biography of his grandfather that the subcontinent's newer generations would want.

In that conversation with Asfandyar Khan, which took place while Afghanistan was yet under Taliban control, we also discussed Indo-Pak relations, Kashmir and Musharraf, and religious extremism and terrorism as well. Two nights later, on the morning of 11 September, my wife and I flew back to Delhi. That evening, on TV, we saw the crumbling of New York's Twin Towers.

In the new phase ushered in by that event, Badshah Khan's life, it was obvious, had taken on additional meaning. I knew I had to write the biography.

Here it is, with all its imperfections. Whether it will fully satisfy Asfandyar Khan I do not know. I have written it for the subcontinent's newer generations, but also for the many everywhere who are being pressurized to believe in an unbridgeable gulf between Muslims and the rest.

Among those to whom I am indebted for this book are several descendants of Badshah Khan and of his older brother, Dr Khan Sahib, including Wali Khan and Mehr Taj, son and daughter of Badshah Khan. I will not name all the others, but I must refer to the wonderful hospitality and help, when in May 2003 I again visited the Charsadda valley and Islamabad, of Anwar Khan, grandson of Dr Khan Sahib, his wife Rashida, and their children. Several others interviewed by me and named in the text also provided valuable facts and insights. My sincere thanks to them.

I am grateful, too, to the University of Illinois at

Urbana-Champaign, which hired me as a visiting professor from the Fall of 2002 but allowed me to squeeze time out to research and write this study.

Finally, I offer thanks to two persons at Penguin, Kamini Mahadevan, who commissioned this study, and Malini Sood, who has edited it with patience and skill.

Rajmohan Gandhi

Copyright Acknowledgements

Grateful acknowledgement is made to the following for permission to reprint copyright material:

Orient Paperbacks, New Delhi for Ghaffar Khan, *My Life and Struggle,* 1969.

Geoffrey Moorhouse for *To the Frontier*, London: Phoenix, 1984.

Camerapix, Nairobi, Kenya for Mohamed Amin, Duncan Willetts and Graham Hancock, *Journey through Pakistan*, 1982.

Cambridge University Press for J.S. Grewal, *The New Cambridge History of India: The Sikhs of the Punjab*, 1991.

The Progressive for Amitabh Pal, 'A pacifist uncovered (Abdul Ghaffar Khan, Pakistani pacifist)', February 2002.

Rajmohan Gandhi

Harold Gould

Hiro Shroff

Dilip Simeon

Sher Zaman Taizi for *Bacha Khan in Afghanistan: A Memoir, June 2002*.

Nilgiri Press, Tomales, Calif. for Eknath Easwaran, *Nonviolent Soldier of Islam*, 1999.

J.N. Dixit for *An Afghan Diary: Zahir Shah to Taliban*, 2000.

Hindustan Times Press, New Delhi for Mahadev Desai, *Two Servants of God*, 1935.

Oxford University Press, Pakistan for M.S. Korejo, *The Frontier Gandhi: His Place in History*, 1993, and Sayed Wiqar Ali Shah, *Ethnicity, Islam, and Nationalism: Muslim Politics in the North-West Frontier Province 1937-47*, 1999.

Princeton University Press for Louis Dupree, *Afghanistan*, 1973.

The Setting

Fifty years ago or thereabouts, Badshah Khan of the Peshawar valley was, for most people of the subcontinent and for the British who had recently vacated it, *the* Pathan, or, to use preferred contemporary (and rather more accurate) expressions, *the* Pakhtun or Pashtun.

In the 1940s and the 1950s—times that surrounded freedom's pain-filled glory—the word Pathan never failed to conjure up the image of this man coming from a region that classical India knew as Gandhara, an immensely tall figure with an absolutely straight back, a great nose, kindly eyes, and a permanent aura of nonviolent defiance. Exercising an undeniable right, a subsequent generation in Pakistan, India, and elsewhere chose, however, to forget him.

This process was aided by turbulence in Afghanistan, which always affects the Pathans of the Frontier. In the 1970s the Afghans, regarded by Badshah Khan as his kin, turned, as they had often done in their history, to infighting and a coup. Then began an absorbing sequence of occupation by the Soviet Union, resistance to that occupation, liberation, civil wars, and Taliban rule. It was not easy, during this long phase, to retain a focus on Badshah Khan's life. Even though he had lived until 1988, by when the end of Soviet occupation was a matter only of time, his leadership of the Pathans' struggle against the British and his post-1947 striving for Pakhtun dignity seemed distant achievements, unconnected with what was happening in Afghanistan and, as a result, in the NWFP, which harboured thousands of Afghan mujahedin and hundreds of thousands of Afghan refugees.

But 9/11 recalled Badshah Khan to the public mind, and not on the subcontinent alone. The *New York Times* wrote (on 7 December 2001, in an Op-Ed piece by Karl E. Meyer) about 'The Peacemaker of the Pashtun Past', who not so long ago symbolized peace and tolerance and seemed an antithesis of a later Pashtun, Mullah Omar of Kandahar (a place frequently but erroneously confused with Gandhara), the fanatical Taliban leader, foe of the USA, and Osama bin Laden's host in Afghanistan.

Yet Khan Abdul Ghaffar Khan—aka Badshah Khan, Bacha Khan, Baba, Khan Sahib, and the Frontier Gandhi—lived for more than peace and tolerance; he lived also for justice. Which is how he became a political prisoner for about twelve years under the British, and for an additional fifteen years after the founding of Pakistan, into which his Peshawar valley and the rest of the North-West Frontier Province had been merged. However, the contrast with Mullah Omar is dramatic enough, from a variety of angles.

One, the struggle for which Badshah Khan mobilized his fellow Pathans was nonviolent.

Two, in him a passion to find an answer to the code of revenge to which Pathans appeared to be sworn seemed to equal a passion for independence from foreign rule. To this Muslim, forgiveness was part of Islam.

Three, non-Muslims seemed as important as Muslims to Badshah Khan, who said that he and his Pathans would protect the Hindus, Sikhs and Christians living in the overwhelmingly Muslim North-West Frontier Province. One man who had touched his life was a white Christian schoolmaster called Wigram; another was a Hindu called Mohandas Gandhi.

Four, Badshah Khan wanted Pashtun women to study, work and lead; in 1932 he sent his daughter Mehr Taj, who had just entered her teens, to study in England.

Five, this devout and loyal Muslim was also enthusiastic about his region's older Buddhist history.

Six, as against the politics of 'me first' and double standards, he asked his Khudai Khidmatgars ('Servants of God'), participants in his reform movement, to serve the society they wished to improve, and practise the values they espoused.

There is more, but what has been said may suffice to suggest Badshah Khan's topicality to any serious-minded resident of the twenty-first century's opening years. To a knowledgeable Indian, however, guilt rather than a sense of relevance is what the name Badshah Khan first triggers, for when in 1947 power was finally sighted by the Indian National Congress, the body long fighting to end British rule, promises given to Badshah Khan were promptly forgotten. He who in hard times had stood for Indian unity was dropped. The sacrifice of a faithful friend was part of the price of power. Quietly, swiftly, matter-of-factly, leaders in India paid the price.

Perhaps betrayal is part of every human enterprise, be it ever so noble. Still its memory hurts, especially when the one betrayed was kingly, true to his word, and long-suffering. Even now, in the year 2004, it is impossible for an Indian aware of the depth and length of Badshah Khan's ties with India and her leaders to recall their 1947 severance without tremors of shame.

Those tremors were responsible for some important Indian books on Badshah Khan, notably one by Tendulkar and another by Pyarelal. Yet the world has moved on, and though guilt will continue to influence any Indian study of Badshah Khan, we must look at him with the spectacles of today rather than those of 1947. The fact that Badshah Khan was let down will be squarely faced by this study. Yet today that fact may be less significant than the fact that Badshah Khan's life has the capacity to speak meaningfully to an inhabitant of our times—to one who is young, or Muslim, or both, or neither.

*

On the subcontinent, the term 'Pathan' is sanctioned by widespread usage. The West has opted for the more proper 'Pakhtun' or 'Pashtun' (or 'Pakhtoon', 'Pashtoon' or 'Pushtun'), which seems the preference also of some scholars from the North-West Frontier Province (or

NWFP or, simply, the Frontier). Though, strictly speaking, 'Pakhtun' and 'Pashtun' refer to adjacent tribes that are similar without being identical, and without their languages being identical, this study will take the liberty of switching freely, for the sake of simplicity, between 'Pathan', 'Pakhtun' and 'Pashtun', and of treating the three words as synonyms.

Traditionally Badshah Khan and his Pathans have been viewed by Indians in the setting of history's great *triangular* clash involving Indian nationalism, Muslim separatism and British imperialism. Claiming to view something different, some Pakistanis speak of Badshah Khan in the setting of a *quadrangular* clash involving Muslim nationalism, Hindu nationalism, British imperialism and Pathan separatism.

Whether triangular or quadrangular, the clash was superimposed on, and intertwined with, another clash, that *between the imperial thrusts of Britain and Russia*, resulting in the so-called Great Game between the Russian Bear and the British Lion, which was played out largely on the 'buffer' territory of Afghanistan. While Russia's Sovietization for seventy-plus years did not alter the nature of this clash, the British side became, after the onset of the Cold War, the American–British side.

Some Indian and Pakistani historians of the Frontier ignore the Great Game. Their natural concerns have focused on where the Frontier stood on two questions: the fight against the British and the call for a Muslim homeland on the subcontinent. But happenings to their west could not be ignored by Badshah Khan and his Pakhtuns, whose links to the people of Afghanistan were of the profoundest kind. To the Frontier's Pathans, the Great Game was a constant and forceful reality, and the question they always had to wrestle with was the nature of their relationship with the Pakhtuns across the 'border' sketched on a map in 1893 by a young British officer named Henry Durand, and hence known as the Durand Line.

After Pakistan was founded, with the Frontier province as one of its constituent parts, it became natural for Pakistanis to view Badshah Khan and the Pathans in *the setting of Pakistan's uneasy relationship with Afghanistan*, a relationship affected by the closeness that had often marked the India–Afghan link. Hence the frequent occurrence in Pakistani writings of the fear or bogey of an Afghan–Pathan–Indian axis.

Today, however, with images of Osama bin Laden and Mullah Omar, of the Taliban and of 9/11, prominent on most minds, many will want to see Badshah Khan and his Pathans not so much in their encounter with Britain, India, Pakistan or Afghanistan, but *in their face-off with modernity*. Placing contemporary Pashtuns, whether resident in Pakistan, Afghanistan or elsewhere, in *the setting of the real or imagined clash between Islam and the West-dominated modern world*, they may ask whether Badshah Khan has anything to offer to an understanding of this presumed clash.

Related to this clash is the discussion in which adherents and scholars of Islam are currently engaged. Does Badshah Khan contribute anything of value to *the modern debate within the world of Islam?*

Inhabitants of India and Pakistan, including those

in the Frontier, may in addition ask whether, through his life, Badshah Khan suggests anything relevant for *the future of the Indo-Pak and Hindu–Muslim relationships*.

*

In the seventeenth century, Khushal Khan Khattak, perhaps the greatest poet of the Pakhtuns and a warrior as well, expressed this yearning for peace among his people:

> In days gone by Pathans were Kings of Hind,
> And still in deeds the Mughal they outdo;
> But concord they know not, and they have sinned
> Against God's unity; so come to rue:
> Ah God! Grant them but concord, sweet refrain,
> And old Khushal will rise, a youth again. [1]

During the twenty-six-year period between 1920 and 1946, many Pathans thought that an answer to Khushal Khan's yearning had finally been found. It was found, it seemed, in and through Abdul Ghaffar Khan, who was born in 1890 in the family of Behram Khan, the khan or chief of the village of Utmanzai in Charsadda tehsil in the Peshawar valley.

Even in the twenty-first century Pathans are not wanting who see Ghaffar Khan as one in a troika of history's great Pathans, along with two personalities of a wholly different kind: Sher Shah Sur (the sixteenth-century King of Hind, who Khushal Khan had in mind) and Ahmed Shah Abdali (or Durrani), who warred and ruled in the eighteenth century. In his lifetime Ghaffar Khan was called Badshah or 'King' Khan by his people, who deemed his bearing and ideas noble.

Two decades before he died, Badshah Khan expressed his own longing. It was in prose but reminiscent of Khushal Khan:

I have one great desire. I want to knit the divided tribes of the Pakhtuns, spread out from Baluchistan to Chitral, into one community, one brotherhood, so that they can share their sorrows and sufferings and play a vital role in serving humanity . . .

The doors are shut upon us, none is allowed to reach us, and we have been presented as a collection of uncivilized, wild tribes.

The courage of our tribal brothers is described as wildness, passion for freedom as lawlessness, their proverbial hospitality as an irrepressible urge [for] begging, borrowing and pillaging . . . Like untended, wild daisies they bloom and fade away in mountain ridges . . .

I want to create for them a free world, where they can grow in peace, comfort and happiness. I want to kiss the earth heaped on the ruins of their homes devastated by brutal people. With my own hands I want to wash their blood-stained clothes. I want to sweep their lanes and humble mud huts . . . I want them to stand on their legs with heads erect, and then want to throw this challenge: 'Show me another decent, gentle and cultured race like them!'[2]

After Badshah Khan's death in a Peshawar hospital on 20 January 1988, the Pathans' feeling for him was shown when about 20,000 of them accompanied his coffin through and beyond the Khyber Pass to Jalalabad in Afghanistan, where he was buried. In doing so, the Pathans also demonstrated their feeling for Pakhtun unity and disdain for an artificial border; without carrying either a Pakistani passport or an Afghan visa, they had crossed the Durand Line.

But Badshah Khan had foes, too. After having him arrested and removed to Sindh in April 1961, Ayub Khan, Pakistan's military ruler at the time and a fellow Pathan, told a press conference in Rawalpindi that Badshah Khan had made 'unreasonable demands'. Added Ayub Khan:

> Abdul Ghaffar Khan wanted the Frontier area to become a part of India. Having failed in that venture, he demanded a separate province in Pakistan, where he wanted to be the king. Later, he wanted to make this Frontier region a part of Afghanistan.[3]

To Pakistan's military ruler, Badshah Khan seemed, in 1961, a traitor, vainglorious, an Afghan agent, and unreasonable.

*

Aspects of Badshah Khan's appearance and personality, and of his conflict with the authorities of Pakistan, are conveyed in a portrayal by an American called James W.

Spain who interviewed him in Karachi, then Pakistan's capital, in 1954. Badshah Khan was sixty-four at the time, and ill.

We found Abdul Ghaffar Khan lying on a rumpled bed. Tall and gaunt, he looked like a sick Jeremiah outside the gates of a King of Israel. He wore a simple, long garment of homespun, something like an old-fashioned night-shirt, and his grizzled head was bare. Above his prominent Pathan nose, dark eyes glistened and charged the otherwise dim and dingy room with a sense of urgency. He did not rise but offered his hand; he gripped mine so strongly that I was unable to withdraw it . . .

'I am loyal to my people. That is all I will be loyal to. You Americans should help us, instead of listening only to these people in Karachi. The Russians should help us . . .'

'Does this freedom you want have to be outside of Pakistan? Can you not be free within Pakistan?' I asked.

'This is a matter of no importance. What matters is that we be free to develop ourselves, to tear down our own Khans who have oppressed us, to make our own laws, and to speak our own language. For this they say I am an agent of Afghanistan. For this they call me traitor. It is false!'

To my great surprise he had slipped into English after our first few words. His vocabulary seemed not to exceed a few hundred words but he used them with extraordinary force and all the skill of a polished orator. He dropped my hand to spread forth his arms in an impassioned plea for freedom. He took it again to demonstrate the sincerity of his denial of being an Afghan agent. It was easy to imagine the impact he would have, speaking in Pakhtu, on an audience of the Pathans, great admirers of the spoken word.[4]

The pages that follow will attempt to understand the battles, inner and outer, that Badshah Khan, a son of the Muhammadzai tribe of the Pakhtuns, fought. But first we must look at the land, the history, and the psychology of the Pakhtuns.

ONE

The Pakhtuns

Millions of years ago, after a large floating island crashed into the Asian continent, joined it, and became the Indian subcontinent, the Himalayan, Karakoram, Hindu Kush and Sulaiman mountain ranges were produced. Also a product of the collision was the river Indus, which sprang from Tibet and flowed turbulently through the Karakoram into what we know of as the Frontier province.

For centuries, Pakhtun tribes have inhabited the diagonal space (north-east to south-west) between the grim range of the Hindu Kush and its rocky associates (starting south-west from the Pamir Knot and culminating in the Sulaiman range near Kandahar), and, on the eastern edge of this space, the Indus. Though with time some Pakhtuns spilled over from this space across both natural boundaries, the bulk of the world's Pakhtuns live here.

If this space, hard of access, between the Hindu Kush

and the Indus is the Pakhtun heartland, it needs also to be said that scenes within this heartland can alter dramatically from one mile to the next. Forbidding cliffs, narrow river gorges, sudden passes and gateways, mountainsides of ice, fir or bush, deep ravines, bare hills, grazing grounds, and, closer to the rivers Kabul, Swat and Indus, lush green valleys—all are contained in the Pakhtun country.

Observers have marked the daring and strength that the Pakhtun country demanded, and evidently secured, from its inhabitants: 'They come down hillsides like falling boulders, not running but bounding; in crags they literally drop from foothold to foothold.'[1]

Origins: If this tract seems isolated from the world, pockets within it have also remained cut off from one another, cliffs and ravines forming almost impenetrable barriers. Hence it is that different physiognomies greet a visitor, who finds that Pakhtun eyes may 'vary in shade from black through burning amber to green'.[2] Hence, too, the conflicting opinions among Pakhtuns as to their origin.

The belief of the subject of our book, Abdul Ghaffar Khan, was that 'the Aryan race first saw the light of the day in this country'.[3] When some Pakhtuns insist on Aryan ancestors, others on Hebrew, and some others on Greek, while a few scholars see a link to the White Huns who erupted from Central Asia in the fourth century AD, it is not impossible that all may be right. Confined within its particular unreachable redoubt, a Pakhtun tribe could remain sealed off for long periods from a possibly unrelated tribe living close to it.

Yet contact did occur. Despite nature's barriers, linkages were made and felt. A common language grew, Pakhto or Pashto, or Pakhtu or Pashtu, spoken differently in different tracts but in significant ways shared by all Pakhtuns.

Scholars identify Pashto as an Indo-Aryan speech, along with other languages such as Sanskrit and Iran's Zend, and if this suggests a link with Vedic times, that link is confirmed by references in Vedic texts and in the Mahabharata to Gandhara. There is irrefutable evidence also of an early presence in the Pakhtun country of Zoroastrian and Buddhist influences and of Greek generals who became rulers, in the process adopting some Buddhist or Hindu practices.

The most famous of half-a-dozen passes that connect the subcontinent to Afghanistan and Central Asia, the Khyber Pass runs twenty-five miles on Pakistani land and another ten miles on Afghan territory. This pass has a lower altitude than generally realized, Landi Kotal, its highest point, being only 3,500 feet above sea level. The pass is also wider than sometimes thought, and it is this low altitude and sufficient width that, over the centuries, allowed the flow of armies, including that of Alexander in the fourth century BC, of Genghis Khan in the thirteenth century AD, Tamerlane in the late fourteenth century, Babur in the early sixteenth century, and Nadir Shah in the eighteenth.

Images: Guarding the Khyber Pass has for centuries been the self-assigned task of one of the Pakhtun tribes, the Afridi, famed for instancy in battle. According to Sir Robert Warburton, a British army officer who served

in the Khyber in the nineteenth century, this swiftness
with a blow has simple roots:

> The Afridi lad from his earliest childhood is taught
> by the circumstances of his existence to distrust all
> mankind, and very often his near relations, heirs to
> his small plot of land by right of inheritance, are his
> deadliest enemies. Distrust of all mankind, and
> readiness to strike the first blow for the safety of
> his own life, have therefore become the maxims of
> the Afridi. If you can overcome this mistrust, and
> be kind in words to him, he will repay you by great
> devotion, and will put up with any punishment you
> like to give him except abuse.[4]

Riled by British road-making, which seemed to
them a hostile act, the Afridis were treated to dozens of
military expeditions and, in 1897, to an attack by some
40,000 soldiers. They were eventually restrained but
never subdued. Even today, the high walls of mud, stone
and timber behind which an extended Afridi family lives
bring a medieval fortress to mind.

A stereotypical story of Afridi ease with the trigger,
no doubt made up but suggestive nonetheless, is this:

> A holy man came to the Khyber Pass many years
> ago from the south. He preached to our fathers of
> their sins and upbraided them. He pointed out that
> in all our country we did not have a single tomb of
> a saint at which we might make our devotions . . .
> Our fathers were much impressed with this holy

man's words. So they killed him and ever since his
tomb has been a noble shrine.[5]

At times imperialist literature presented the Pathan
warrior in ghoulish if awed terms, as in the following:

Between the dust-layered blue turban and a shaggy
black beard (usually dyed when it began to whiten)
were fixed the eyes of a hawk, the beak of a vulture
and the mouth of a shark . . . Here was a creature
whose whole purpose and pleasure in life was the
inflicting of a death as uncomfortable and prolonged
as it might be possible to arrange.[6]

The seemingly violent Pathan is also seen as a
member of a feudal society where leaders—the khans—
feuded with one another unless there was a common
non-Pathan foe, and where 'impoverished tenants
provided menial services and manpower to magnify the
status of their Khan'.[7]

If famous for drawing their guns, the Pakhtuns are
also portrayed as over-draping their women and
privileging a woman's modesty over her survival. A
Western writer who went in 1984 to a Pakhtun area
field clinic during the Afghans' battle against Soviet
occupation claims that the

patients were all men. If a woman was injured, she
would only be brought to the field hospital if she
had been hit in the arm or the face; the husband
would not countenance the attention of a male

doctor if it was necessary to remove any of her
clothes. Most wounded women therefore died.[8]

Adds Geoffrey Moorhouse:

No women in the world can be more jealously
possessed by their menfolk than the women of the
Pathans, and it is both rare and dangerous for a male
outside her family so much as to look upon a Pathan
woman's face. The most innocent exchange of this
kind could mean death for them both, and a simple
touch of the hands most certainly would. Human
nature being what it is, illicit unions do sometimes
occur; and what happens thereafter is absolutely
sure unless the couple manage to fly from the tribal
territories to some city where they can lose
themselves, though they may be pursued even there.
The custom is for the woman to be shot by her own
father or brother, the man to be executed by his
father or uncle. The honour of two families is
thereby cleansed of all stain. The one thing . . . that
a westerner can envy is that molestation of Pathan
women is virtually unknown.[9]

A way of life refusing to alter over time constitutes
the third popular image of the Pakhtuns. In his classic
study of the Pathans, Olaf Caroe, one of the Raj's
Frontier-based officers, writes: 'Could one awake in
Talash to see Alexander or Babur pass with their clatter
of arms, the waker, likely as not, would find the men of
the villages much as he knows them now.'[10] Adds Caroe:

The persistence of the Pathan tribal tradition has produced a society at all levels, starting from the nomad and the herdsman, through the articulated tribe and the sponsors of an Asian dynastic principle, to the modern lawyer, engineer, doctor, administrator and politician. Standing over against the tribal village and the tents of the caravan are men for a century imbued with Western thought . . . Anyone who cares to move in a twenty-mile radius around Peshawar . . . [can] daily enjoy a bodily translation into earlier phases of human society and life . . . [and witness] a congeries of peoples engaged in a long march through the centuries from the fifth to the twentieth.

Other tribal societies [*proceeds Caroe*] have shattered like brittle glass; individuals have become alienated and schizophrenic; once-sacred customs have been touted on the streets before tourists for a few pennies. Why have the Pathans remained unaffected?[11]

One part of Caroe's answer to his question was the terrain preventing adjacent kingdoms or empires from controlling the tribes, or taxing them. Another was the Pakhtuns' granite-hard code of honour. Pathans may or may not have some common ethnic characteristics; they may all be Muslims; they may all speak a Pashto variant; they may inhabit a common terrain; but the final definition of a Pakhtun, no matter what his tribe, or his clan within that tribe, is that he lives by the code of Pakhtunwali.

*

History: However, before addressing this code we should glance at the Pakhtuns' history over time. For a start, the Pakhtuns impeded Alexander, who nonetheless walked in Charsadda, the Peshawar Valley town with which Badshah Khan and his Muhammadzais were intimately tied.

Ruling from Peshawar city in the first and second centuries of the Common Era, the Greco-Buddhist king Kanishka had built there a relic tower of carved wood that rose in thirteen storeys to a height of 400 feet and was capped by an iron pinnacle. Visiting Peshawar in the sixth century, Sung-yun, a Chinese pilgrim, had seen this tower, apparently in its fourth version. A Buddhist monastery of rare magnificence, visited by the scholar Vira Deva, seems to have flourished in Peshawar in the ninth century.

By this time many Pakhtuns had accepted Islam. In the Arab thrusts that quickly followed Islam's emergence in the sixth century, the Pakhtun country too was invaded by fired-up Arabs, who, en route, had easily defeated the Persians. The Pathans repulsed the Arabs but, west of Kabul, took Islam from them.

At the end of the tenth century, kings who were possibly Pakhtun but also Hindu ruled on both sides of the Khyber Pass—the Hindushahis. Kabul, Jalalabad and Peshawar were under Hindushahi control. Writing in the eleventh century, al-Biruni, the brilliant scholar who joined the court of Mahmud Ghazni, named several princes with Hindu names, 'Samand, Kamalu, Bhim,

Jaipala, Anandapala, and Tarojanapala (Trilochanapala)', adding that the last was killed in 1021 and 'his son Bhimpala five years later'. Claiming that 'this Hindushahiya dynasty is now extinct', al-Biruni added that in 'all their grandeur' the Hindushahis 'never slackened in the ardent desire of doing that which is good and right, that they were men of noble sentiment and noble bearing'.[12]

Writing of the period around AD 1000, al-Biruni said that 'in the mountains to the west of India there live various tribes of the Afghans which extend up to the neighbourhood of the valley of the Sindh (Indus)'. He 'designate[d] these tribes as Hindus'.[13] In the 1940s, genealogies of the Pakhtuns' Yusufzai tribe would yield names of Hindu or Sanskrit origin, for instance, Sarbanr (Suryabans) and Krishyun (Krishna).

About 130 years before the time of Mahmud of Ghazni and al-Biruni, an Iranian called Yaqub-i-Lais enlisted Afghan tribesmen in a successful bid to convert many in the Kabul, Ghazni and Khyber areas to Islam. In AD 870 he captured Kabul from the Hindushahis, but the latter soon recovered the city.

Sabuktagin, father of Mahmud of Ghazni, Turkic by race, strove to expel Hindus from Kabul. Bolder was the aim of his son Mahmud, who resolved to oust the Hindus from Gandhara and also to cross the Indus. In the year AD 1000, Mahmud defeated Jaipal in an unknown field close to Peshawar. Eight years later, a bigger battle was fought, perhaps on the same field, between Mahmud and Anandpal, who was supported by Hindu rajas coming all the way from Gwalior and Kannauj and also by a large number of unconverted

Pakhtuns. But Mahmud won. He also drafted many of
the vanquished in his later forays beyond the Indus.
According to al-Biruni, Anandpal offered support to
Mahmud to quell a Turkish revolt, saying, 'I have been
conquered by you and therefore I do not wish that
another man should conquer you.'[14]

Conqueror, raider and destroyer, Mahmud, who
died in AD 1030, raised magnificent buildings in Ghazni
and courted scholars such as Firdausi and al-Biruni. One
hundred and twenty years after his death, a Ghor
chieftain of Iranian and possibly Turkish blood called
Alauddin took Ghazni by storm and burnt it to the
ground. Later Alauddin also wrecked Bust, the second
city of the Ghaznavids, destroying everything in it and
not even sparing the tombs of the rulers.

A nephew of Alauddin was Muhammad Ghori, also
known as Muizuddin and Shahabuddin. Ghori crossed
the Indus in 1178, captured Lahore in 1186, was defeated
by Prithviraj at Narain near Karnal in 1190, and defeated
Prithviraj in 1191 on the same battlefield. Afghan
mercenaries had aided Ghori's conquest. In 1206, he was
assassinated by a local Muslim on the banks of the Indus.

The Khaljis or Khiljis, an Afghan dynasty, governed
Delhi from 1290 to 1321, with one of them, Alauddin,
ruling a large territory indeed. The Khaljis, the Lodis
(1451–1526) and the Surs (1539–55) were all Afghans/
Pakhtuns. No wonder Khushal Khan Khattak would
write:

I hear the story of Bahlol (Lodi) and Sher Shah
That in days gone by Pathans were Kings in Hind;

For six or seven generations theirs was the Kingdom,
And all the world wondered at them![15]

The greatest of these Pakhtun Kings of Hind was
Sher Shah of Sur, but he had been preceded into Delhi
by Babur, a Turk with Mongol and also some Persian
blood in his veins. During his forays across the Peshawar
Valley, Babur studied the Pakhtun country and
encountered the Pathan tribes. It seems he also fell in
love with Mubarikah of the Yusufzai tribe and married
her. From Mubarikah and other Pakhtuns Babur learnt
of the customs and histories of different Pakhtun tribes,
which he incorporated in the *Baburnama*.

For a short period displacing the Mughals from their
Indian throne and welding together, in a foreign land,
all his Pakhtun mercenaries, Sher Shah seemed to bring
order to the Indian subcontinent in five years. Also, he
appeared to show mercy to the poor and the needy,
cherished the cultivator, and built roads and inns. Delhi's
Old Fort and the Rohtas fortress on a hill north of
Jhelum are credited to him.

Shortly before dying, Sher Shah, ruler of Hindustan
and one who had stunned the Mughals, spoke of his
unfulfilled wishes. One of these, disclosing the builder
in him, was a desire to construct fifty inns for travellers
to Mecca. Another was even nobler, and less expected:

I designed to raise a tomb to Sultan Ibrahim at
Panipat, but on condition that opposite it another
should be erected to the Chaghatai Sultan Babur,
who rendered him a martyr. These wishes, so close

to my heart, I now take with me to the grave.[16]

In wanting to honour Babur the Turk, who had defeated Ibrahim Lodi the Pakhtun, Sher Shah showed the value that he, the greatest of the Pathan heroes, attached in the sixteenth century to reconciliation.

Born in 1525 of Pathan parents, Bayazid or Bazid Ansari or the Pir-i-Roshan became famous for rallying tribes and assembling armies to fight Akbar, the Great Mughal, and notorious for preaching or condoning beliefs in a pantheistic Sufism, in the transmigration of souls, and the veneration of holy souls, including himself. In Caroe's assessment, despite their heretical views, 'Bazid and his descendants for two generations were men of genius' who contributed to the Pakhtun spirit of autonomy, which harried the Mughal emperor Aurangzeb (d. 1707) as much as it had vexed Akbar. 'Bazid the Roshani left a great name', and his followers, including the Afridi swordsman Yusuf, continue to be recalled in ballads 'today'.[17]

Writing several decades after Bayazid's death, Khushal Khan Khattak (1616–91) swore of his own orthodoxy, adding, 'Only one King I know, His orders I obey, His yea and His nay alike rule my life.'[18] Yet Khattak praised the mystical poetry of Mirza Ansari, a Roshani descendant, and criticized that of Akhund Darwezah, who had satirized Pir-i-Roshan:

The Mirza who wrote sweet verse is long since dead,
The book of Akhund Darwezah I have read from
end to end,

And in it found no poetic measure for delight . . .[19]

In another verse, Khattak said that though his contemporary, the Mughal emperor Aurangzeb, might prostrate numerous times a day, and fast until the navel joined the spine, a ruler would only be judged by how just he was. The failure of his Pakhtuns to unite embittered Khushal Khan:

No great deed will be wrought by the Pathans,
Heaven ordains that petty should be their achievement;
I seek to straighten them, they straighten not.[20]

Khattak is followed in the Pakhtun story by Ahmad Shah Abdali or Durrani, hero to the Afghans and something else to Sikhs, Mughals, Marathas and others in India. Ruling over the Pakhtuns from 1747 to 1773, with Kandahar as his capital, he swept eight times across the Indus, ravaged the Punjab, obtained Mughal recognition of his rule over trans-Indus areas including Peshawar, annexed Lahore and Multan, reached Sirhind, and captured Kashmir. As a result he bequeathed to his people a pull towards Kashmir, which however is countered by the Pakhtun proverb, 'Unto every man his own country is Kashmir.'[21]

Peshawar became Durrani's winter capital. Though his raids into India incurred deep hostility, Durrani or Abdali is remembered by Pakhtuns as a king who never lost the common touch, wrote poetry in Pashtu and knew how to manage men and tribes.

But this goodwill in the Pakhtun country, including Peshawar, was matched by the ire that Abdali engendered among the Sikhs, the Marathas and the Mughals. In 1756 he desecrated the Sikhs' holiest shrine, the Golden Temple; in 1761 he defeated the Marathas at Panipat (a Mughal faction backed the Marathas but the Sikhs were neutral in this battle); and in 1762 Abdali's forces 'killed more than 5,000 Singhs in a single day in a running battle in the present district of Ludhiana'. The 'great carnage' is marked every year by the Sikhs.[22] However, Abdali also appointed Hindus as governors in a few of his Indian territories, and Hindu traders flourished in Kandahar.[23]

In 1819, sixty-seven years after Abdali had taken it from the Mughals, the Sikh ruler, Ranjit Singh, captured Kashmir. Four years later, after a bitter battle in Nowshera, Ranjit Singh entered Peshawar. While acknowledging Sikh boldness and valour under Ranjit Singh in Nowshera and elsewhere, Caroe provides a harsh account of what occurred next in Peshawar. Since Pathan–Sikh cordiality was hardly the first thing desired by the empire's chief officer in the Frontier, this account has to be taken with caution. Yet it is the sort of narrative that Pathans have been raised on, even as Sikhs are brought up on stories of Abdali's depredations in the Punjab.

> After the battle (of Nowshera, March 1823) Ranjit Singh advanced to Peshawar, slaying and plundering as he went. He battered down the Bala Hissar and sacked the fair palace within . . . He cut the cypresses

and muddied the basins of the garden of Shah Leman below the Fort, and allowed his cavalry to ravage the square miles of delicious orchards, plum, peach, apricot and pear, the glory of Peshawar. The name of the Sikhashahi—the Sikh rule—is a synonym for misgovernment and oppression in the mouths of teachers and children to this day . . . That Peshawar contains no architectural monuments of any value is due mainly to the devastations of 1823.[24]

We will look next at Sayyid Ahmad Shah Barelvi, a Hindustani with links to UP and Bihar, who reached Peshawar in 1827. Puritanical and charismatic, seen by some as a zealot and by others as a *mujaddid*, or one entitled to reinterpret the faith, Sayyid Ahmad Shah fanned the flames of revolt against the Sikhs and left a legacy of jihad against the British, who at the time of Sayyid Ahmad's death were in the final phase of their conquest of India.

Sayyid Ahmad, whose defiance was launched from Charsadda, helped the Pathans defeat the Sikhs in some daring battles, but in May 1831 he was surprised by a band of Sikhs and killed at Balakot. By now his influence among the Pathans was in decline. For one thing, the Pathans could never, in the end, wholly trust a Hindustani. For another, Sayyid Ahmad demanded an end to the dowry system that the Pathan chiefs were practising. Also, it seems that 'when Ahmad was accused, as many say unjustly, of assigning maidens one by one to his needy Hindustani followers, the people were greatly incensed'.[25]

Having eventually distrusted every stranger entering their land, be he an Alexander, an Arab, an Akbar, an Aurangzeb, a Ranjit Singh or a Sayyid Ahmad, the Pakhtuns were now to face strangers of a kind they had never seen before—white men and women arriving from a far island with, so the British thought, a heaven-sent mandate to impose order.

An early contact occurred in 1809, fifty-two years after the British had won, in Plassey in Bengal, their first major battle in India. A young British officer, Mountstuart Elphinstone, called on the Afghan ruler, Shah Shuja, a grandson of Abdali, in Shuja's winter seat, Peshawar, and held cordial talks. By 1838, however, the British had created an 'army of the Indus' consisting of 15,000 troops and an equal number of horses, mules, camels and elephants. Alleging an Afghan threat to peace on British India's frontier, the army moved deep into the Pakhtun country. The British appeared to gain control, yet in the winter of 1841–42 the Afghans stormed the British Residency in Kabul, killed the Resident, and forced out the British army.

Four thousand and five hundred soldiers and 12,000 camp followers retreated from Kabul towards the frozen passes to their south-east but could not complete the journey. In mid-January, a half-dead doctor called William Brydon rode alone into Fort Jalalabad to tell of the rout and death of an entire army. In the summer of 1843, however, the British swept across to Kabul, set the city on fire, and returned to Peshawar.

By the end of the 1840s, the British had overcome the Sikhs, annexed the Punjab, and inherited the lands that Ranjit Singh had conquered between the Indus and the Afghan 'border'. The Frontier's towns, Peshawar included, and some of its roads, were administered as an extension of the Punjab, but the Pakhtuns continued to control the countryside, the mountains and the Khyber.

During the 1857 Revolt, a daring diplomacy won for the British the neutrality of the Pakhtuns and the support of the Sikhs, two critical factors in saving the British position on the subcontinent. And in the 1870s a fiercely-implemented 'Forward Policy' secured British control over the north-west's passes, though no position was won without a bitter fight or freed from future Pakhtun challenges.

To the border Pathan there appeared (*a British commentator acknowledged*) a vision of a great mailed fist, the fingers of which, in the nineties, seemed to be closing around him. Isolated forts garrisoned by the British troops commanded the trade routes or frowned upon his native hamlet or terraced fields. Dazzling white roads wound their way like serpents towards his fortress in the mountains . . . Long lines of boundary pillars enclos[ed] his country threatening his independence which was his proudest boast.[26]

Every Pakhtun tribe was up in arms. The Pakhtun tradition of hospitality and sanctuary was abandoned; British civilians were ambushed and killed. The British answer was to send some Pathans to the black water of the Andamans, burn villages and crops, destroy wells and fruit trees, and starve the Pakhtuns, including women and children, by blockading.

More than forty military expeditions took the field between 1858 and 1902. The British were gaining. Abdur Rahman, obtaining the Afghan throne in 1879, was pro-British. In 1893 Kabul acquiesced in British dominion east and south of a line drawn by Lieutenant Henry Durand and cutting right across Pakhtun territory; and in the Frontier the ranks grew of suitably placated tribal chiefs willing to share control with the British.

Yet a year of great trauma was at hand. In 1897, thousands of tribesmen attacking with swords, knives and a few obsolete rifles were gunned down by British and Sikh soldiers in Malakand and Chakdarra. Next, the Afridis and the Orakzais took the Khyber Pass by surprise. Finally, in reprisal, the British devastated the homes, fields and orchards of the Afridis and the Orakzais, and recaptured the Pass. Forty thousand troops of the British had quelled the 1897 Pakhtun rebellion. And 1903 would see the promulgation of the Frontier Crimes Regulation Act, under which a person could be sentenced for life without being brought before a court of law or the right to a counsel.

The British justified their Forward Policy by citing Tsarist Russia's incursions into Central Asia, through Tashkent, Samarkand and Bukhara and towards Afghan lands. As the Great Game intensified, and 'security' became the British watchword, the Punjab province's 'frontier districts', the tracts lying along the Indus on an eastern belt of the Pakhtun country, seemed to demand new arrangements.

In 1901, Curzon, the viceroy, announced that these 'settled' districts on the north-western frontier would be detached from the Punjab and henceforth constitute a new province, the North-West Frontier Province, or the NWFP. If they did not harass the British, the Pakhtun tribes living in the large, mountainous and sparsely populated 'tribal' space between the new province and the Durand Line (the Afghan 'border') would be left alone.

The start of the new century thus saw, on the subcontinent's north-west, a 'settled' yet largely illiterate and predominantly agricultural Frontier province with a peasant–tribal society. Beyond that province lay a rocky 'tribal' space that the British hoped would act as a buffer between India and Afghanistan, and beyond the tribal space an Afghanistan expected to serve as a buffer between the British and Russian empires. Two additional (and contiguous) Pakhtun or Pashtun spaces were, firstly, the 'princely' territories of Dhir, Chitral and Swat, to the north of the 'settled' districts, managed under British oversight by chiefs, and, secondly, to the south, the Pashtun-speaking portions of British-run Baluchistan (or Balochistan).

*

The Pakhtun psychology: We can start with the opening lines of Louis Dupree's classic study, *Afghanistan* (1973), in which he mentions the 'insolence' of the Pakhtuns, adding that it is not the frustrated insolence of urbanized, dehumanized man in western society but insolence without arrogance, the insolence of harsh freedoms set against a backdrop of rough mountains and deserts, the insolence of equality felt and practised (with an occasional touch of superiority), the insolence of bravery past and bravery anticipated.[27]

More than seventy years before the appearance of Dupree's work, the Frontier's 1897 battles were sketched for the British public by a twenty-three-year-old correspondent-cum-officer called Winston Churchill, who also described the battle terrain and his adversaries' mindset:

Valley walls rise steeply five or six thousand feet on every side . . . Fierce snow-fed torrents foam under skies of brass . . . Except at harvest time, when self-preservation enjoins a temporary truce, the Pathan tribes are always engaged in public or private war. Every man is a warrior, a politician and a theologian. Every large house is a real feudal fortress made, it is true, only of sunbaked clay, but with battlements, turrets, loopholes, flanking towers, drawbridges, etc., complete . . .

Every family cultivates its vendetta; every clan its feud . . . Nothing is ever forgotten, and very few debts are left unpaid.

For the purposes of social life, in addition to the convention about harvest time, a most elaborate code of honour has been established and is on the whole faithfully observed. A man who knew it and observed it faultlessly might pass unharmed from one end of the Frontier to another. The slightest technical slip, however, would be fatal.[28]

This *Pakhtunwali*, or the way of the Pakhtuns, cannot of course be seen as static. As several modern scholars emphasize, it is subject to negotiation and innovation.[29] Decades earlier, the poet Iqbal had called 'the Afghan conservatism' a 'miracle', for it was 'adamantine, yet fully sensitive to and assimilative of new cultural forces. And this is the secret of the eternal organic growth of the Afghan type.'[30]

Dynamic yet stubborn, *Pakhtunwali* had several elements. It implied, first, obedience to the *jirga*, or assembly (or group) of elders. Discussions at a *jirga* were frank and democratic, though the village chief, who normally held a quantity of land and was called a khan, was likely to be more equal than the others. A *jirga*'s rulings followed a mix of Islamic law and Pakhtun custom. Only a senseless man defied his tribal *jirga*, in which case he was ostracized, fined, or had his property burnt.

Second, there was the principle of *melmastia* or hospitality, generally offered in the *hujra*, the bachelors' den which functioned also as the guest-house of a clan or village. Strangers and guests were served food and offered the *chilum*, or water-pipe, by the khan or chief himself. Importantly, *melmastia* extended to offering protection to the visitor, whatever the cost or risk.

Third, there was *nanawatee*, which is the application of *Pakhtunwali* when hostility had to give way to peace. It involved supplication by the defeated, with the Qur'an in his hands. If the vanquished, abasing himself, offered a pair of sheep, or said, straw in mouth, 'I am your ox', his victor *had* to be magnanimous. [31]

Fourth, though this could have been named first, there was *badal*, or revenge, a concept intimately linked to the notion of honour. As young Churchill quickly noticed, no injury was to be forgotten and no debt left unpaid. *Badal* dismissed blood ties and could target a brother or a cousin; in fact enmity between first cousins had a precise name, *tarburwali*. And *badal* of course applied to a rival *khel* (clan), a rival tribe and an alien intruder.

In a powerful little book written in the mid-1940s, the poet and artist Ghani Khan, who was Badshah Khan's oldest son, described the working of *badal*:

[If dishonoured, the Pathan] must shoot. He has no alternative. If he does not, his brothers will look down upon him, his father will sneer at him, his sister will avoid his eyes, his wife will be insolent and his friends will cut him off . . . One day he goes out and never comes back. He has laughed his way into a bullet that was fired by another of his own blood and race. His wife inherits from him a moment of joy, two sons and a lifetime of sorrow. [32]

The Pakhtuns always knew that their code had a

flaw: the thrusts of *badal* and *melmastia* were opposed
to each other. But the contradiction was not squarely
faced until Badshah Khan appeared on the scene. It is to
this man that we now return.

TWO

The Sons of Behram Khan
1890–1919

In that year of trauma, 1897, Ghaffar was a seven-year-old boy, the youngest of four siblings, girl-boy-girl-boy being the order in which they had arrived.[1] His father, Behram Khan, a chief of the village of Utmanzai on the eastern bank of the river Swat, was close to sixty when Abdul Ghaffar was born. Though ignorant of the year of his birth, he remembered well the subcontinent's 1857 Revolt.

Behram Khan was a scion of one of the smaller Pakhtun tribes, the Muhammadzai, smaller but influential, for the Muhammadzai lands in a tract known as Hashtnagar or Ashtnagar ('eight towns') were rich.

These lands were bounded in the north and the west by the river Swat, in the east by the river Indus, and in the south by the close-by river Kabul. To the north rose the Malakand range of mountains. Normally wanderers rather than settlers, and always in pursuit of seasons,

the Pakhtuns who found this tract, however, stayed put.
Continuous settlement gave the Muhammadzais several
advantages: their agriculture flourished, they felt secure,
their language was preserved (the Muhammadzais are
proud of the pure accents of their Pakhto), traditions
were bequeathed and remembered. In short, they
became well established.

If wonderfully fertile, with British-built canals
enhancing nature's gifts, their land was appealing as well,
especially when the fields were green and the trees were
in flower or heavy with fruit. Throughout his long life
Ghaffar Khan would offer an unqualified verdict: 'There
is no spot on earth so beautiful.'[2] How Behram Khan
came into his holdings of land is not clearly known, but
he owned a piece in Utmanzai and larger pieces in the
Ashtnagar village of Muhammad Naray, about five miles
north of Utmanzai.

Four miles south of Utmanzai lay the ancient city
of Charsadda, once the Gandhara capital, where
Alexander had walked. Later, Kushan kings moved
twenty miles south-west, and across the Kabul river, to
Purushapura or Peshawar, destined to become the
headquarters of the British effort to subdue the
Pakhtuns. The Khyber Pass started twelve-and-a-half
miles west of Peshawar.

From Utmanzai, the forts of Malakand and
Chakdarra, attacked by Afridis in 1897, were, respectively,
only about twenty-eight and twenty-three miles to the
north. The Tirah Valley orchards and gardens that the
British destroyed in 1897 were about thirty miles to
the south-west.

Fierce though the Pakhtuns' family, clan and tribal rivalries were, these were forgotten in the clash with the British, justifying the Pashto proverb that a much-hated cousin is of use in a crisis. Behram Khan, his tall and beautiful wife, their eldest son Abdul Jabbar,[3] who was eight years older than Abdul Ghaffar, and even seven-year-old Ghaffar would have been shaken to pieces by the close-by events of 1897, and roused to fury against the British.

This was not a new experience for the family, for, as we saw, 1897 had been preceded by happenings as chilling even if not on the same scale. When occurring in the lifetime of Behram's father Saifullah Khan, such events had made Saifullah indignant, too, and victims of British wrath found sympathy and support from him. There was, as well, a family legacy of fighting for justice; prior to the British arrival, Behram's grandfather, Saifullah's father Ubaidullah, had been hanged for his stand by a Durrani regime.

But there were problems on Behram's mind. For one thing, he knew that the canals were not the only good thing the British had done in the Pakhtun country. He liked the Edwardes Memorial Mission School in Peshawar that Rev. E.F.E. Wigram was conducting and was thinking of enrolling Jabbar in it. He liked, also, the brother of Rev. Wigram who ran a hospital. Different British officers were friendly towards Behram, addressed him as 'Uncle', and derived amusement by challenging Behram to remember their names; he was apt to name someone dead for decades.[4] And Behram did not forget that during the 1857 Revolt an older brother of his had loyally served the British side and, in fact, had commanded the armed men guarding the Charsadda treasury.

Moreover, his instincts told Behram that a Pakhtun victory over the British was unlikely. The Afridis attacking the forts at Malakand and Chakdarra had thought that the forts' garrisons constituted the whole of the British army; when British reinforcements turned up, the Afridis were shocked. Behram knew better.

Then again, Behram was unimpressed by some foes of the British in Utmanzai and Charsadda. Mostly uneducated mullahs, they claimed religious grounds for opposing the few schools the British had started in the Frontier province and threatened the parents of school-going children with excommunication. Yet they seemed incapable of setting up alternative schools. A mullah who had taught Ghaffar, when the boy was five or six, to recite the Qur'an could not explain its verses to Ghaffar because he himself did not know their meaning; he knew, however, how to hit pupils.

Whether or not aware that the Prophet of Islam had prescribed learning, the illiterate Behram coveted it for his sons. He made his choice. Defying the threats, he sent both his sons to a British-launched municipal school in Peshawar, a decision that ought to be set against the fact that in the entire Frontier province, only fifteen students had matriculated in 1891; twelve years later, in 1903, only seventy-one would do so. In an autobiography he dictated in 1965, Ghaffar Khan would claim that his brother Jabbar 'was the first to go to school in Hashtnagar'.[5]

Though comprising only 7 per cent of the Frontier province's population and mostly residing in towns, Hindus and Sikhs were more willing to send their children to the Raj's schools. Ghaffar would later recall that Hindu 'untouchable' boys were some of his playmates at the Peshawar municipal school.

Sharper objections were raised when, around 1898 or 1899, Behram sent Jabbar to Rev. Wigram's school and again when, around 1902, Ghaffar too was sent there, decisions never to be regretted by either boy or by their father.

Here we may pause to recognize two unconnected things. One is that the North-West Frontier Province was ruled by a Chief Commissioner answerable to the Viceroy, not by a Governor, and was unhindered by committees or councils that in other provinces gave natives ringside seats for observing governance. The other is that much of what we know about Behram Khan and his wife is limited to the loving and brief pictures provided at different times by their devoted and oft-independent son, Ghaffar Khan. This is a pity, for what is known about the parents begets a curiosity to know more.

The son called his father 'influential, powerful and popular'. We are informed that Behram, the highly-placed Khan of Utmanzai, laughed and swore merrily; that he carried food on his head for visitors in the Utmanzai *hujra*; that he rode horses until he was ninety and was an adept farmer; that he never told a lie and many poor Pathans left their savings with him; and that he did not dance attendance on British officers who had the capacity to ruin him or rain wealth on him.

Especially significant, perhaps, was the son's assessment that the father 'had no feuds because he had forgiven all his enemies. He knew no revenge.'[6] All descendants have heard that Behram Khan, dedicating himself to his family and his lands, had decided not to spend any time or money on feuds or for guns, and had even declared, rejecting *badal*, that past killings against his clan would not be avenged.[7]

As for the 'tall and beautiful' mother, she tended to live in the world of the spirit, 'often sit[ting] down after her namaaz to meditate in silence', and was said to be especially fond of her youngest, Ghaffar, who returned this feeling and was also close to the sibling nearest in age to him. 'There was great love between this sister and me', he would recall when he was seventy-eight.[8]

Let us pause again to mark something that must astonish most modern readers: neither Ghaffar's mother, nor his sisters, nor the two women he would in due course marry are named in his memoirs or in books about him. In the summer of 1968, when Badshah Khan was seventy-eight and living in Kabul, he was asked by the Indian scholar, Haridev Sharma, 'What were the names of your sisters?' Badshah Khan replied: 'Why speak their names now?'[9]

The unwillingness to name or talk about the women featuring in their lives has been, and remains, a characteristic of Pakhtun males, and of several communities elsewhere on the subcontinent. When, in the late 1980s, this author was researching the life of Vallabhbhai Patel (1875–1950), his effort to discover whether Patel's wife

Jhaverba (a character entirely ignored in most studies of Patel) was tall or short, dark or light-skinned, or good-looking or not, or what her personality was like, proved largely in vain.

Another subcontinental figure researched by this writer, Chakravarti Rajagopalachari (1878–1972), like Patel a close colleague of Badshah Khan in the independence movement, was found to be a good deal more forthcoming regarding the women central to his life, but more so about his mother than about his wife. When it comes to expressing feelings publicly about one's mother or wife, Pakhtun society is more discouraging than the Tamil world in which Rajagopalachari was raised, yet Rajagopalachari too was reluctant to name his wife even in that most private of spaces, a prison diary.

'Why speak their names now?' We may detect irritation in the reply; no doubt Badshah Khan had been asked that sort of question before, and he may have disliked its repetition from Sharma. But there was also the Pakhtun convention against naming or discussing women outside a closed family circle, which was an extension of the custom of restricting women physically to the interior of a home, a domestic space where, often, the women were indeed honoured.

But behind 'Why speak their names now?' there may have also been, apart from irritation and convention, suppressed sorrow related to the hard and anonymous lives—and, as we shall see, the sudden and early deaths—of the women close to Ghaffar Khan, and perhaps connected also to the premature and unrecorded deaths of numerous female cousins, aunts and nieces.

Only a journey all the way from Delhi (via Dubai and Islamabad) to the Frontier province, made in the summer of 2003, and enquiries there from Behram Khan's descendants unearthed the names of Behram Khan's daughters (Shama and Quresha)[10] and of the wives of his sons.

To return to our story: unable either to prevent Behram Khan from sending the boys to the mission school or to excommunicate Utmanzai's powerful Khan, his conservative foes said that ostracism would follow if the boys learnt the English language, or, it was later said, if they read the Christian scriptures. But the punishment never materialized.

The boys lodged in Peshawar with Barani Kaka, a family servant, in a boarding house close to where the Wigram brothers lived. It is probable that the boarding house was chosen for just that reason by Behram Khan. Ghaffar seemed to do well at school in mathematics and particularly in geometry, played some cricket and football, carried stumps and other boys' bats, and went out hunting with his mates but, apparently, 'killed no beast or bird'.[11]

Continuing to bet on the West and its institutions, Behram Khan sent Jabbar, who had matriculated in 1905 and was by now a husband (of Khurshid) and a father, to study medicine in Bombay. In 1909, he did something bolder; Jabbar, also called, as the Khan's elder son, Khan Sahib, was sent to London, where, courtesy of Dr Wigram, he found a chance to train at St. Thomas's Hospital. Left behind in the Frontier were Khurshid and three small boys, Sadullah, Ubeidullah and Hidayatullah.

In 1908 or thereabouts, when Ghaffar Khan was a strongly-built yet reserved Pathan lad of eighteen or so and rising to six-foot-three, he was urged by his helper Barani Kaka to apply for a commission in the British army. A few of Ghaffar's acquaintances had obtained this commission, and Ghaffar Khan was drawn (he would later say) by the glamour of an officer's life.

He applied to the office of the Commander-in-Chief of India. Word that he had been accepted reached him while he was writing his matriculation finals in Peshawar; the next day he went to the Recruiting Office where, after an examination, he was enrolled for direct commission in the Frontier Guides. First recruited in 1846, the Guides were the eyes and ears of the British in the Pakhtun country. A serious-minded, physically strong son of the highly-respected Khan of Utmanzai was an excellent acquisition for the Raj's custodians in the Frontier.

But Ghaffar's life as a Guide for the Empire was not to be. He was in Peshawar, visiting a cavalry Guide who, like him, came from a family of khans, when a British subaltern turned up and gave a tongue-lashing to Ghaffar's friend. The friend's offence was not donning a Pathan's customary turban and, moreover, parting his hair in the style of an Englishman. Ghaffar saw that his friend 'turned pale and had no courage to retort back'. Ghaffar Khan could not stomach either the subaltern's rebuke or his friend's silence. There and then his plan to join the Guides was aborted. 'I had flattered myself',

Badshah Khan would later say, 'that I was specially fitted to look like and enjoy an equal footing with Englishmen. But Allah had willed otherwise.'[12]

The refusal to join as a Guide greatly upset Behram Khan, but the father was partially calmed after Jabbar, on Ghaffar's request, wrote from London urging Behram Khan not to remain angry. The Mahomedan Anglo-Oriental College at Aligarh, later to become the Aligarh Muslim University, was the next destination for Ghaffar Khan, who spent about a year there. But Khan Sahib had thought up another option for a younger brother good in mathematics: a journey to England to study engineering.

Behram Khan was enthusiastic and handed 3,000 rupees to Ghaffar; there was not, and a hundred years later there is not, a shortage of subcontinental parents dreaming of a doctor-engineer pair among their progeny. On his part Ghaffar seemed pleased and booked a berth on a P&O steamship.

But this plan too was blocked. The three male Khans had reckoned without the boys' mother. She said she did not want her second son also to leave the Frontier and India. Those going to England never returned, she insisted. If Ghaffar went, he would become a Christian or marry an English girl or both. Indeed, Jabbar, in England, had by this time married, or was about to marry, a second wife, May, a British girl. In 1935 Badshah Khan would say to Mahadev Desai: 'The fact of my brother having married an English girl finally sealed the fate of my visit to England.'[13] The mother was adamant, and Ghaffar, who loved her deeply, would not defy her to go to England.

Those familiar with Gandhi's early life, which was spent by the sea even as Badshah Khan's was lived against the mountains, will have noted hints of similarities: doting parents in both cases who were also diligently served by the sons; signs of leadership mixed with reserve; in each youth a strong sense of dignity; and some passing desire, again in both cases, to cultivate strength, even armed strength. Mohandas, born twenty-one years before Ghaffar, also played some cricket, and we are informed that he tried to settle disputes on the field, a characteristic not dissimilar to Ghaffar's readiness to carry stumps and his friends' bats.

In both cases, the conflicting pulls of nationalism and the West formed the background for at least some personal or family choices, though 'nation' and 'nationalism' may have meant different things to Mohandas and young Ghaffar. The confrontation with the mother over a trip to England is also almost identical. Gandhi's mother, too, had raised the question of an English girl. We know that Mohandas resolved it through the device of a vow, while Ghaffar Khan chose to sacrifice the idea of going to England.

It is a fair surmise that the Wigram brothers were involved in the now-abandoned thought of Ghaffar studying in England, for in later recalling the impact of his mother's successful remonstrance with him, Badshah Khan would dwell on the brothers:

The teacher who had created in me the spirit of service to the creatures of God was the Britisher,

Rev. E.F.E. Wigram. His brother was a doctor. They came from a well-known family and both the brothers were dedicated to the mission. All their expenses were borne by their parents . . . I was a witness to the love and the spirit with which both the brothers used to serve the people . . .

Our headmaster, Rev. Wigram, used to give scholarships to three or four poor students and that too had a great effect on me. I said to myself, 'We Pakhtuns have no sympathy for our poor brothers, and they who came from a foreign land, how much sympathy they have!'

When my mother did not give her consent to go to England, I made up my mind to serve . . . my people, who, at that time, due to their stupidity and backwardness, were heading towards disaster and chaos.[14]

In his old age, Ghani, Badshah Khan's older son, would recall his father's warmth for missionaries: 'He used to say they are wonderful people, they will not get married, they have no ambitions, they just want to serve.'[15]

Taking a cue from the example of his former headmaster, Ghaffar Khan and a friend opened a school in Utmanzai in 1910 and sought to enlist support for a network of schools elsewhere. Of Ghaffar Khan's mind at this stage we have few clues apart from the statement quoted above; our knowledge of Ghaffar Khan's youth, like our knowledge of his parents, is confined to what a much older Ghaffar Khan would disclose in response to questions from someone like Mahadev Desai or, later still, in a dictated autobiography. No record of what schoolmates or friends of his youth said about him seems to have survived.

Some inferences, however, are undeniable. The journeys that he would undertake before long show a Ghaffar Khan who comprehends his Pakhtun country's terrain, its sloping hills and hidden passes, and a recognition he would receive from Pakhtuns around him suggests his interest in their lives.

But we must return to the school in Utmanzai that Ghaffar Khan and his friend opened. In this venture he received encouragement from Haji Fazli Wahid Sahib of the village of Turangzai, which was a mile away. Enjoying a high reputation in the Pakhtun country, the Haji also wanted to set up schools. Ghaffar Khan's sentiment for the Wigram brothers notwithstanding, he seems to have envisioned, as did the Haji of Turangzai, schools that would promote not only reform among the Pakhtuns—the ending of feuds and of wasteful expenditure on weddings and funerals—but also autonomy vis-à-vis the British. These would be *azad madrassas*, independent Islamic schools.

In fact, the Ghaffar Khan who did not go to England increasingly becomes (or, perhaps, merely reveals) a nationalistic Ghaffar Khan. Quietly, in fact secretly, he makes visits to faraway Deoband in the UP, the Muslim institution designed to counter the seemingly pro-British impulses of the Aligarh college. He meets and likes the principal at Deoband, Maulana Muhammad-ul Hasan, and, in Delhi, Maulana Obeidullah Sindhi, who sought to acquaint English-knowing Muslims with their religion. He subscribes to the radical Urdu newspaper started in 1912 by Abul Kalam Azad, *Al Hilal*, knowing well that the Raj was keeping a tab on *Al Hilal*'s readers.

This seemingly abrupt radicalism is not explained either in the Badshah Khan autobiography or in any of the books on him or by his sons. All we know is that the radicalism appeared to follow the cancellation of his England plan, which had followed his refusal, despite his father's urging, to become a Guide. There is no evidence, however, that Ghaffar Khan would have become pro-British had he gone to England. On the contrary, a desire to know the Pakhtuns' foe might well have been (we are speculating) one reason for his wanting to go there. We can only conclude that in the years preceding the Great War it was perfectly possible for a Pathan in his early twenties to be stirred by a British teacher and, at the same time, to resent bitterly a British connection, congenial one day and brutal the next, that the Pakhtuns had never asked for.

Two decades later Ghaffar Khan would use language disclosing shame at Pathan support for some of Britain's imperial exercises and bitterness at its reward, but the shame and the bitterness probably dated from his late teens. 'We Afghans helped the English to loot Delhi, attack Baghdad and Jerusalem', he would say in Ahmedabad in June 1931, 'but . . . we got in return the Frontier Crimes Regulation, which is like a slow poison to us.'[16]

Howsoever triggered or developed, the radicalism troubled old Behram, who by now had crossed eighty.

He applied a time-tested remedy. In 1912, at the age of around twenty-three, Ghaffar Khan was married to Mehr Qandh,[17] a girl in whom he seemed interested, given some land to manage, and advised to settle down.

He appeared to adore his wife, 'a whimsical, lovable, generous creature, . . . from a fine old family'.[18] After their child Abdul Ghani was born the next year, Ghaffar worked hard in the fields. 'He went to the field like an ordinary farmer in the last part of the night. Then tea and breakfast [would] follow him and he ploughed there and kept his bullocks and buffalo and in the evening came home . . . He was a tough sort of fellow.'[19] Yet, 'very often, when he sat by the fire, he would stop cuddling [the child] and get engrossed in his own thoughts.'[20]

Mehr Qandh, who came from the close-by Ashtnagar village of Rajjar, lived with more and more of these moods and long silences and hated them, and she also disliked Ghaffar Khan's habit of suddenly leaving for a trip. In 1913 he went all the way to Agra, for he had read that the All India Muslim League was meeting there, and that Abul Kalam Azad and the Aga Khan would be speaking. The talks in Agra were mostly about the targeting of the Turks by the Europeans.

Something was cooking in his mind, something not known to his wife or parents. In the next year, 1914, he made another secret visit to Deoband. Two of his Pakhtun friends accompanied him; there were sombre discussions; plans were hatched. A centre in support of India's liberation would be opened in the Frontier's tribal areas. Ghaffar Khan and his Pakhtun friend Maulvi Fazle

Mohamed would go first to Fazle Mohamed's village on the edge of the Malakand territory and thence to the territory of Bajaur, where they would select a safe base. Maulana Obeidullah Sindhi would soon join them in Bajaur and confirm the choice.

Returning to Utmanzai, Ghaffar Khan announced that he was going on a pilgrimage to the Chishti dargah in Ajmer, but in fact left with Fazle Mohamed by train to the Frontier town of Dargai and thence on a tonga and on foot towards Fazle's village on the Malakand rim. The Raj's guards were active and once or twice Ghaffar Khan was stared at with well-merited suspicion, but the two managed to reach the village two days after they had left Peshawar.

While Fazle waited there for Maulana Obeidullah Sindhi, Ghaffar Khan, accompanied by one of Fazle's relatives, set out for Bajaur, a large tract on the Afghan border with an area of 5,000 square miles and a population at the time of about 1,00,000. To the west of the Bajaur country was the river Kunar, which formed the border with Afghanistan; the river Panjkora meandered in the north. The Mohmand tribal territory lay to the east and south of Bajaur.

Ghaffar Khan walked to as many Bajaur villages as he could but finally chose a Mohmand village, Zagai. There, in a cell in a small mosque, he waited for Obeidullah Sindhi. As far as the villagers were concerned, this mystical young Pakhtun was performing the *chilla*. The long intense prayer ended, the waiting continued, but there was no sign of the Maulana. Reluctantly and slowly, Ghaffar Khan and Fazle's relative trudged back to Fazle's village, and Ghaffar Khan returned to Utmanzai. What he told his family about Ajmer is not known!

With the World War starting, the plan for a revolutionary centre in the tribal hills was abandoned. The Deoband principal was arrested in Mecca, where he had gone for a hajj, and handed over to the British. Maulana Obeidullah Sindhi went into exile in Afghanistan. The Haji of Turangzai made for the Buner territory, where some pro-British mullahs tried to have him arrested; however, he escaped to the Mohmands. Accompanying the Haji to these secluded areas were some of Ghaffar Khan's close comrades.

We may note or deduce the following about the elusive base for liberty. One, there is no hint that it was to be a nonviolent centre. Although we have no record of a plan to collect weapons or train men in armed warfare, the secrecy that, in Badshah Khan's own account, marked every stage of the Bajaur expedition suggests a possibly violent project. Badshah Khan would never claim that the planning in Deoband was for a nonviolent base, and in 1981 he would admit, 'In my youth I also thought [of] violence.'[21]

Second, the bid for the centre shows the depth of young Ghaffar Khan's passion for liberty. Later in life he would recall 'the seed I had sowed in 1912'.[22] If he was accurate about the date, then we must surmise that he burnt his boats in 1912, the year of his marriage. This would explain the moods and silences.

Tragedy struck in December 1915, soon after the birth of Ghaffar Khan's second son, Abdul Wali. The older child, Ghani, went down with a deathly flu and seemed near his end. At this point, while Ghaffar Khan was on his knees on a prayer mat, Mehr Qandh did what only a mother can do, and what mothers in all climes and times have done.

'Tears were streaming down her face', her husband would later recall, 'as she raised her hands towards heaven and humbly began to pray [for the boy's recovery], adding, "Let me be ill in his stead."' Sadly, it pleased the Almighty to grant both wishes. Ghani recovered and Mehr Qandh, Ghaffar Khan's beautiful young wife, died. 'They covered her with flowers and took her to the burial ground [in Utmanzai] in her wedding robe.'[23]

Whether it was because of the way he took his wife's passing, or because of the schools he had started, or because he had said 'no' both to the Guides and to England, or because he seemed called to solemn if undisclosed missions, or simply because he was warm and strong and considerate, or for more than one cause, the khans of Utmanzai and the neighbouring villages met in a mosque and declared that Ghaffar Khan, the twenty-six-year-old son of the old chief Behram Khan, was their Badshah, their king. The name would stick.

But the Badshah was not at peace. His wife was dead, and so was the dream of a Pakhtun base for liberty. He had gone against the wishes of his apparently pro-British father, but what had his independence achieved? The Raj's men seemed to cover every square inch of the Frontier and had driven off people like his friend the Haji of Turangzai. Ghaffar Khan wanted to bring peace to his beloved, divided, feuding Pakhtuns, but his attempts to seek liberty seemed capable of bringing the Raj's wrath, and destruction, on their heads. He liked the Wigram brothers and did not wish *badal* on British heads, but could not possibly offer *melmastia* to men who had entered the Frontier at gunpoint. His questionings represented the Pakhtun dilemma, but unexpected events were near at hand.

Before looking at them, we should note Badshah Khan's answer, given when he was seventy-eight, to the question, 'Whose writ ran at home?' 'Of both of us', he claimed, adding, 'I started the practice of eating together with my wife. As you know, with Pathans and many Indians, the men eat first and then, separately, the women. I broke other useless customs.'[24]

Here we may also observe that the warmth and considerateness that his fellow Pakhtuns noticed in Ghaffar Khan would not always be experienced by his own children. What he gave to the community would seem to restrict, at first sight at any rate, the affection he offered to the immediate family.

The Frontier province had not been excited by the Great War that ended in 1918 and for which the Punjab had provided a great many recruits. What drove passions in the NWFP was its exclusion from reforms announced by the British in 1918. The Montagu–Chelmsford Report recommended a sharing between Britons and Indians of provincial power, but not in the NWFP. For the Pathans there would be no franchise, no elections, not even for local bodies, and of course no legislature or ministry.

The Frontier's resentment coincided with restiveness across India as hopes raised by the War's ending were belied, and as prices rose. Early in 1919, the British countered the rising discontent with the Rowlatt Bills under which, among other things, the police could detain without trial a man carrying a seditious pamphlet on his person while denying him a lawyer. The chief mobilizer of the sentiment against Rowlatt was Mohandas Gandhi, who in 1915 had returned to India after two decades in South Africa. Calling for a nationwide demonstration against Rowlatt, Gandhi invited Indians to take a pledge to disobey the Rowlatt law, and, significantly, to disobey nonviolently. The pledge read as follows:

> The [Rowlatt] bills are unjust, subversive of the principles of liberty and justice, and destructive of the elementary rights of individuals on which the safety of the community as a whole and the state itself is based. We solemnly affirm that in the event of these bills becoming law and until they are withdrawn we shall refuse civilly to obey these laws . . .
>
> We further affirm that in this struggle, we will faithfully follow truth and refrain from violence to life, person and property.[25]

The Frontier province was familiar, through the Frontier Crimes Regulation, with provisions of the Rowlatt kind. Even so, Badshah Khan felt a stirring. He saw a chance to join a movement that seemed capable of threatening British rule on the subcontinent as a whole.

More than that, the combination of defiance and nonviolence appealed to Ghaffar Khan. Consciously or unconsciously, he had been feeling after the very thing. It was a combination that might resolve part of the dilemma of the Pakhtuns, enabling them to fight the British without inviting terrible destruction, and without feeding the fires of violence and revenge that Ghaffar Khan, and his father, had always longed to douse.

As luck would have it, Gandhi's intriguing call coincided with a significant development in Afghanistan. In February 1919, the Amir of Afghanistan, Habibullah, of Pakhtun descent and a distant cousin of the Durranis, was murdered. Pakhtuns in Afghanistan and in the NWFP believed that Mustafa Saghi, a Tajik, was behind the deed. Saghi was quickly arrested and, three years later, executed, though a few others were also punished for the crime, and the case was never fully resolved. Yet the arrest of Saghi in February 1919 and, immediately thereafter, the ascension of Amanullah, Habibullah's son, to Kabul's vacant throne thrilled all Pakhtuns, including those in the Frontier.

Buoyed by sounds of promise from two horizons, one marked by the Khyber and the other by the Indus, Badshah Khan decided on a public meeting in Utmanzai to protest Rowlatt. It was called on Sunday, 6 April 1919, the day on which meetings had been invited across India. The response in Utmanzai was staggering, and it launched Ghaffar Khan into the pages of history.

THREE

Fire of Hope
1919–37

Ninety-year-old Behram Khan, attending a political meeting for the first time in his life, listened uneasily as his son condemned the Rowlatt legislation. A month later he had greater cause for anxiety. On 5 May 1919, a border dispute not far from the Khyber Pass sparked off a series of skirmishes that historians would call the Third Anglo-Afghan War. Martial law was declared in Peshawar district, and yet Ghaffar Khan set forth, a group of Pathans following him, towards Afghanistan, to offer support—it is not clear in what form—to King Amanullah. Forgetting his age, Behram Khan chased the group and at Mohmand stopped it from proceeding further.

Denouncing Rowlatt was not in itself an illegality. Neither was sympathizing with Amanullah. Taken together, however, the two attitudes added up to sedition in British eyes. Badshah Khan was arrested when he returned to Utmanzai and taken to a jail in Mardan. The next day the Police Superintendent of Mardan ordered that Ghaffar Khan be fettered and driven to Peshawar under an escort comprising, among others, the Police Superintendent himself and Mardan's Assistant Commissioner.

After a night in a lock-up in Peshawar's military cantonment, Badshah Khan was taken, his fettered feet bleeding, to a court where three or four Britons interrogated him. He was asked whether he was stirring up an agitation against the government and also whether he was a 'Badshah of the Pathans'.

'I don't know the answer to that', Ghaffar Khan answered, 'but I know that I am a servant of the community. Also, we cannot take the Rowlatt bills lying down.' Viewed as 'a most dangerous convict' and ordered to remain in prison and in fetters, Badshah Khan was in addition sought to be implicated in a case of damage to telegraph wires.

A Pathan convicted for the damage told a court that Badshah Khan had inspired him to oppose Rowlatt. 'Didn't Ghaffar Khan instigate you to cut the wires?' the Pathan was asked. 'No, sir', was the clear answer.

*

All of Utmanzai was punished for Badshah Khan's independence. Troops herded residents into the azad school that Ghaffar Khan had started, ringed the school compound with field guns, and 'vigorously started loading the cannons'. Thinking that the end had come, the villagers took to praying, but the British aim was to terrify, not shoot. A punitive fine of Rs 30,000 was imposed on Utmanzai but over one lakh rupees was seized in cash and other movables.

Behram Khan was not spared. The old man, hitherto pro-British, was taken to a jail where, to his huge relief, he found his son. Along with other residents of Utmanzai, Behram Khan had assumed that Badshah Khan had been hanged. After three months Behram Khan was released; after another three months Badshah Khan, too, was let out. It was the doing of the province's Chief Commissioner or boss, a wise officer called Sir George Roos-Keppel.[1]

The half-year in jail in 1919 would be a mere start to a bitter career of imprisonment that altogether would swallow twenty-seven years of Badshah Khan's life.

*

'A new wife has been found for you', Behram Khan and his wife informed their son, now weighing much less than the 220 pounds he had registered when arrested, and carrying broad scars on his feet, a lifelong legacy of the fetters that for six months had bound him night and day. But before remarriage—with Nambata,[2] also from Rajjar—there was to be another spell in prison for Ghaffar Khan, for the British authorities imagined his hand behind a bomb that had exploded in the town of Nowshera. There being no evidence at all, he was released after spending a week in a cold dark Peshawar cell where, largely starved, he 'slept' on a cement floor with blankets full of lice as his covering.

Surviving from the record of this arrest is a conversation that reveals what will be noticed several times in these pages: Badshah Khan's defiant, and often harsh, humour. Needled by Badshah Khan's firm answers, a Mr Short, Peshawar's chief CID officer, seems to have shouted, 'Speak gently!' Replied Badshah Khan: 'When I speak loudly you ask me to speak softly, and when I speak softly you ask me to speak loudly. You please demonstrate to me how to speak.' That evening Badshah Khan was denied his dinner of two slices of bread.[3]

Parental hopes that marriage would domesticate Badshah Khan were wholly belied. His appetite for defying the British whetted by his prison experience, Ghaffar Khan also saw that Rowlatt and Afghanistan had been joined by a third lively issue—Britain's treatment of Turkey. Turkey, an ally of the defeated Germany in the late war, was also the world's principal Muslim nation whose Sultan was seen by all Sunni Muslims as their khalifa or chief.

Assured by Britain that Turkey and its Sultan would be justly dealt with, Pathans and other Indian Muslims had soldiered on the side of the allies, yet 1919 and 1920 saw contrary signs. The subcontinent's Muslims became extremely restive over khilafat, or the position of the khalifa. To Gandhi, this restiveness offered a once-in-a-hundred-years, not-to-be-missed opportunity to forge a Hindu–Muslim front for swaraj, or independence, and in defence of khilafat. To Hindus and Muslims he proposed nonviolent non-cooperation as the means.

Early in 1920, Badshah Khan travelled to Delhi for

a Khilafat conference in which Gandhi, the Ali Brothers, Shaukat and Muhammad, Hakim Ajmal Khan, Abul Kalam Azad, and others were taking part. There is no record of Ghaffar Khan meeting Gandhi in Delhi, where, it has been claimed, Badshah Khan was influenced by an argument that India, ruled by an anti-khilafat Britain, had become a *dar-ul-harb*, or land of war, and that good Muslims should therefore exile themselves to Afghanistan through hijrat, or pilgrimage, to a *dar-ul-salam*, or land of peace.

It is certainly true that Ghaffar Khan, now thirty years old, was among about 18,000 Pathans who moved to Kabul in 1920, a hijrat the British allowed, reckoning it would impose a desirable strain on Amanullah's government while ridding the Frontier of troublesome Pathans.

In any case, he had a meeting in Kabul with Amanullah. The king asked Badshah Khan to return to India and take his Pathans back with him. Badshah Khan urged Amanullah to learn Pashto, the language of his ancestors. Each took the other's advice. Ghaffar Khan tried to open schools for tribal Pathans in the Bajaur area, on the British side of the Durand Line, but, persuaded by the British Political Agent, the tribal chiefs denied support to Badshah Khan, who was obliged to return to Utmanzai. Years later, in his autobiography, Badshah Khan would regret his and others' 1920 hijrat and admit that 'it did enormous damage to the Pathans'.[4]

*

But if Afghanistan did not yield much, India promised a lot in December 1920. The tide of non-cooperation was advancing, and the Indian National Congress was meeting in the city of Nagpur, located in India's geographical centre, to decide how far to go in defiance of the British. Badshah Khan journeyed to Nagpur, saw Gandhi (again only from a distance), and liked the programme of action that Gandhi announced and the Congress accepted.

Returning to the Frontier, he raised the Utmanzai school to high-school level. Talented teachers joined him in instructing pupils in a range of subjects including Pakhtun history and Islam. Pakhto was the language of instruction. In order to take educational, social and economic reform to other parts of the Frontier, he founded the Anjuman-Islah-ul-Afaghina (Society for the Reform of the Afghans) and toured the region. But he also became the president of the Khilafat Committee of Peshawar, and the British continued to see him as a seditionist.

Disliking Badshah Khan's schools and tours, the Chief Commissioner, Sir John Maffey, told Behram Khan: 'Your son is visiting village after village and establishing schools. Ask him to stop this work and stay at home like the others.' Otherwise, said Maffey, there would be trouble for son and father both.

Behram Khan liked the advice. Why shouldn't his happily remarried son settle down with his two bright boys? To Ghaffar Khan he said, 'What the others are not doing, you should not do. Sit comfortably at home.' 'If others stop offering namaaz', the son replied, 'would you want me to stop it too?' 'Of course not', said the father. 'Well, Father', said Badshah Khan, 'My schools are like offering prayer.'

When a British officer directly confronted Ghaffar Khan, the latter answered that he wanted his schools to be like the missionary school he had attended. 'This is not service but rebellion', he was told. The opinion of an officer sufficed. On 17 December 1921, Badshah Khan was seized, taken to Peshawar Jail, and thrust into a solitary cell. As he would later recall:

> The cell was stinking—the earthen sanitary pan there was full to the brim with faeces. I stepped out of the cell and told the officer that the stink was unbearable. He pushed me inside and locked the door. After my arrest the other Khilafat colleagues too were arrested. All the twenty-four hours we were confined to the solitary cells. Food was pushed through the bars . . . The cells were guarded to prevent anyone communicating with us. The harsh treatment drove most of [my] colleagues to furnish security. [5]

After ten days Badshah Khan was taken out of his cell and produced before the Deputy Commissioner. One of the policemen present told the British officer that Badshah Khan's offences were that he had gone on hijrat to Afghanistan and, after returning to the Frontier, opened an azad school. The Deputy Commissioner asked the policemen why they had allowed Ghaffar Khan to return to the Frontier. Not receiving a satisfactory answer, he repeated the question several times.

Badshah Khan interrupted the Briton and said, 'You have occupied our country and now want to bar us from entering it.' Infuriated, the officer ordered the police to take Badshah Khan away, adding, 'I am sentencing him to three years' rigorous imprisonment.'[6]

About this interview a story has been related by the mystic Gurdial Malik, a friend of Gandhi and Tagore, which may be apocryphal yet suggestive. According to Malik, the Englishman expressed his scepticism about Ghaffar Khan's professed nonviolence. Badshah Khan linked it to Gandhi. 'And what would you have done', the Deputy Commissioner is supposed to have asked, 'without nonviolence?' Badshah Khan, in this story, placed his large hands around two iron bars and slowly pulled them apart. 'That is what I would have done to you', he said without a smile.[7]

Whatever the truth of this story, it seems fairly certain that Badshah Khan's conversion to nonviolence occurred in the 1919–21 period. Almost two decades later, in remarks made after he and Badshah Khan had spent over a month together in the Frontier province, Gandhi would date the conversion. Speaking, in Ghaffar Khan's presence, in Abbottabad in the Hazara district in 1939, he would say:

As early as 1920, Badshah Khan had come to recognize in nonviolence a weapon, the mightiest in the world, and his choice was made.[8]

In 1981, speaking in Delhi to an old Frontier

colleague, Ghaffar Khan would confirm that it was only after 1920 that he started telling Pakhtuns that 'their condition would never improve [as long as] they believed in "blood for blood". Violence, I explained, creates hatred and fear. Nonviolence generates love, makes one bold.'[9]

*

All of Ghaffar Khan—body, mind, and soul—was sorely tested during these three jail years, 1921–24, which were divided first between Peshawar and Dera Ismail Khan in the Pakhtun country, and then between Dera Ghazi Khan, Lahore and Mianwali in the Punjab. The big strapping son of a khan was proud of his family's lands, his clan, his father's status and the Pakhtun race. His parents' special love had built self-confidence into him. His older brother was now a doctor in Britain where he had acquired a Scottish wife, May. Nambata, Ghaffar Khan's new wife, and his young sons loved and honoured him. And the Pathans of Utmanzai had called him king. Badshah Khan certainly thought of himself as at least the equal of the Frontier's British officers.

Yet these officers had shackled him, barred him from daylight, from the sun in the Frontier's bitter cold, from sleeping for more than two hours at a stretch, from his wife and children and parents, and, much of the time, from contacts with fellow prisoners or any company. Before the eyes of Pathans who honoured him and his father, he had been shoved into and out of the police's vehicles, into and out of 'servants' compartments' of trains, and into and out of prison cells. He was given filthy food, ordered to grind twenty kilos of corn each day by rotating a heavy stone chakki, and abused by lackeys of prison officials. And again and again he was invited to find relief through petty bribing, an apology or a surety.

He passed the test, spurning every demeaning offer and countering discomfort with his will. He found loneliness very hard but tried to tackle it with reading when possible or with prayer. The humiliations he answered with indifference, a blunt remark or even kindness, but mostly by preserving his self-respect.

In Peshawar Jail in December 1921,

> when I donned the jail clothes, the trousers hardly reached my calf and the shirt did not even reach the navel. And when I did my namaaz, the trousers often got torn and the shirt clung to the ribs . . . [My] cell faced the north; the sunlight never entered it. It was intensely cold . . . During the night, the watchman on duty changed every third hour and, making noise, shouted at us . . . until we woke up to respond to his call.[10]

Decades later, asked how his father 'survived mentally in jail', Ghani Khan would reply:

> It was . . . faith. The feeling that you are doing the right thing, that even by being in jail you are serving your people, you are serving your country, you are giving an example . . . In those days you just had to

apologize, say I will not do it again, and out you [went] and your property was returned. But he would not say it. He just would not say it.[11]

A surprise visitor at Peshawar Jail was the older brother, Dr Khan Sahib. After receiving an MRCS certificate from St. Thomas's Hospital in London, he had gone during the War to the front in France. Of what was happening back in the Frontier to his old father or younger brother, Jabbar was entirely ignorant. After the War ended, it took him six months to obtain embarkation orders, and it was only in March 1920 that he returned to India, with his British wife May. He was made a captain in the Indian Medical Service and posted to Mardan with the Guides Regiment, the very unit that Ghaffar Khan had rejected.

However, when in 1921 Dr Khan Sahib was ordered to proceed to Waziristan for action against the Waziri Pakhtuns, he refused. Resigning his commission, Dr Khan Sahib started private practice in Peshawar. Also a factor in the resignation was the disrespect the British officers' wives apparently showed to May Khan.[12]

To his younger brother in prison Dr Khan Sahib took a message from Peshawar's British officers: if he promised not to tour the Frontier, Badshah Khan would be allowed to run his schools. The deal was turned down.

At the jail in Dera Ismail Khan the superintendent was an Englishman who only knew English, the jailor an aged and inert Muslim, and the deputy jailor, who was the prison's real boss, a Hindu called Gangaram. Badshah Khan described Gangaram as 'a veritable rogue'. In his autobiography he would say about Gangaram: 'In order to extract bribes he made the prisoners fight among themselves and supplied young boys to the prisoners.'[13]

Claiming that he could not admit before Allah that he had asked Badshah Khan, 'a man of God', to work the chakki, the old Muslim jailor quietly brought wheat already ground to Badshah Khan. 'But please don't tell the superintendent', the jailor said. 'I will lose my job.' 'Give me corn to grind', Badshah Khan replied, 'I cannot lie.' The jailor's offer of food and milk from his house was also declined.

Despite an oft-acknowledged struggle with loneliness, the one thing that Badshah Khan did not evidently do during this or any other prison term was to write. While Tilak, Gandhi, Nehru, Abul Kalam Azad, Rajagopalachari, Jivatram Kripalani, Pattabhi Sitaramayya and Narendra Deva were among those who used some of their time in British jails to write, Ghaffar Khan— like Vallabhbhai Patel—did not.

A disdain for intellectuals who wrote at length but failed at crucial moments to act was an attitude he shared with Patel, but there may have been another factor in Badshah Khan's unwillingness to wield in prison the weapon with which others fought loneliness: the pen. For the reflection that writing entails can add emotional pain to the loneliness of a solitary cell.

We have already suspected that accompanying Ghaffar Khan's pain at British injustices against the Pakhtuns was an inner sadness: the loss of a lovely wife and other personal tragedies, to which was now joined the separation from Nambata and from his children. If he took pen to paper and reflected, this pain, more intimate than what the British had inflicted on him and something this stoic man did not wish to face, could burst out of his soul; and perhaps it was this suppressed sorrow that in the first place made isolation so hard for him.

When visible, the moon surely stabbed Ghaffar Khan with reminders of his children, of Nambata and the deceased Mehr Qandh, and of his parents, brother and sisters. Yet he did not dwell on the pangs or transmit them to paper. Neither did he record his extended companionship with his cell's walls, ceiling, floor and insects.

Gangaram sent word that for a small bribe Badshah Khan could be moved out of his solitary cell to a room with other prisoners. Moreover, he would not have to pay the bribe himself; other Pathans would do it for Badshah Khan. Ghaffar Khan's reply was that he would rather furnish security to the British.

One day the jail's British superintendent entered Badshah Khan's cell while he was grinding corn. Pointing to a bowl of cooked vegetable beside him, Ghaffar Khan said to the officer: 'I put this before a cat but it would not touch it, and you give this to human beings.'

The next day Badshah Khan was asked to stop grinding and instead make envelopes in a workshop. In this workshop Badshah Khan found Pakhtun prisoners who 'used to quarrel among themselves and fight over the boys'. According to Ghaffar Khan, he tried to 'dissuade' the prisoners.[14]

Thanks to Badshah Khan's presence in the jail, Gangaram's income from bribes shrank. The deputy jailor's response was to plot Badshah Khan's transfer. He told the superintendent that Badshah Khan was 'creating trouble in the workshop'. Perhaps Gangaram was hinting, among other things, at Badshah Khan's reaction to the 'fight over the boys'. All we know is that the superintendent accepted Gangaram's argument that 'he would not be able to maintain discipline among the prisoners if Badshah Khan was not removed'.

Badshah Khan was in fetters and handcuffs when a police van, screened on all sides, took him from the jail to Dera Ismail Khan's railway station. Ringing his neck was an iron hoop from which dangled a piece of wood bearing his name, prison number and sentence. He was placed in a servants' compartment on a train that steamed southward along the eastern bank of the Indus. At Ghazi Ghat station he was shifted to a boat, ferried across the waters, and taken in a tonga to the jail in Dera Ghazi Khan in the Punjab country.

Badshah Khan liked this prison. 'My fetters were removed when I was taken inside the jail—a very pleasant experience for me.' The superintendent, a Muslim, was 'a decent' man. Though Badshah Khan was placed, with criminals, in the 'C' class, there were many political types in the jail, Muslims, Hindus and Sikhs, with whom he was glad to talk. For the first time, he came 'in close contact with the people of the Punjab'. For the first time also he read the Gita (finding it, at this stage, 'beyond me'), the Granth Sahib and the Bible. 'It was indeed by the great grace of God', Badshah Khan would later say, 'that I was transferred to this jail, otherwise I might not have survived.' He had profited from Gangaram's little triumph.

At the previous jail he had lost fifty-five pounds, contracted scurvy and lumbago, and damaged his teeth. For treatment, the Dera Ghazi Khan superintendent sent Badshah Khan to the jail in Lahore. Here, in the jail office, a Dr Premnath extracted two of Ghaffar Khan's teeth. 'I am a man of means', Badshah Khan said, 'I will pay your fees.' Dr Premnath would have none of it. When Badshah Khan insisted, the doctor replied, 'I cannot match your sacrifice, let me do this much', picked up his bag and went away.

During this Lahore Jail interregnum Badshah Khan met the Congress leader, Lala Lajpat Rai, exchanged views with other Congress and Khilafat activists, and 'studied the holy Qur'an diligently' with a Muslim scholar, Malik Lal Khan. However, this religious scholar 'soon dropped out, accusing me of giving my own interpretation to the text. He was a blind follower of tradition and [could not] appreciate an independent interpretation.'[15]

Here we have a clear indication of the kind of Muslim Ghaffar Khan was in 1922, and no doubt earlier. Sent back to Dera Ghazi Khan, Ghaffar Khan found that Gurdittmal, 'our respected teacher in my barrack' who ended his Hindu prayers with 'shanti, shanti' ('peace, peace'), was 'not a man of peace'. 'He used to lose his temper easily.' But the Sikh prayers impressed Badshah Khan, including the line chanted enthusiastically in Punjabi, 'Let me lose my head, let my body perish, but not my Sikh faith.' He drew the interesting conclusion that

> The Sikhs were more spirited than the Hindus and the Muslims because their scripture, composed in their mother tongue, touched their hearts . . . The Hindus and the Muslims do not understand the meaning of their prayers because they are recited in Sanskrit and Arabic and not in their mother tongue.[16]

Since the Punjab of the early 1920s was witnessing the nonviolent Gur-ka-Bagh struggle for the autonomy and cleansing of Sikh gurdwaras, many of Badshah Khan's prison companions in Dera Ghazi Khan were Sikh satyagrahis, none more impressive than Sardar Kharak Singh, who was often penalized for standing up for prisoners' rights. Badshah Khan would later recall:

> Through a hole in the door of the hospital barrack, we used to have a glimpse of each other. Kharak Singh had become very weak and at times I passed some food for him through the hole. He was a brave man. All the difficulties and miseries did not rob him of his fine sense of humour.[17]

At the peak of one summer Badshah Khan was transferred again, this time to the jail at Mianwali in the Punjab. Here the jailor controlled prisoners by offering them access to a cool spot next to the jail well. 'Our jailor was a queer fellow, he used to take the prisoners to the well for bathing.' Badshah Khan was 'deeply hurt', he would later write, when he noticed that despite insults some prisoners pleaded for permission to visit this spot.[18]

*

Every three months during this sentence, someone from Badshah Khan's family was allowed to visit him and also to receive a letter from him.

> My mother was greatly disturbed by my arrest. Whenever I was allowed to write a letter, once in three months, I wrote to her. She was most keen on visiting me in jail, but she was very old, and Dera Ghazi Khan was far away and the Indus lay between us. To spare her discomfort, I always entreated her not to come for the interview.[19]

She died in 1923, but neither rulers nor family members dared give her favourite son the news. A year later, while still in jail, a stunned Badshah Khan read a reference to her death in a newspaper. After his release his sister would inform him that their dying mother's last question was, 'Where is Ghaffare?'[20]

We are reminded of the delay in Gandhi's learning of his mother's death. Gandhi was twenty-two, returning to Bombay after three years of study in London:

> I was pining to see my mother. I did not know that she was no more . . . The sad news was now given

me . . . My brother had kept me ignorant of her
death, which took place whilst I was still in England.
The news was a severe shock to me. But I must not
dwell upon it . . . Most of my cherished hopes were
shattered. (*Autobiography*)

Neither would Ghaffar Khan 'dwell upon' his
feelings on learning of the death of his mother, whom
he too, at thirty-four, was pining to see. Shortly before
the release was due, Badshah Khan was moved to
Peshawar Jail and produced before the Deputy
Commissioner, who ordered the police to take him at
once to Utmanzai and free him there. The tactic pre-
empted a Pakhtun plan to receive their leader at Attock
Bridge, place him on a horse, and bring him in a
procession to Utmanzai.

The ordeal was over. We do not know whether, in
1924, he suspected the repetitions that lay ahead. But
we know what he told Gandhi in 1931 about his first
imprisonment: 'I am deeply thankful that God imposed
on me that severe discipline in the very beginning of
my career. What would have happened to me if I had
had an easy life?'[21]

*

Utmanzai's schoolboys were the first to sight Badshah
Khan. The cheeks of the thirty-four-year-old Pathan had
hollowed but his blue eyes were proud, determined and
cold. Hundreds came to see him at the hujra at Behram
Khan's house. The old man poured out tea for all of

them and said 'some complimentary things about Englishmen'.[22] After all they had enabled the Pathans to find a leader.

The azad school had flourished during the incarceration of its founder (though in his old age Ghani, who studied and boarded there, would recall its harsh feel, 'scorpions under the mats' and meagre food),[23] and the imprisonment had popularized his cause. Thousands attended the meeting, held on the grounds of the school, to welcome his return. At the meeting he was presented with the title 'Fakhr-e-Afghan', 'Pride of the Pathans'. To those gathered he said:

> Once a pregnant tigress attacked a herd of sheep, gave birth to a cub, and died. The cub grew up among the sheep and adopted their ways and manners. One day a tiger attacked them and discovered that there in the herd of sheep was a tiger cub bleating while running away with the sheep. The tiger separated the cub from the herd and dragged it to a pool in which it could see its own reflection and realize it was a tiger and not a sheep. 'You are a tiger and not a sheep,' the tiger told the cub. 'Do not bleat but roar like a tiger!'
>
> You Pakhtuns are not sheep but tigers. You have been reared in slavery. Don't bleat, roar like a tiger.[24]

From a perch amidst the Frontier's mountains, the returned prisoner lit a fire of hope in the hearts of his people.

*

Meanwhile, the subcontinent and the world had changed. A great Hindu–Muslim front had stunned India's British regime in 1920, 1921, and 1922, but Turkey discarded the khilafat for which India's Muslims had seemed willing to die. With the death of khilafat as an issue, the Muslims no longer needed Hindu support and were inclined to suspect swaraj as an enterprise of and for Hindus. The joint front collapsed, and Hindu–Muslim conflicts erupted in different places, including in the Frontier's Kohat town, which all Hindus vacated.

Differing in their reading of the events in Kohat, Gandhi and the Ali brothers drifted apart, but Badshah Khan saw Hindu–Muslim unity as an inescapable goal. Told by a village cleric that unity with 'idol-worshipping Hindus' was impossible, Ghaffar Khan replied:

If they are idol worshippers, what are we? What is the worship of tombs? How are they any the less devotees of God when I know that they believe in one God? And why do you despair of Hindu–Muslim unity? Look at the fields over there. The grain sowed therein has to remain in the earth for a certain time, then it sprouts and in due time yields hundreds of its kind. The same is the case about every effort in a good cause.[25]

Two years after his son's release, Behram Khan died. Even in his nineties he had ridden horses and bantered with clansmen and with the British. Not long after his father's death, Badshah Khan went with Nambata and his eldest sister on hajj. An attack of flu during the voyage from Karachi nearly killed Badshah Khan, who travelled on deck as all cabins had been booked, but an Arab took him into a cabin and saved his life.

Riding overnight on camels across the desert, the party visited Mecca, Medina, Jeddah, the resort town of Taif, and Jerusalem. It was a wonderful experience for Ghaffar Khan and young Nambata, the mother by now of a girl, Mehr Taj or Tajo, and a younger boy, Abdul Ali or Lali. But in Jerusalem the young wife and mother, who had only recently endured Badshah Khan's three-year absence in prison, fell over the edge of a stairway and died.

A shaken Ghaffar Khan looked back and faced what his prison term had wrought for his wife. It was a factor in his refusal, hereafter, to remarry. He would later say:

After her death I was under pressure from . . . friends and others to marry again. I thought: 'For my pleasure, why should I send a poor woman to trouble? All the time I am courting jail, difficulties and suffering. Why should another person be dragged into all that?' I did not marry again.[26]

Henceforth his bereft children would be chiefly looked after by Dr Khan Sahib and even more by his wife May, the mother herself of a son, Jan, and a daughter, Mariam.

*

Before returning to his children Badshah Khan also visited Lebanon, Syria, and Iraq and saw that the Middle East's urge for freedom from European control was no different from what his Pathans desired. Seeing, too, that the Middle East's nationalists had their Arabic journals, Badshah Khan realized that the Pakhtuns needed something in printed Pashto.

Though their homeland was in the Frontier and in Afghanistan, Pakhtuns had gone to distant parts of the subcontinent and beyond—as workers in dockyards and on ships, as watchmen, as moneylenders, as traders, as farmers, as police officers. They were to be found in South-east Asia, in Australia, in California. With his new monthly journal, *Pakhtun*, Badshah Khan hoped to reach them wherever they were.

Until *Pakhtun* was started in May 1928, the Frontier only had English or Urdu papers. Many Pathans had internalized the view that Pashto or Pakhto was not a 'proper' language, and some mullahs even alleged that Pakhto was the language of hell. (To this Badshah Khan's response was to ask where the mullahs obtained this information.) Urged to subscribe to *Pakhtun*, some educated Pakhtuns demanded to know if there was anything worth reading in Pakhto.

But the forty-four-page monthly, edited by Ghaffar Khan and costing four rupees a year, met a real need. It was political, literary, educational, and reformist. The first issue covered twenty-five subjects in prose and verse, and the opening editorial addressed India and Afghanistan both:

The Pakhtuns, including those in Afghanistan, form one nation. It is unfortunate that in Afghanistan there is no journal published in Pakhto, the language of all Pakhtuns ... Quality journals are not produced overnight. Some of the renowned journals are nearly two centuries old, for example *The Times* of London, which was first published in 1785. We are sorry to say that we are disappointed with our Afghan brethren. [Afghanistan] is a Pakhtun nation by language, tradition and customs, but their state language is Persian.

Pakhtun's topics ranged from threats to tribal Pakhtuns, the visit to India by the Simon Commission and a journey to Europe by King Amanullah to cures for plant diseases. An early piece by 'Nagina, a Pakhtun sister' was blunt:

Except for the Pakhtun, the women have no enemy. He is clever but ardent in suppressing women. Our hands, feet and brains are kept in a state of coma ... O Pakhtun, when you demand your freedom, why do you deny it to women?[27]

Other articles said that the purdah practised by many Muslim women in India 'can never be called Islamic' and asked Pathans to examine 'why we are downtrodden, why we lag behind other nations [and to] search within in the light of Islamic teachings'. Except for the periods when Badshah Khan found himself in jail, the journal would appear for about twenty years.

Many early issues carried these lines by Badshah Khan's son, Ghani, now fifteen years old, whose name, however, was kept out:

If I a slave lie buried in a grave, under a resplendent tombstone,
Respect it not, spit on it.
When I die, and not lie bathed on martyr's blood,
None should his tongue pollute, offering prayers for me.

Impatient for items from the son, his father, Ghani would recall in the future, sometimes sent 'a letter abusing me that I could not write ten lines for my country and that I was a disgrace to the nation and so forth'. The result would be another column entitled 'Nonsense', signed by 'The Mad Philosopher'.[28]

Amanullah, who nursed modernizing ambitions, admired *Pakhtun*, saw that it created pride in the Pakhto language in Afghanistan, and came out with his own *Pakhtun Jagh*. But only nine issues of *Pakhtun Jagh* had been published when Amanullah was forced to leave Afghanistan. Clerics had criticized him as a kafir. Badshah Khan suspected the British, who disliked Amanullah's independence, of encouraging the opposition to the Afghan ruler.

A Tajik freebooter, Habibullah, also known as Bacha-i-Saqao, seized power in Kabul. Badshah Khan said that God was punishing Afghanistan's Pakhtuns for their failure to protect Amanullah's throne, and he also supported the bid by Nadir Khan, a relative of Amanullah, to recover the throne. Badshah Khan raised men, money and sympathy for Nadir Khan; among those he approached for Nadir Khan's cause was the poet Iqbal. Some of the Frontier's tribesmen, especially among the Mahsuds and the Waziris, also backed Nadir Khan's bid, which succeeded. Assassinated in 1933, Nadir Khan was succeeded by his nineteen-year-old son, Zahir Shah.

*

As in 1919, Badshah Khan was again, in 1928-29, inspecting both horizons. Gandhi's moves interested him as much as those of Amanullah and Nadir Khan, and he was also curious about the thinking of the Ali Brothers. In December 1928 he went to Calcutta where Muhammad Ali was presiding over a Khilafat conference and Gandhi overseeing a Congress session. Ghaffar Khan found Muhammad Ali losing his temper at a Punjab delegate. At the Congress gathering, Badshah Khan noticed that Gandhi reacted with apparent enjoyment to interruptions from a haughty young man.

Unable to keep the contrast to himself, Ghaffar Khan blurted it out to Muhammad Ali, adding, 'You are our leader, and we wish you to grow in stature. How nice it would be if you cultivate some tolerance and self-restraint.' The Khilafat leader shouted, 'Oh, wild Pathans have come to teach Muhammad Ali!' Then he got up and left.[29]

At Calcutta, the Congress threw out a challenge to the British. If self-government as a dominion was not conceded to India by end-1929, Congress would (a) raise its goal from dominion status to complete independence and (b) launch a nonviolent defiance towards the achievement of the new goal. The challenge was of considerable interest to Badshah Khan.

In the summer of 1929, Badshah Khan visited Lucknow, where Congress leaders were having a get-together, and met Gandhi and Jawaharlal Nehru for the first time. Nehru, a year older than Badshah Khan, and Dr Khan Sahib had known each other as students in London, and the older brother had given Ghaffar Khan a letter of introduction. Jawaharlal and Ghaffar Khan discussed Afghan affairs, and then Nehru took Ghaffar Khan to Gandhi. Ten years after Gandhi's call for defying Rowlatt nonviolently had attracted Ghaffar Khan, the Pakhtun and the Gujarati had their first face-to-face meeting.

Not much is known about what occurred during this encounter in Lucknow, but it produced a bond and also, possibly, some ideas. After he returned to the Frontier, Badshah Khan received a cable from Nadir Khan announcing his capture of Kabul. To celebrate the restoration of the Pakhtun dynasty, Badshah Khan called for two processions, one setting forth from the north and the other from the south, and for the two to converge at Utmanzai.

A mammoth gathering resulted in Utmanzai. The Badshah Khan who addressed it was fired up—as ten years earlier—by what had happened, or was likely to happen, across both boundaries of his Pakhtun country. Beyond the Khyber, to his north-west, a regime to his liking had obtained power, and beyond the Indus, to his

south-east, preparations for a nonviolent war of
liberation seemed afoot. To his Pakhtuns Ghaffar Khan
spoke of Amanullah as 'the revolutionary king of the
Pakhtuns'. He added:

> There are only two ways for a nation to progress:
> religion and patriotism. Though America and Europe
> have neglected religion, they are full of national
> spirit and have prospered. The cause of our
> degradation is that we are lacking in national and
> religious spirit.
>
> A great revolution is in the offing and you are
> not even aware of it. During my recent visit to the
> subcontinent, I noticed that men and women were
> fully prepared to serve the nation. Leave aside
> women, even our men are not aware of the interests
> of the country and community.
>
> A nation progresses that produces people who
> deny themselves leisure and comfort and stake their
> social status and future prospects for the advancement
> of their nation.
>
> A concern for isolated existence is the way of
> the beasts. The animals create their own shelters,
> choose their mates and rear their progeny. How
> are we superior beings if we do the same? If you
> want the progress and prosperity of your country,
> you should lead a community life instead of an
> individual existence. [30]

There was quite a response, the moment was ripe,
and lines were quickly laid for a Pakhtun organization

that would go beyond the Anjuman-Islah-ul-Afaghina, which was confined to education. The new organization would address the feuds, litigations and enmities among the Pakhtuns, their spirit of vengeance, their tendency towards violence, 'and that too not against aliens but against their own brethren', and their harmful customs, and 'infuse among the Pakhtuns the spirit and consciousness for the service of our community and country in the name of God'.[31] An unconcealed suggestion was that, if necessary, the new body would struggle on behalf of the Pakhtuns.

*

Thus were born, in September 1929, the Khudai Khidmatgars, or the Serving Volunteers of God. While the vast majority of those joining were Muslims, a Hindu, Sikh, or Christian could also become a Khudai Khidmatgar. Through this decision, Badshah Khan gave a greater-than-ethnic territorial definition to Pakhtunness and, simultaneously, acknowledged that non-Muslims too could serve God. It was hoped that the volunteers would be supported by elected jirgas or committees at the village, tappa (cluster of villages), tahsil and district levels and all the way up to a Provincial Jirga, which was seen as an unofficial Pakhtun parliament. One wishing to become a Khudai Khidmatgar had to take the following oath:

> I am a Khudai Khidmatgar, and as God needs no service I shall serve Him by serving His creatures selflessly.

I shall never use violence, I shall not retaliate or take revenge, and I shall forgive anyone who indulges in oppression and excesses against me.

I shall not be a party to any intrigue, family feuds and enmity, and I shall treat every Pakhtun as my brother and comrade.

I shall give up evil customs and practices.

I shall expect no reward for my services. I shall be fearless and be prepared for any sacrifice. [32]

As Badshah Khan and his comrades walked from one village to the next to talk to the Pathans about the Khudai Khidmatgars, their white clothes got dirty in no time. One companion took his shirt, trousers and turban to a village tannery and dipped them in a solution of pine bark, where the clothes became a deep, brownish red. The others followed, the clothes of the party drew attention, and the Khudai Khidmatgars, or the KKs, also became known as the Red Shirts.

The KK volunteers were organized in military fashion, with a Salar-e-Azam or commander-in-chief who nominated officers in the body's units at village, tappa, tahsil and district levels. Badshah Khan appointed the Salar-e-Azam. But neither the commander-in-chief nor his officers nor their men carried any arms, not even a lathi.

This commitment to nonviolence, which was new and significant in the public life of the Frontier province, did not however erase the fact that the KKs had emerged in direct consequence of the forceful crushing, led by Pakhtuns, of a non-Pakhtun attempt to seize the throne in Kabul. In the words of a critical Pakistani admirer of Badshah Khan, 'a violent event in Kabul was celebrated in a nonviolent setting in Utmanzai, giving birth to a nonviolent movement.'[33]

*

Within a few months, at the end of December, the Congress held its annual session in Lahore, on the banks of the Ravi. To this session, where Jawaharlal presided and Gandhi moved a resolution authorizing the All-India Congress Committee to launch civil disobedience for attaining complete independence, Ghaffar Khan took hundreds of delegates from the Frontier. It was the first time that a Congress session had seen a substantial Pathan presence.

At the stroke of midnight on 31 December 1929, the resolution for nonviolent defiance was declared carried and the tricolour raised amid shouts of 'Inquilab Zindabad'. As the Frontier volunteers danced with delight, Jawaharlal donned a Pathan turban and joined them.

Between January and April 1930, Badshah Khan and his unarmed band again walked from village to village in the Pakhtun country amid expectations of an India-wide revolt. KK ranks swelled. Anxiety in the Raj did likewise. Summoning Badshah Khan, the Frontier's Chief Commissioner asked him to stop raising what the Raj saw as a private army. Ghaffar Khan replied that he could not; the nonviolent KKs aimed at social work but their future role depended on the policies of the Raj.

To the bafflement of many, Gandhi announced that the Congress's revolt would begin over the salt tax; led by him, the people of India would pick up, sell or buy salt without paying the tax. Each act would violate the law and invite a prison sentence or a lathi blow, but Indians would not hit back.

The 1930 salt defiance, which caught the world's imagination, was nowhere more resolute than in the Frontier. Aware of Badshah Khan's rising charisma, the British arrested him and several of his colleagues early in the morning of 23 April, when he was on his way to Peshawar from Utmanzai. Thousands surrounded the prison in Charsadda where Badshah Khan was kept, and the city of Peshawar erupted.

That day, in the KK version, 200 to 300 Pathans were killed by British bullets in Peshawar and elsewhere in the Frontier. Armoured cars, horses and machine guns were let loose, and lathis viciously brought down. Yet the KKs and their supporters, who were chased down the streets and lanes of Peshawar, all of them Pathans raised on the code of revenge, did not hit back. Even more dramatically, soldiers of the Raj's Garhwal Rifles refused to obey their officer's order to fire at a crowd of unarmed Pathans. Later the soldiers were court-martialled and given long prison terms, but the Raj's demise had been scripted by *their* nonviolent revolt in Peshawar's Kissa Khwani Bazaar.

The spirit of the Frontier in 1930, and the mix of bafflement and admiration it produced in the British, is conveyed in what an officer called Bacon told Ghani in the late 1930s. Relates Ghani:

He told me, 'Ghani, I was the Assistant Commissioner in Charsadda. The Red Shirts would be brought to me. I had orders to give them each two years rigorous imprisonment. I would say, "Are you a Red Shirt?" They would say yes. "Do you want freedom?" "Yes, I want freedom." "If I release you, will you do it again?" "Yes."'

[Bacon] said, 'I would want to get up and hug him. But instead I would write, "Two years."'[34]

The Peshawar bloodshed drew the older brother, Dr Khan Sahib, into the public gaze. As a doctor he tried to save life and limb, as a Pathan he was horrified that the Guards whom he had once served opened fire on unarmed citizens in Peshawar, and as the brother of the arrested leader he demanded forbearance and restraint from Badshah Khan's followers.

Earlier, in the summer of 1929, Dr Khan Sahib had sent his nephew, Ghani, to England, where the lad stayed 'in a priest's family', friends or relatives, possibly, of the Wigrams. Ghaffar Khan endorsed this plan for his older son.[35]

Repression escalated. *Pakhtun* was banned; Utmanzai was once more targeted and its residents beaten and humiliated; Wali, Badshah Khan's second son, now fourteen and wearing the KK uniform, was threatened and almost killed; and the KK office was burnt down. But KK ranks continued to grow and defiance continued throughout the Frontier, which in consequence was kept under martial law from August 1930 until the following January.

*

However, Badshah Khan was enjoying what he would later call 'a blissful life' in his jail in the town of Gujrat in the Punjab. He liked his companions, who included Dr M.A. Ansari, Dr Saifuddin Kitchlew, Maulana Zafar Ali Khan, and Gandhi's youngest son, Devadas. Ghaffar Khan conducted a Qur'an class while Pandit Jagatram from the Andamans taught the Gita. (Both classes lost students as the months passed, Badshah Khan would afterwards recall.) He joined volleyball sessions and helped with the cooking.

After visitors at permitted interviews told him of the ongoing 'inhuman oppression' in the Frontier, Badshah Khan seems to have asked two of them, Mian Jafar Shah and Abdullah Shah, to obtain help from Muslim League leaders in Lahore, Delhi and Simla. According to Badshah Khan's autobiography, the League leaders were found to be unresponsive, whereas the Congress was willing to back the Pakhtuns. In consequence, the Pathans in Gujrat Jail, led by Badshah Khan, sent a message asking the KKs who were at large to convene their apex body, the Provincial Jirga, to consider joining the Congress. The Jirga met and announced that the KKs had joined the Congress. Fulfilling the Raj's fears, a social reform body had become a political body.

Korejo, Badshah Khan's Pakistani critic, asks how proper it was for Badshah Khan, an enthusiastic participant at the Congress session in Lahore, to approach the League first. The answer perhaps lies in a communiqué sent in May 1930 by the Frontier's Chief Commissioner to the leading khans and tribal chiefs of Peshawar district, about which, in Gujrat Jail's relatively open atmosphere, Badshah Khan would certainly have heard.

Warning the big khans and chiefs that the Congress, which had presented a socialistic programme in Lahore, posed a danger to their landed properties, the Chief Commissioner added that the KKs were the servants not, as they claimed, of God but of Gandhi the Hindu, and also of the atheistic Bolsheviks, whose red colour was sported by the KKs. Recognizing the potential for mischief in the Raj's propaganda, Badshah Khan may have thought it prudent to approach the League first.

According to Badshah Khan's autobiography, following the Jirga's decision to join the Congress, the British sent word to him in Gujrat Jail that all reforms proposed for India could at once apply to the Frontier as well—provided the Pathans disowned the Congress. Many of his Pathan colleagues in Gujrat wanted, it would seem, to grab the offer, but Ghaffar Khan firmly rejected it. The men making or carrying the offer are not named in the autobiography; yet British eagerness to snap the Pathan–Congress link would be evident throughout the 1930s and the 1940s.

When, in January 1931, Gandhi and other Congress leaders detained for their role in the 1930 defiance were released, the Frontier's Chief Commissioner, Sir Steuart Pearson, prevented the discharge of Badshah Khan. However, in talks with Irwin, the Viceroy, Gandhi insisted that Badshah Khan should be treated like other Congress leaders. On 11 March he was let out.

To the accompaniment of Winston Churchill's

famous lament, Gandhi strode up the steps of the Viceregal Palace, parleyed on equal terms with the representative of the king emperor, and helped produce a truce under the so-called Gandhi–Irwin Pact. But the freed Ghaffar Khan was not inclined to be charitable or restrained towards the British. In more than one speech he said:

> One horn of the *firangi* (foreigner) is already broken. Now you arise and get ready to break the other horn. This is your land, but owing to your disunity the *firangis* are occupying it. Your children die of hunger and thirst while their children are enjoying everything they want.[36]

*

How nonviolent was Badshah Khan in 1931? The question was on many minds including Gandhi's. He invited Ghaffar Khan to Bardoli in Gujarat, where, organized by Vallabhbhai Patel, peasants had won a great nonviolent battle in 1928. In Bardoli, Devadas Gandhi, Ghaffar Khan's recent companion in prison and ten years younger, frankly asked Badshah Khan if the latter's nonviolence was not 'mere expediency'. Added Devadas, 'What about the propaganda in the Anglo-Indian press about the Red Shirt plan of a violent offensive against the British?'

He had prized ahimsa for some time, Badshah Khan replied,

but the unparalleled success of the experiment in my province (*a reference, no doubt, to the 1930 events*) has made me a confirmed champion of nonviolence. We know only too well the bitter results of violence from the blood feuds . . . We indeed have an abundance of violence in our natures. It is good in our own interests to take training in nonviolence. Moreover, is not the Pathan amenable only to love and reason? [If you win him,] he will go with you to hell, but you cannot force him even to go to heaven. I want the Pathan to learn to do unto others as he would like to be done by.[37]

Significantly, Badshah Khan linked nonviolence to Islam. At a Bardoli meeting chaired by Kasturba, he said:

There is nothing surprising in a Musalman or a Pathan like me subscribing to nonviolence. It is not a new creed. It was followed fourteen hundred years ago by the Prophet, all the time he was in Mecca . . . But we had so far forgotten it that when Mahatma Gandhi placed it before us we thought he was sponsoring a new creed or a novel weapon . . . [38]

To Badshah Khan, nonviolence, or *adam tashaddud*, the Pakhto expression he favoured, literally meaning 'no violence', was the twin of patience, a virtue stressed again and again in the Qur'an. If nonviolence was Islamic, so too, in Badshah Khan's view, was the freedom struggle:

According to the teachings of the Prophet, jihad is to say the truth to tyrant kings.[39]

The Congress aims at liberating the people from slavery and exploitation. It aims to feed India's hungry millions and to clothe India's naked millions. The Prophet's mission was to free the oppressed, to feed the poor and to clothe the naked. And, therefore, the work of the Congress is nothing but the work of the Prophet.[40]

And he saw Hindu–Muslim unity as fundamental:

There are influences enough to divide us. You in India are familiar with the cry of the Afghan bogy. We have been made familiar of late with the cry of a Hindu rule—a rule of the rich Hindu, of the educated Hindu, of the nationalist Hindu. To those who come to warn me against a Hindu rule, I say, perhaps it may be better to be slaves under a neighbour than under a perfect stranger.[41]

Informed by Irwin's successor, Lord Willingdon, that Ghaffar Khan might be arrested for his outspoken speeches, Gandhi replied that in that case the truce could terminate. He offered to visit the Frontier to assess the scene, or to depute Nehru. When the Viceroy rejected the proposals, Gandhi sent Devadas to the NWFP in the last week of July 1931.

A truck in which Ghaffar Khan and Devadas had left Peshawar for Utmanzai was fired at near Sardaryab Bridge and an occupant was wounded, but only after

Badshah Khan and Devadas had shifted into a friend's car. Ghaffar Khan seemed convinced that the assailant, a well-known dacoit called Kazi, had been 'hired to shoot at us'.[42] After a six-day visit, Devadas reported to the Congress Working Committee of humiliations and torture by the Raj's police, of the Pathans' apparent resolve not to retaliate, and of 'the fullest emphasis on nonviolence'.[43]

Yet Ghaffar Khan's nonviolence coexisted with a strong anti-British emotion. When, in August, Gandhi and Ghaffar Khan found themselves in Simla, along with Patel, the Congress President for that year, and Nehru, to meet Willingdon and other British officials, Badshah Khan refused to meet Howell, Foreign Secretary to the Government of India. At Howell's instance, Gandhi asked Badshah Khan about his refusal. The latter replied: 'I am a weak human being and I do not want to slip walking on a slippery ground.' Roaring with laughter, Gandhi said, 'Don't I meet the *firangis*?' 'You are a Mahatma', said Badshah Khan, who however agreed to meet Howell.

In the event, Badshah Khan liked the conversation with Howell, if only because the official had served in the Frontier. While he was with Howell, the phone rang. Howell said that Emerson, the Home Secretary, wished to meet Badshah Khan. 'I cannot meet him', Badshah Khan replied. 'But his office is right on your way back', said Howell.

Badshah Khan met Emerson, who, from his own account of the meeting, told Ghaffar Khan that 'if it came to a fight, the Government would have no difficulty in dealing with his movement', and also, 'if he wanted a fight he could have a good one.' In his autobiography, Ghaffar Khan calls Emerson 'pompous' and adds, almost implying a link, that the official had 'spent the major part of his career in the Punjab'.[44]

One comment in Emerson's record of the interview, followed by a prophecy, is perhaps of particular interest:

> Whenever I mentioned events in any other province, either by way of illustration or comparison, he at once interrupted, [saying] he was not interested and concerned with the Frontier only. This was very marked, and sooner or later he will certainly split with the Congress.[45]

Despite several indications that Willingdon and his team had no wish to recognize Badshah Khan's place in the Frontier, or concede any significant Indian demand, Gandhi went to England for the Round Table Conference held in the autumn of 1931. He wanted at least to reach the British people. This he did quite effectively but in India the truce collapsed. In Bengal there was violence from the Indian side and repression from the British; in the UP and the Frontier there was strong repression without sufficient provocation.

Economic hardship sharpened the Frontier face-off. Property was seized because land tax was not paid. The KKs were certainly marching and asking fellow Pathans to be ready to defy the government, but they carried no weapons and attacked no one. The Raj, however, was infuriated.

By December, the *Daily Express* of London was linking Badshah Khan with jihad and the Red Shirts with Bolsheviks. Equally colourfully, the *Daily Mail* called the Frontier 'an outpost of the Soviet Republic' and 'the spearhead of an attack on India'. It spoke of 'Russian gold pouring in across the Khyber Pass' and of 'Muslims being armed with Russian weapons'. Their leader, according to the paper, was 'the terrible Abdul Ghaffar Khan, a jailbird and a relentless enemy of the British'.[46]

A Liberal MP, Robert Bernays, visited the Frontier, talked with Badshah Khan, and offered a different assessment. Quoting what Ghaffar Khan had told him ('I do not hate the British; I have received no money from Russia; I teach the Red Shirts to love their neighbours and speak the truth; I am doing my best to teach the gospel of nonviolence to the Muslims.'), Bernays added:

> The impression of him that I recorded in my diary that night is: Abdul Ghaffar Khan is a kindly, gentle and rather lovable man. As well think that old George Lansbury is a dangerous revolutionary.[47]

In his autobiography, dictated years later, Ghaffar Khan would contrast the Frontier's violent upheavals of the 1890s with the nonviolent struggle of the early 1930s:

> The British crushed the violent movement in no time, but the nonviolent movement, in spite of

intense repression, flourished . . . If a Britisher was killed, not only the culprit was punished, but the whole village and entire region suffered for it. The people held the violence and its doer responsible for the repression. In the nonviolent movement *we* courted suffering, and the community did not suffer but benefited. Thus, it won love and sympathy of the people.[48]

Shortly after his rearrest, which took place on Christmas Eve, 1931, a former British missionary, Verrier Elwin, who was a friend of Gandhi's, went to the Frontier and wrote down what people thought of Badshah Khan. A senior British official spoke to him of Badshah Khan as 'that old rascal', while an Afridi in a village fortress told Elwin that Ghaffar Khan was 'no good' because he 'could not shoot'. But 'an English lady who had lived in his family for eight years', as Elwin described her—none other, surely, than May Khan— said to Elwin that Ghaffar Khan was 'a Christ'.[49]

Elwin had met Ghaffar Khan in Bardoli in the summer and thought that 'the very spirit of nonviolence [shone] in his face'. Describing Ghaffar Khan as 'a very competent organizer' and as one whose 'name is usually linked with that of the Mahatma', Elwin added: 'His speeches are more fiery and he has not the Mahatma's power of winning the hearts of his enemies . . . He is an autocrat, essentially a leader.' Badshah Khan reminded him, Elwin went on, 'of Wordsworth's lines on another great highlander':

In him the savage virtue of the race,
Revenge, and all ferocious thoughts were dead.[50]

The 'autocrat' remark should be seen alongside Badshah Khan's frank statements in 1931 that the Pathans needed a single leader who should however be periodically replaced, and also alongside his reaction to a verse in November 1931 that expressed a wish for Badshah Khan to become 'our king':

This wish and this thought of yours is a direct cause of your servitude. You want to cast off the British yoke to fall into my servitude. Please give up this idea of kingship. This country belongs to all Pakhtuns . . . We shall choose our *Mashir* for three years only, and if he proves himself fit for the task, then we may retain him. Otherwise he shall be removed.[51]

The noticeable role of Pakhtun women in the 1930–31 movement (among the women addressing meetings were the sisters of the Khan brothers) was connected to that movement's nonviolence. At a meeting organized by women, in June or July 1931, in the Frontier village of Bhaizai, Badshah Khan said:

Whenever I went to India and saw the national awakening and patriotism of the Hindu and the Parsi women, I used to say to myself, 'Would such a time come when our Pakhtun women would also awake?' . . . Thank God today I see my desire fulfilled.
In the Holy Qur'an you have an equal share with

men. You are today oppressed because we men have ignored the commands of God and the Prophet. Today we are the followers of custom and we oppress you. But thank God we have realized that our gain and loss, progress and downfall, are common.[52]

We may conclude that in 1931 Badshah Khan was blunt, anti-British, charismatic, Islamic, bold, innovative—and nonviolent.

*

In December 1931 he declined a summons from the Frontier's new Chief Commissioner, Sir Ralph Griffith, who then asked his police to produce Ghaffar Khan. The resulting interview seemed cordial enough and even encouraging when Griffith jotted down Badshah Khan's complaints. Three days later, however, on the night of 24 December, Ghaffar Khan and his brother were surprised by the Frontier police and arrested under Regulation 3 of 1818. Also taken into custody that night were Dr Khan Sahib's two sons, Sadullah and Ubeidullah, the sons of Badshah Khan's sisters, several other nephews and cousins, and all committed KKs.

Put, along with Dr Khan Sahib and some others, on a train going east, Ghaffar Khan found that 'a Punjabi police inspector promptly closed the shutters' whenever these were opened. 'Well, young man', Badshah Khan said to him, 'we are not women that you are closing the windows for screening us from public gaze.'

When, after eighteen hours, the train entered the

UP, a British officer opened the door of the prisoners' compartment, invited them to stretch their legs on the platform, and even offered Badshah Khan a glass of liquor. Saying, 'I don't drink', Ghaffar Khan declined, but later he recalled the Briton's 'sympathy and concern' and marked 'the difference between this Englishman and the Punjabi Muslim police officer'.[53]

The prisoners were separated. Ghaffar Khan was taken to the jail in Hazaribagh in Bihar, the older brother to Allahabad, and the latter's sons to two other jails. Placed in a solitary cell, Badshah Khan found this term much harder to endure than the previous one. Though Hazaribagh Jail would soon hold numerous other political prisoners, none was allowed near Badshah Khan's cell:

> I live alone in a third-class barrack. Nobody can come to me, nor can I go to see anybody. There is neither volley-ball nor badminton, nor a letter nor an interview. In my opinion [the British] are taking revenge.[54]

Written five weeks after arrival in Hazaribagh, the letter containing these remarks was addressed by Badshah Khan to the Congress leader, Dr M.A. Ansari, who was in Gujrat Jail, where the two had been companions in 1930. The letter was never delivered. For six months Badshah Khan was not allowed to see a newspaper or receive a letter or a visitor, even though, or possibly because, the British were aware, as an officer of the Raj put it in April 1932, that 'the loneliness of separate confinement' always affected Badshah Khan.[55]

After six months Dr Khan Sahib was brought to Hazaribagh from Allahabad. The brothers walked, cooked, and raised flowers, vegetables and papaya. In a letter not allowed to be sent, Ghaffar Khan claimed that he had grown 'a small, beautiful garden'.[56] But as one wearying month followed another, jail officials thought that the brothers were inclined to be 'irritable' or 'impatient and restless' and less able to hold on to their 'sense of dignity or self-respect'. The brothers' requests for books that could claim their interest and for companions for games were turned down.

In Multan Jail, Ubeidullah, Dr Khan Sahib's son, survived a long hunger strike. The doctor's children by his British wife, May, a boy and a girl, were studying in England. Perceiving, in the phrase of a Government of India note, 'advantages in keeping the son and daughter away from India and free from any contamination', the British provided for the two an allowance of Rs 400 a month, and an additional allowance of Rs 200 for the maintenance of May Khan.[57]

There were no allowances for the younger brother's family. Significantly, Mehr Taj, Ghaffar Khan's daughter, for a spell a boarder in a Murree convent, was also in England, in May Khan's care, an arrangement backed by her father.[58] 'I always told Mehr Taj', Badshah Khan seems to have commented at one point, 'that she was not to allow her brothers to touch her share of any treats.'[59] Ghani, the oldest boy, had gone on from England to a university in Louisiana in the USA to study chemical engineering, though shortage of funds would soon force him to return to the Frontier.

Badshah Khan found the Hazaribagh jailor, 'Chhota Sahib' as the prisoners called him, 'decent and sympathetic'. At times Chhota Sahib permitted the brothers to give a farewell party for a Bihari political prisoner about to be released. On one such occasion, Ghaffar Khan would later recall,

> I served tea and pakodas and my brother served him fried brinjal. Our guest relished the eatables and suddenly burst into laughter. He told me that once a Muslim postman delivered a postcard to him by carefully holding one corner of it. He took it by holding the other corner. And yet his brother made him wash his hand saying, 'You are polluted.'[60]

In another revealing incident, Ghaffar Khan offered a papaya he had grown to a fellow inmate at Hazaribagh, a Bihari Brahmin, who, however,

> would not cut the papaya with my knife, because I was a meat-eater. When I asked him why he was jailed, he replied innocently that he was involved in a murder case.[61]

*

Outside, a great all-India defiance, as widespread and strong in 1932 as it had been in 1930, was suppressed. Though roughly punished before and after imprisonment, the KKs had played a major role and continued to grow.

Badshah Khan would later say, 'The British considered a nonviolent Pathan more dangerous than a violent Pathan, and that is why in 1932 they inflicted heinous acts to goad them to violence. But they failed.'[62]

The Frontier arrests of December 1931 had been followed by the captivity of Gandhi and of every significant Congress leader. Released in the summer of 1933 but ordered not to enter the Frontier province, Gandhi switched his strategy. Until the moment became ripe for another confrontation, he would advise the Congress to suspend disobedience and use the political reforms the British were offering. Also, he would focus on a great Indian liability: the practice of untouchability.

Inside, the Khan brothers followed events as best as they could; they were allowed some newspapers from the autumn of 1932. In August 1934, after he heard that Gandhi was on one of his fasts, Badshah Khan fasted for a week himself. It was the sort of gesture that would popularize an appellation, dating from 1930, that neither the humility nor the independence in Ghaffar Khan could approve of—'the Frontier Gandhi'.

At the end of August 1934, the brothers were released but banned from entering the NWFP or the Punjab. Gandhi and his friend and backer, Jamnalal Bajaj, invited the brothers to Wardha in central India, and Badshah Khan was also asked if he would accept the presidency of the Congress, which was to meet for an annual session in Bombay. Declining, Ghaffar Khan replied, 'I am a soldier, a Khudai Khidmatgar.' He added that there were 'other ways of rendering concrete help' to the Frontier.[63] The Frontier was his primary concern.

Modesty apart, a fear of entanglements beyond the Indus may have dissuaded Badshah Khan.

En route to Wardha, Badshah Khan made strong speeches in Patna, Gaya, and Allahabad, saying that slavery was a curse and that 'when a Pathan child saw an Englishman, it exclaimed, "Oh, you are still here."'[64]

In Wardha, he, Dr Khan Sahib and Gandhi saw a lot of each other during walks, meals and prayer sessions. Often, at Gandhi's instance, Ghaffar Khan, now forty-four, would read from the Qur'an, at times using Gandhi's reading glasses. All, including Gandhi and the Khan brothers, picked up stones from village fields and stored them for use in future construction; and Dr Khan Sahib became a sought-after physician in the Wardha community.

The Khan brothers grew close also to the Bajaj family, hosts in Wardha to Gandhi and his guests, and to Mahadev Desai, Gandhi's secretary. Desai drew the brothers out on their lives and soon produced, to the advantage of contemporaries and future researchers, a valuable little book, *Two Servants of God*.

The Wardha conversations were frank. Gandhi asked Ghaffar Khan whether his sister-in-law May had converted to Islam. 'You will be surprised that I cannot say whether she is a Muslim or a Christian', Badshah Khan replied. 'She was never converted', he added, 'that much I know. And she is at complete liberty to follow her own faith . . . I have never so much as asked her about it.'

'What you say about your brother's wife does surprise me agreeably', Gandhi remarked, adding,

'What would other Muslims say? Many do not think like you in this matter.' Acknowledging that many Muslims disagreed, Badshah Khan said that very few knew the true spirit of Islam. The Holy Qur'an had said that God had sent messengers to all peoples. As far as he was concerned, Hindus, too, were *Ahl-e-Kitab*, or people of the Book. To him the Books named in the Qur'an were illustrative; there could be others.

In the Frontier they had been told, Ghaffar Khan added, that Gandhi had become a communalist, and that his fast over untouchability showed that he was putting Hindus first. But he had 'stoutly refused to countenance any such criticism', Badshah Khan said.[65]

'The brothers' friendship seems to me to be a gift from God', Gandhi would say in a letter.[66] Dr Khan Sahib, however, was candid with Mahadev Desai about his lapses in Islamic observance, adding, 'My brother offers the namaaz on my behalf also.'[67] Struck by what he described as Ghaffar Khan's 'submission or surrender to God', Desai wrote:

I have the privilege of having a number of Muslim friends, true as steel and ready to sacrifice their all for Hindu–Muslim unity, but I do not yet know one who is greater than or even equal to Khan Abdul Ghaffar Khan in the transparent purity and the ascetic severity of his life, combined with extreme tenderness and living faith in God.[68]

We can contrast this with a comment made at about the same time, in Britain's *Morning Post*, by Michael

O'Dwyer, who was the Governor of Punjab when Jallianwala occurred and who had served in the Frontier:

Abdul Ghaffar is in close touch with the hostile Frontier tribes and is the son-in-law of the Haji of Turangzai, who has so often in recent years roused the Mohmands, Afridis and other tribes to attack Peshawar itself . . . The daring revolutionary Abdul [Ghaffar] Khan . . . is known as the Frontier Gandhi, though he openly sneers at Gandhi's nonviolence cant and makes no secret of his intentions to expel the British and organize on the NW Frontier a Communist republic on the Soviet lines.[69]

As Desai would point out, Ghaffar Khan's father-in-law was not the Haji of Turangzai but Sultan Mohammad Khan of Rajjar, a Justice of the Peace and a close friend of British officers.[70]

The brothers informed Gandhi of the hostility they had invited, including in sections of the Punjab's Muslim press, by sending their children abroad for education. According to Desai, the brothers had laughed out the opposition.[71] However, the girls receiving training in a Wardha school created by Gandhi, Bajaj and their associates impressed Ghaffar Khan, who asked Gandhi if Mehr Taj could join the school. At Gandhi's request, his British associate, Madeleine Slade, or Mira Behn, as she was known in India, brought Mehr Taj from England to India.

Barred from the Frontier, Badshah Khan visited Tagore in Santiniketan and Muslim peasants in Bengal, attended the Bombay Congress, and tried to reduce ignorance about the Frontier. In a speech in Nagpada in Bombay, he commented on 'the knowledge of a Congressman', a prison companion, who two years earlier had asked Badshah Khan, 'Is it true that the Pathans suck the blood of human beings?' 'I replied', Ghaffar Khan recalled, 'that it was quite true. Human blood is very delicious, you have never tasted it.'[72]

In Nagpada, apart from again displaying his caustic humour, Badshah Khan also made remarks that the Raj would pounce on. Invited by the Indian Christian Association, Badshah Khan spoke on 27 October 1934 of how much Rev. Wigram had meant to him. His own view, Ghaffar Khan added, was that Christ had come for the poor and the oppressed. He described the April 1930 deaths from police bullets in Peshawar and spoke of repression throughout the Frontier. He said that British police had 'fired bullets, ruined and looted the houses of the people, broken into pieces all the utensils used for drinking tea and eating food'. And he again mentioned the children of the Frontier who, spotting an Englishman, were apt to exclaim, 'You are still here!'[73]

In November Ghaffar Khan went to Delhi and the UP. There, in north India, his youngest son, Abdul Ali, joined him. With Ali, now twelve, he returned, on 5 December, to Wardha, his home for the moment, where, escorted by Mira Behn, Mehr Taj had just arrived from England. Ghani, twenty, and Wali, eighteen, were already in Wardha. After three long years, all four children were with their father. A conversation that

Ghani recalled when he was seventy-five may relate to this period:

> I used to talk to [Gandhi] about my shikaar, about girls. Once he said to Father, 'Have you been bloodthirsty like [Ghani] when you were young?' Father said, 'No, no.' He told him a lie and said, 'I have never shot a bird even.' Because Father used to go for shikaar.[74]

Some grains of salt may be in order here, for a wish to shock was part of the character of Ghani, who, not long after the dream-like reunion in Wardha, had a spell in Tagore's Santiniketan, where a fellow student was Indira, Nehru's daughter, and where would be discovered Ghani's gifts in poetry, painting and sculpture.

Sadly, the Wardha reunion lasted a mere two days. On 7 December, the Superintendent of Police of Wardha, accompanied by a police officer from Bombay, turned up at Gandhi's Satyagraha Ashram, produced a warrant for arrest for sedition under Section 124-A of the Indian Penal Code, and asked for Ghaffar Khan, who was with Gandhi. 'I am ready', Badshah Khan said. Gandhi remarked that if the police chief would not mind, Ghaffar Khan would first see his family, who were in Bajaj's home.

Gandhi walked with Badshah Khan to the police van, which took its prisoner to the Bajaj home. The children were in tears when farewells were made, but not the father. To Jamnalal Bajaj and his wife Jankidevi, Ghaffar Khan said: 'It is all God's doing. He kept me out just for the time He wanted to use me outside. Now I must serve from the inside. What pleases Him pleases me.'[75]

*

This time, in line with the new Congress strategy, defence was offered in the Bombay court, where Badshah Khan was represented by the brilliant lawyer, Bhulabhai Desai.

Case law in British India held that words that brought the government into hatred and contempt were seditious. Badshah Khan told the court that having 'accepted the Congress policy of not seeking arrest and imprisonment at the present moment', he 'had no desire whatsoever to utter words of sedition'. Still, he added, if he had made remarks that others construed as seditious, he was sorry.

H.P. Dastur, the Chief Presidency Magistrate, who was a Parsi, ignored the expression of regret, and he ignored as well the tribute that Badshah Khan had paid in Nagpada to Rev. Wigram. Holding that there was enough in the speech to invite contempt and hatred towards the government, he awarded a sentence of two years' rigorous imprisonment.

But the records of the Raj reveal that plans for Badshah Khan's re-arrest were drawn up from the moment of his release from Hazaribagh, and possibly firmed up following his visit to the Muslims of rural Bengal. 'There is reason to believe that, in particular, he might devote attention to Bengal', reads a confidential note by the Home Secretary, Sir Henry Craik.[76] This note was written after the arrest and in order to provide grounds against an early release, but the records show that re-arrest was being considered right from end-August 1934.[77]

Ghaffar Khan was first sent to Sabarmati Jail in Ahmedabad, where warders were instructed not to speak to the prisoner. He slept on the floor and there was none to talk with, though Badshah Khan derived some amusement from the monkeys that were around. Following a visit to the jail that Gandhi was allowed to make in May 1935, Ghaffar Khan was shifted to a better barrack but could not stomach the food.

Later a cook from Peshawar Jail was brought but he was a TB patient and Badshah Khan felt sure 'the intention was to infect me with tuberculosis.'[78] In August 1935 the prisoner was sent, along with the cook, to Bareilly in the UP, where he bore 'the hot wind that incessantly blows there' and came out in boils in his solitary cell. But the cook was finally removed, and then Badshah Khan was moved to a jail in Almora in the UP hills, where he completed a garden that Jawaharlal Nehru, who had served a term in Almora, had begun.

After nineteen months, towards the end of July 1936, he was released. Part of the five-month remission, he was informed, was due to his efficient gardening. But he was again barred from the Frontier and the Punjab. Rejoining Gandhi in Wardha in the middle of November, he recalled the latest arrest in language that suggests an input from Gandhi:

I certainly do not regard as violence the desire and demand for independence . . . There was nothing violent in my speech. I was charged with sedition which is a statutory crime but is not, on that account, necessarily a violent activity. But I know that if there is violence in me, want of evidence produced by [the government] cannot exculpate me from it. And if there is real nonviolence in me, no amount of evidence that [the government] can produce can make me violent. It is a matter between my Maker and me, for He alone can read men's hearts.[79]

*

It looked, however, as if the new Congress strategy was bearing fruit. The British, on their part, had offered provincial elections with a fairly wide franchise and significant if partial power to provincial legislatures and ministries. Many in the Congress felt disinclined to 'cooperate' in any British scheme, but with Gandhi's backing the Congress agreed to take part in elections that were to be held early in 1937 in provinces across India.

For two reasons the Khan brothers were interested. First, the British had finally conceded the Frontier province's right to have an elected assembly and ministers. Second, after great hesitation, the Raj allowed the Khudai Khidmatgars to contest the Frontier elections. While Dr Khan Sahib could imagine himself as an elected leader, and a useful one, the younger brother wondered about the impact of power and pomp on the discipline of the Khudai Khidmatgars.

Jawaharlal Nehru, president of the Congress in 1936 and 1937, proved the party's star campaigner while Vallabhbhai Patel raised campaign funds and chaired the board that selected candidates. Along with Badshah Khan and Gandhi, Nehru, too, was kept out of the NWFP by the Raj, though Patel was permitted to enter the province for five days.

There was much warmth but not perfect harmony in Ghaffar Khan's relationship with Jawaharlal, who was older by a year. In the autumn of 1931, after the Gandhi–Irwin truce had given way to repression in the Frontier, an offer made by Jawaharlal, who was the Congress general secretary at the time, to raise from Rs 500 to Rs 1,000 the monthly help to the Peshawar Congress Committee from the central office did not go down well with Badshah Khan, who seems to have said:

Panditji, we don't need your money. Why should we take money from you? You carry your load, we shall bear ours. If you want to help us, then build a girls' school and a hospital for our women.[80]

For a while Nehru was put out by what he saw as a proud and prickly reaction, but Ghaffar Khan's suffering and steadfastness stayed in his mind. One night in 1936 he dreamt that Ghaffar Khan was being attacked on all sides, and that he, Jawaharlal, was fighting to defend

Badshah Khan. Nehru woke up exhausted and found
his pillow wet with tears.[81] When, at the end of 1936,
the Congress met for its annual session in the village of
Faizpur in Maharashtra, Jawaharlal referred to Badshah
Khan in his presidential address:

> We offer a cordial welcome to Khan Abdul Ghaffar
> Khan for his own brave self as well as for the sake
> of the people of the Frontier province whom he
> has so effectively and gallantly led in India's struggle
> for freedom. But though he is with us, he may not,
> so the orders of the British Government in India
> run, go back home or enter his own province or
> even the Punjab.[82]

Even without Badshah Khan, and without a visit
by Nehru, the Frontier province sent the Khudai
Khidmatgars, representing the Congress, to power at
the head of a coalition, with nineteen seats of its own in
a house of fifty, including fifteen out of the thirty-six
seats reserved for Muslims. Though the British had
permitted Jinnah, the Muslim League president, to visit
the province in October 1936 and even to meet a
delegation of chiefs from tribal areas closed to Indian
politicians, the League did not win a single seat in the
NWFP. However, several independents, including some
of the big khans, were elected from Muslim
constituencies.

Ominously for the Raj, Khudai Khidmatgar
candidates humbled four titled khans, Sir Sahibzada
Abdul Qayyum (who, before the elections, had been

nominated to serve as the Frontier's First Minister),
Nawab Sir Mohammad Akbar Khan, Nawab Sher Ali
Khan and Khan Bahadur Quli Khan.

A Muslim–Congress alliance ruling the Frontier was
the last thing the Raj desired, and the Governor seems
to have asked at least one independent Sikh MLA, Rao
Sahib Parmanand, who was beholden to the British, not
to support a Khudai Khidmatgar ministry. Encouraged,
however, by another British officer, Lionel Jardine, the
Revenue Commissioner, who asked him 'to go by your
conscience', Parmanand supplied a crucial vote in favour
of the Khudai Khidmatgars.[83]

Congress victories in other provinces were even
more compelling, but was it honourable to assume
office under the British umbrella? It was not until July
and August 1937, after Gandhi had secured a public
commitment from the Viceroy that the Raj would not
interfere in their day-to-day functioning, that Congress-
led ministries took office, replacing caretaker
governments. In Peshawar, Dr Khan Sahib, older brother
and close if independent associate of the 'terrible rebel',
Ghaffar Khan, found himself the premier of the NWFP.

It was no longer possible to keep Badshah Khan out
of the Frontier. At the end of August 1937, after six
years of exile, he returned to the province. To the
mammoth gathering that welcomed him in Peshawar,
he said:

Thank God, I am once again with you to share your
joys. But . . . our happiness is meaningless until we
have achieved our goal of independence . . . As for

my part, let me tell you once again that I will continue to struggle for liberty until we have shaken off the foreign yoke and set up a true people's government in this country.[84]

FOUR

Journey to Freedom
1937–46

Though their influence had spread right across the settled districts of the Frontier (these were, from north to south, Hazara, Mardan, Peshawar, Kohat, Bannu, and Dera Ismail Khan), the Khudai Khidmatgars were strongest in Peshawar and Mardan and weakest in the only Frontier district east of the Indus, Hazara, which was also the sole district where Pakhtuns were in a minority. Also, the KKs were more popular in villages than in towns, and with smaller rather than titled or large-estate Khans.

Dr Khan Sahib's ministry was quick with new legislation. Pakhto became the medium of instruction in primary schools. Agriculturalists were given tax relief. The practice of nominating 'eminent' Pathans to various boards or offices was abandoned and replaced by open competition. The hated Frontier Crimes Regulation was repealed. And new rural primary schools for girls and boys were launched.

Following the KKs' victory at the polls, it was at last possible for Indian leaders to visit the Frontier province. Arriving in October 1937, Jawaharlal Nehru, the Congress President, told a cheering gathering of about a lakh in Peshawar that Badshah Khan was also Fakhr-e-Hind, the Pride of India. In a letter to Rammanohar Lohia, a leader of the Congress socialists, Nehru observed that the Pakhtuns' identification with the Indian freedom struggle was a recent development, occurring 'since the noncooperation movement'. Nehru also recognized that the Pakhtuns 'have a strong feeling of kinship with . . . the border tribes in the semi-independent area beyond India' and 'even with the Afghans proper'.[1]

Badshah Khan's candour was recorded when, in 1938, Mahadev Desai, Gandhi's note-taking aide, visited the Frontier. Badshah Khan told him: 'Pathans will waste any amount of money over entertaining guests, but if you ask them to contribute any hard cash, they will not do so. They are temperamentally incapable of giving any cash.'[2] When Ghaffar Khan and Desai drove past a knot of Afridis, the former commented: '[Among the Afridis] adultery is non-existent, for the penalty is death.' He added:

These Afridis are plain, simple fellows like the Pathan, hospitable to a fault. They speak Pakhtu, and apart from their blood feuds are well organized and close-knit. Why should it be difficult to make up with them? Why should they be bribed or bombed? If we can solve the problem of their bread,

they will live peacefully and amicably. But we are
not allowed to go near them.[3]

For long Ghaffar Khan had felt close to the Afridis
and the other Pakhtun tribes, and wished to integrate
them with the Pathans of the NWFP and of Baluchistan.
Yet no 'settled' Pathan was allowed to enter a tribal
territory without British permission. Apart from three
brief forays, Ghaffar Khan himself had never known a
tribal territory from within. (The three exceptions were
the aborted Bajaur experiment of 1914, his 1919 dash
to the Mohmand territory, when his father chased him
and brought him back, and the fruitless hijrat of 1920,
for which Ghaffar Khan had to cross tribal lands.) The
inability to live with the tribals and enlist them for
fulfilling his vision would vex him all his life.

Desai noticed that the KKs wore red kurtas and
pyjamas while on duty and grey ones, increasingly made
of khadi, the handspun, handwoven cloth popularized
by Gandhi and the Congress, when not. Training the
volunteers was a major goal for Badshah Khan, who
told Desai of a three-day fast he had undertaken because
some KKs had attempted to seize knives and spears from
maulvis who had called Badshah Khan names.[4] At a
Buddhist site in Mardan district, Desai said to Badshah
Khan, 'You are preaching the gospel of ahimsa where
centuries ago the same gospel was preached.' Ghaffar
Khan's response was a silent smile.[5]

He was forty-eight now. Photographs of him from
this time suggest a mountain of a frame, a youth's
strength, a general's ramrod bearing, and a bright kindly

face where a broad smile contradicts deep lines, carved by the bitter waters of captivity, that mark the forehead. The head is getting to be almost completely bald, but the hair still there and on the brow is a lot darker than the beard, which has whitened.

*

Making his first visit to the Frontier in 1938, Gandhi spent a week there in May and then, in the autumn, five more weeks. In July the next year, accompanied by his wife, Kasturba, he made another short visit. We may, in this study of Badshah Khan, spend a little time on what Gandhi said or did in the province, for his interactions there add to our understanding of the Khan brothers, the KKs, the Pakhtuns, and Gandhi himself.

For one thing, Gandhi matched Badshah Khan's candour; the Frontier's air and happenings and the company of the Khan brothers and of the KKs elicited frank as well as revealing remarks from him. In the heart of the Pakhtun country, he contested the notion that the sword was central to Islam:

> I claim to have as much regard in my heart for Islam and other religions as for my own, and I dare say with all the emphasis that I can command that though the sword has been wielded in the history of Islam and that too in the name of religion, Islam was not founded by the sword, nor was its spread due to it.[6]

After an address was presented to him at Peshawar's famed Islamia College, founded in 1908 through the efforts of the civil servant George Roos-Keppel and Sahibzada Sir Abdul Qayyum, Gandhi asked his audience to reflect on the boundaries of their community:

> Islam . . . believes in the brotherhood of man. But you will permit me to point out that it is not the brotherhood of Muslims only but universal brotherhood . . . The Allah of Islam is the same as the God of Christians and the Ishwar of Hindus.[7]

To the province's Hindu and Sikh minorities, troubled by raids and abductions carried out by tribes descending into the settled areas, Gandhi prescribed the duty of self-defence. 'Self-defence is everybody's birthright. I do not want to see a single coward in India', he said in the walled city of Bannu. Yet he also asked the Hindus and Sikhs to realize that the tribesman was 'a human being, just like you and me, and capable of responding to the human touch'.

He had met several tribesmen following his arrival in the province, Gandhi added, and he 'did not find that their nature was essentially different from human nature elsewhere'. Then he challenged the Hindus: 'You are a community of traders. Do not leave out of your traffic that noblest and precious merchandise, love. Give to the tribesmen all the love you are capable of, and you will have theirs in return.'[8]

The Gandhian candour did not spare the Premier, Dr Khan Sahib. Noting that border raids had become more serious since the ministry's assumption of office, and acknowledging that British help in checking the raids was not forthcoming, Gandhi said, 'Unless Dr Khan Sahib can cope with the question of the raids, it might be better for him to tender his resignation.'[9]

At Mardan, where three Sikhs had been killed, Gandhi told the Pakhtuns: 'There were Khudai Khidmatgars in the village . . . It was their duty to catch the culprits. It is their duty to prevent the recurrence of the deed. It is also your duty to befriend the bereaved and to assure the fear-stricken of your sympathy and succour.'[10]

A remark made in Bannu revealed the relationship in Gandhi's mind between the spinning wheel and nonviolence. 'God whispered into my heart', said Gandhi, 'If you want to work through nonviolence, you have to proceed with small things.'[11] A week later, addressing Khudai Khidmatgars in the town of Tank in Dera Ismail Khan district, Gandhi offered an observation that would be quoted often in the future:

A small body of determined spirits fired by an unquenchable faith in their mission can alter the course of history.[12]

Even more interesting were two other statements Gandhi made in the Frontier. One addressed the gender question in the Pakhtun country. Gandhi took an indirect approach, narrating, with great honesty, his personal experiences with Kasturba.

I have disciplined myself sufficiently never to feel angry with the enemy, but I sometimes lose my temper with friends . . . I used to be a tyrant at home . . . I used to let loose my anger at Kasturba. But she bore it all meekly and uncomplainingly. I had a notion that it was her duty to obey me, her lord and master, in everything.

But her unresisting meekness opened my eyes and slowly it began to dawn upon me that I had no such prescriptive right over her. If I wanted her obedience, I had first to persuade her by patient argument. She thus became my teacher in nonviolence. And I dare say, I have not had a more loyal and faithful comrade in life.

I literally used to make life a hell for her. Every other day I would change my residence, prescribe what dress she was to wear. She had been brought up in an orthodox family, where untouchability was observed. Muslims and untouchables used to frequent our house. I made her serve them all, regardless of her innate reluctance.

But she never said 'no'. She was not educated in the usual sense of the term and was simple and unsophisticated. Her guileless simplicity conquered me. You all have wives, mothers and sisters at home. You can take the lesson of nonviolence from them.[13]

Another memorable statement was made at a public meeting in Abbottabad, in the Frontier's Hazara district, on 24 July 1939, on Gandhi's third (and last) visit to the province. By this time, on the eve of the war in

Europe, the Muslim League's line that Indian independence would mean Hindu rule had gained growing acceptance among the subcontinent's Muslims. Gandhi, whose hosts in Abbottabad were Rai Sahib Parmanand, a Sikh member of the Frontier legislature, and his brother Rachpal Singh, spoke from his depths to the Frontier's Muslims, Sikhs, and Hindus:

> If you dissect my heart, you will find that the prayer and spiritual striving for the attainment of Hindu–Muslim unity goes on there unceasingly all the 24 hours without even a moment's interruption whether I am awake or asleep . . . That dream [of Hindu–Muslim unity] has filled my being since the earliest childhood.
>
> The greatest of things in this world are accomplished not through unaided human effort. They come in their own good time. God has His own way of choosing His instruments. Who knows, in spite of my incessant heart prayers, I may not be found worthy for this great work.
>
> We must all keep our loins girt and our lamps well trimmed. We don't know when or on whom His choice may fall. You may not shirk your responsibility by shoving it all on me. Pray for me that my dream may be fulfilled in my life . . . God's ways are more than man's arithmetic.[14]

Throughout all the three visits, Ghaffar Khan was Gandhi's host, guide, and interpreter. Gandhi found his host 'faithful' in his translations and also 'a born orator who speaks with dignity and effect'.[15]

Unwell when he arrived for his second (and longest) visit, Gandhi quickly recovered in the peace and quiet of Utmanzai, on the bank of a stream, with its timber-roofed mud houses standing against an unbroken stretch of dark green fields of maize, sugar cane, legumes and cotton, and orchards of oranges, peaches, plums, grapes, apricots and pears. At Gandhi's insistence, Badshah Khan had arms taken away from the guards protecting the house where Gandhi was staying, but he refused to dismiss the guards.[16]

A drive past Kohat Pass found Badshah Khan 'in raptures over the ravishing beauty of the landscape', but all of a sudden he exclaimed, 'Look, there is Ajab Khan's home.' In 1923, Ajab Khan had abducted a white woman called Mollie Ellis. Ghaffar Khan told Gandhi of Mollie Ellis's testimony that she was unharmed while in Ajab Khan's custody. Pyarelal, another close Gandhi aide, who was travelling with Gandhi and Badshah Khan, recorded that the latter 'believed Ajab Khan to be guiltless and seemed pleased with the fact that Ajab Khan had eluded the British and was "still alive and settled somewhere on the border of Turkistan".'[17]

Some of the routes on which Gandhi was taken were unsafe, but Badshah Khan was confident of his reputation among the 'wild' tribals. Before setting off on one risky stretch, Badshah Khan told his son Wali, now twenty-three, who was driving: 'If you hear somebody shout out "Stop!", brake at once. Nobody will touch us if they know who we are. But if you try to rush past, you may hear a shot ring out after you.'[18]

During Gandhi's travels across the province, KKs were posted along the route at regular intervals, villages were festooned with arches, and tribal Pathans often stood on perches to watch him. Despite Badshah Khan's, and Gandhi's, pleas, gifts were given. An old Khan stopped the travellers and presented Gandhi with a large coat of handspun wool. Saying he had no means of carrying the gift, Gandhi asked the Khan to keep it until winter, 'when I shall return'. 'Keep it as my property', Gandhi added, making everyone 'shake with laughter'.[19]

When the party approached a village near Utmanzai, Ghaffar Khan said: 'This is Turangzai, the home of the famous Haji. He was a brave soul. The British spread all kinds of stories about him. I was described as the Haji's son-in-law by Sir Michael O'Dwyer.'[20] Everywhere Gandhi spent long periods with KK groups, listening to them, and also advising them. They were asked to conquer idleness, learn punctuality and crafts, and, as Gandhi put it in Tank, 'to become a living wall of protection to your (Hindu and Sikh) neighbours'.[21]

Probed by Gandhi, some KK officers claimed that even if Badshah Khan turned away from nonviolence, they would not. Gandhi asked them to be sure that this was indeed their stand. If they were not convinced, they should revert to violence. 'It was much better for them to be brave soldiers in arms than to be disarmed and cowardly.'[22]

When a Khidmatgar admitted that he would depart from nonviolence in case of 'abuse of their revered leaders', Gandhi said he was reminded of his turn-of-the-century Pathan comrades in South Africa. 'I know

it is no joke for a Pathan to take an affront lying low',
Gandhi added. He told the KKs that they could command
an obedience from love greater than the obedience from
fear extorted by the officers of Hitler and Mussolini.[23]

We have a record of some of the Frontier
conversations between Gandhi and Ghaffar Khan. In
October 1938 Gandhi said to Ghaffar Khan:

> Unless we can develop the capacity to stop these
> Frontier raids without the help of the police and
> the military, it is no use Congress retaining power.
>
> For years, ever since we met each other, it has
> been a pet dream of mine to visit the tribal areas,
> go right up to Kabul, mix with the trans-border
> tribes and try to understand their psychology. Why
> should we not go forth together, present to them
> our viewpoint and establish with the tribesmen a
> bond of friendship and sympathy?[24]

The remark suggests, among other things, that the
border areas and Afghanistan were probably discussed
when the two first met in Lucknow in 1929. Now, ten
years later, Badshah Khan said to his guest, referring to
the Frontier province:

> This land, so rich in fruit and grain, might well have
> been a smiling little Eden upon this earth, but it
> today has fallen under a blight. Violence has been
> the real bane . . . It shattered our solidarity and
> tore us with wretched internal feuds.
>
> The entire strength of the Pathan is today spent

in thinking how to cut the throat of his brother . . .
The nonviolent movement is the greatest boon that
God has sent us. I say this from experience of the
miraculous transformation that even the little
measure of nonviolence that we have attained has
wrought in our midst.

We used to be so timid and indolent. The sight
of an Englishman would frighten us. [Our]
movement has instilled fresh life into us and made
us more industrious. We have shed our fear and
are no longer afraid of an Englishman or for that
matter of any man. Englishmen are afraid of our
nonviolence. A nonviolent Pathan, they say, is more
dangerous than a violent Pathan.

'I have been accused', Ghaffar Khan told Gandhi,
'of having a lashkar of one lakh of Khudai Khidmatgars
to help the Hindus to subdue the Muslim population!'
He would refute the gross libel, he said, not by rebuttal
but by letting his people see his work.[25]

When, in November 1938, the two parted at Taxila,
'our eyes were wet', Gandhi recorded in an article in
Harijan.[26] Earlier he had spoken at a Peshawar public
meeting of

the wonderful and affectionate allegiance of the
people to [Badshah Khan] as their general . . . Not
only the Khudai Khidmatgars, but I noticed
wherever I went that every man, woman and child
knew him and loved him. They greeted him most
familiarly. His touch seemed to soothe them.

[Badshah Khan] was most gentle to whoever approached him. The obedience of the Khudai Khidmatgars was unquestioned. All this has filled me with boundless joy.[27]

We may stay, for a moment, with this picture of Ghaffar Khan's 'gentleness' and warmth, which the tide of his blunt statements can easily erase. The 'record' of his life is replete with the latter, with one harsh if truthful remark following, in endless sequence, another candid comment. His warmth, expressed in his eyes, touch and voice rather than in what he said, was less often 'recorded', though it was invariably felt by the recipient. This warmth or gentleness is the unrecorded 'given' of the Badshah Khan story, a reality to be remembered at its beginning, middle, and end. Also to be remembered, however, is the sense in his children and grandchildren that he suppressed his affection for the family. Perhaps one tap had to be turned off if another was to flow freely.

*

As Premier, Dr Khan Sahib commanded the provincial police while his younger brother led the KKs. The contrast between the brothers—the younger one a rebel, an idealist, a widower and, for all his dislike of solitary confinement, a loner, the other an irreverent, gregarious, and pragmatic doctor with two wives, one of them British—seemed sharpened by Dr Khan Sahib's elevation to the top of what was after all a British-created establishment.

Badshah Khan's egalitarianism, and the KK platform, obliged the older brother to abolish the honorific titles and nominated appointments with which the British had placated the province's big khans and landed aristocracy. The British Governor withheld assent for some of the equalizing measures and invited KK displeasure, but influential rural elements were alienated by the KK ministry's intentions.

A picture of the relationship between the brothers at this time has been provided by Pritam Pal Singh, later a senior officer in the Indian army. Visiting the Abbottabad home of Singh's MLA uncle Parmanand, Dr Khan Sahib seems to have asked, referring to Ghaffar Khan, '*Mera bhai kidhar hai?*' ('Where is my brother?'), using in Hindustani/Urdu the natural form preferred by the Pakhtuns. At this Parmanand said, offering the politer construction, 'You mean "*Mere bhai kidhar hain?*"'

'But he is younger than me', Dr Khan Sahib replied. 'Younger in age, no doubt', said Parmanand. By this time Ghaffar Khan had joined them, and the older brother said, '*Mere bhai idhar hain*', this time using the respectful form for 'My brother is here'. According to Pritam Pal Singh, who was present, 'the eyes of both brothers became wet.' But Dr Khan Sahib may have also smiled.[28]

Dr Khan Sahib's tightrope exercise called for keeping faith with the Pakhtuns without offending the British beyond a limit. Hitler's war terminated the exercise. Without consulting Indian political leaders, the Viceroy declared that India was at war with Germany and demanded the compliance of provincial ministries.

When the Congress asked if Indian independence would follow the end of the war, the British offered no clear reply, whereupon all Congress ministries resigned, including Dr Khan Sahib's in Peshawar. A bitter blow had struck Dr Khan Sahib and his wife May by this time—their young son Jan died of jaundice.

At Jinnah's urging, League leaders in the Frontier attempted to form a ministry to replace Dr Khan Sahib's, but the legislators refused to back it, and from November 1939 to 1943 the province remained under Governor's rule. It does not seem that Badshah Khan regretted the departure of the KKs from power. At a March 1940 meeting of the Congress Working Committee, of which he was a member, he said: 'It is astounding the amount of corruption I saw about me when we came to possess a little power.'[29]

More than one war was now being fought. The British were fighting the Germans, the Congress was fighting the British, and the Muslim League was fighting the Congress. In March 1940, in a watershed move, the Muslim League asked for a separate Muslim homeland on the subcontinent, Pakistan. In the womb of this demand lay a fourth tension, Pakhtuns versus the Punjab, which, given its size and numbers, would dominate any future Pakistan.

The war and its dilemmas, including the Pakistan demand, strained Congress unity. Led by Rajagopalachari from Madras and Vallabhbhai Patel from Gujarat, both of whom argued that despite British control a share in office would be of value, a Congress section sought accommodation with the British in the summer of 1940.

Gandhi asked this section to go ahead and try, but not with his backing. He did not see how he, with his commitment to nonviolence, could support a war; and he did not think the British were going to let the Congress have a dignified share.

Ghaffar Khan agreed with Gandhi's position, and when, following the lead of Rajagopalachari and Patel, the Congress decided to explore a compromise with the British, he resigned from the Congress and its Working Committee. He did not expect the British to respond positively to the Congress offer, and he was troubled by the suggestion that the Congress was condoning violence:

> I should like to make it clear that the nonviolence I have believed in and preached to my brethren of the Khudai Khidmatgars is much wider. It affects all our life . . .
>
> Unless we learn this lesson of nonviolence fully, we shall never do away with the deadly feuds which have been the curse of the people of the Frontier. Since we took to nonviolence and the Khudai Khidmatgars pledged themselves to it, we have largely succeeded in ending the feuds. Nonviolence has added greatly to the courage of the Pathans . . . Because the Pathans were previously addicted to violence far more than others, they have profited by nonviolence much more.
>
> Khudai Khidmatgars must therefore be what our name implies—pure servants of God and humanity—by laying down our lives and never taking any life.[30]

Commented Gandhi:

> [Badshah Khan] is a Pathan and a Pathan may be
> said to be born with a rifle or a sword in his hand.
> But [Badshah Khan] deliberately asked his Khudai
> Khidmatgars to shed all weapons when he asked
> them to join the satyagraha against the Rowlatt Act.
> He saw that his deliberate giving up of the weapons
> of violence had a magical effect.
>
> It was the only remedy for the blood feuds which
> were handed down from sire to son and which had
> become part of the normal life of a Pathan. They
> had decimated numerous families and nonviolence
> seemed to Khan Saheb to have come as longed for
> salvation. The violent blood feuds would otherwise
> have no end and would spell the end of the
> Pathans.[31]

Out of power and out of the war, the KKs needed
an agenda. Badshah Khan offered them a constructive
programme. To train Pakhtuns in village industries,
including spinning and weaving khaddar, he opened a
centre in Sardaryab, which lay between Charsadda and
Peshawar. But he rejoined the Congress when the British
rejected the Congress overtures, and he and Dr Khan
Sahib associated themselves with the campaign of
individual civil disobedience (ICD) that the Congress
carried out from the end of 1940.

Designed to demonstrate opposition to British rule
without embarrassing the British in their war effort,
ICD sent about 25,000 Indians to prison in 1940 and

1941. *Pakhtun* suspended publication and Dr Khan Sahib courted arrest, but he was released within hours.

Ghaffar Khan conducted camps in Sardaryab, including a large one in November 1941, when about 500 persons lived for a week in 'little tents without the side flaps', ate nan, dal and vegetables, and joined in spinning and in cleaning adjoining places, including police stations. Most participants were Pakhtuns, but some also came from Kashmir, the Punjab and Baluchistan, and twenty Hindus took part, as did two women.

By this time Germany had invaded the Soviet Union, and in the following month, December 1941, Japan attacked Pearl Harbour and began its sweep across the Pacific. Once more Rajagopalachari argued that the British, now under greater pressure, would respond to a fresh Congress offer; once more Ghaffar Khan and Gandhi disagreed; once more the British proved less than willing.

Elsewhere in Asia, the British were in retreat. Would they, if it came to that, leave India to the Japanese? Would Churchill, the British prime minister, divide India, as Jinnah was demanding he should, to Churchill's apparent approval? Would India turn to Subhas Bose, who had escaped from detention in 1941 and who was trying to liberate India with the help of Japanese and German arms?

To the swirling events of 1942, which threatened his vision of a free, united, democratic and nonviolent India, Gandhi responded with a new call: the British should 'Quit India'. He did not think they would quit, but the call would restore his vision to centre stage. As soon as the Congress endorsed Gandhi's call, in a meeting in Bombay in August 1942, he and all other leaders present were clapped in jail. But the Indian people responded massively, even if not always nonviolently, to the 'Quit India' cry.

In 1930 and the years immediately following, the Frontier had spectacularly led the Indian defiance. With the Quit India movement in 1942, the Frontier's contribution was significant but not dramatic. There were several reasons for this.

For one thing, Badshah Khan's disagreement with the Congress in 1940 and in early 1942 had weakened the KKs' links with the all-India Congress. For another, Badshah Khan had to bear in mind the Muslim League's charge that Quit India was a Hindu movement. Third, some of Quit India's sting in the Frontier was removed by the British policy of quickly releasing many of the Pakhtuns it had arrested. Fourth, Quit India had to compete with the opportunities for military recruitment that the war offered to the Pathans. A part was also played, finally, by propaganda against some marriages in the brothers' families.

In 1939, Mariam, Dr Khan Sahib's daughter by his British wife, had married Jaswant Singh, a young air force officer from a family of Sikhs converted to Christianity, and Badshah Khan's son Ghani, employed as a technical manager in a sugar mill in the UP, had married Roshan, daughter of Faridoon Rustamji, a Parsi who was a senior figure in the administration of the Nizam of Hyderabad. It was easy for foes to allege a dilution in the Khan brothers' Islam.[32]

For unspecified 'local' reasons[33] Ghaffar Khan did not attend the Bombay meeting of the Congress, which meant that he was not one of those immediately arrested. However, he agreed to lead Quit India activities in the Frontier.

Unlike some Quit India commanders elsewhere in the land, Badshah Khan was determined to keep the stir peaceful, for, apart from anything else, violence would expose the Pakhtuns to greater repression.[34] Firmly opposing proposals to cut telephone wires or railway lines, he first organized the picketing of liquor shops and then, in September, authorized the disciplined recitation of the Quit India message to the secretariat, schools and police stations.

Confined to the Frontier, this unique Quit India style, as well as Badshah Khan's absence from the Bombay meeting, revealed his and the KKs' independence from any central Congress strategies, an autonomy born of an instinctive understanding that the interests of the KKs and the all-India Congress would not always coincide. Even so, the province sent about 6,000 Pathans to British prisons in 1942, out of an all-India total of roughly 60,000, an impressive proportion.

Wearing a red KK shirt and accompanied by a group of KKs, Dr Khan Sahib, now sixty, entered the government offices he had presided over and addressed the staff on Quit India. Another former minister, Qazi Ataullah, led a KK batch that went to local schools, and a third batch took the message to Peshawar's police stations. Later in the month, larger KK batches raided government offices, inviting arrest.

On 27 October, Badshah Khan walked from Charsadda, with fifty KKs, to raid the district court at Mardan. On the way they spoke to villagers and prayed with them. The police ordered them to stop before entering Mardan. Refusing, they kept marching with their hands locked together. 'After some difficulty', the Chief Secretary wrote, Badshah Khan was arrested. According to this officer, Badshah Khan 'fought violently and resisted every effort to remove him' into the police car. Badshah Khan's account, dictated in the 1960s, reads: 'The police beat us mercilessly with lathis. A petty official, Khushdil Khan, beat me and broke two of my ribs. My clothes were bespattered with blood.'[35]

We may pause here for a quick reflection on the recollections of earlier years, frequently cited in this study, that Badshah Khan dictated in Kabul in 1965, when he was seventy-five, for the benefit of his faithful and diligent biographer, D.G. Tendulkar. The man who jotted down the recollections was K.B. Narang, a Pakhto-knowing Khudai Khidmatgar, Hindu by religion, who had been a member of the Frontier legislature and who later published the recollections as Badshah Khan's autobiography. A comparison, where possible, with contemporary documents suggests that in many instances these recollections are remarkably accurate. Yet some caution is in order, for the memories of no human being can remain wholly untouched by the impact of Time.

*

Another long spell in detention followed. For altogether two-and-a-half years, Ghaffar Khan was kept in jails in Abbottabad and Haripur in Hazara district. About this period Badshah Khan would later say, 'Except in the early days of the [Quit India] movement, the British Government, though hostile to me, did not insult or inflict injury on me.'

The 1937–39 stint of Dr Khan Sahib's KK ministry, which several British officers had served, had produced some links between Badshah Khan and the British. We may also suspect that Badshah Khan's attitude towards British officers in the Frontier in the early 1940s was influenced by his awareness that they could affect the developing clash between him and the Muslim League. On their part the British desired an increase in Badshah Khan's autonomy vis-à-vis the Congress.

Ghaffar Khan, for a portion of this time in prison, was permitted the company of his son Wali. Badshah Khan and other prisoners were allowed to make rope for charpoys. 'Many of us', he would later write, 'earned a good sum of money from it and sent it to our centre at Sardaryab.'[36] He also reared hens. Literacy classes were held for illiterate KKs, and the Qur'an and the Gita were read. On Sundays there was scope for 'talks, discussions and story-telling', with Ghaffar Khan dwelling on the lives of two of the earliest Khalifas, Abu Bakr and Omar.

Recalling this period later, Badshah Khan would claim that he made some impact on Colonel Smith, the Inspector General of the province's prisons:

A quick-tempered pakka sahib, he was deeply prejudiced against the KKs. He once even had one KK shot dead inside a locked chakki-cell. During one of his visits of inspection, he came to Haripur prison.

I had reared some poultry in my yard. The birds used to come and sit on my lap. Sometimes they perched on my back and head and shoulders. Colonel Smith witnessed all this from behind me . . . After some time he appeared before me and said, 'Good morning, Khan Saheb, what is all this?' 'Just what you see,' I answered . . .

I explained to him that what he had witnessed was a small illustration of the power of love. 'See how they respond to a little affection!' My remarks plunged him into deep thought. For a while he stood still and uttered not a word. After that, though our movement continued, he was a different man . . .

He had a soft corner for me. Although haughty, he was a man of character. He used to say that he would not live a single day in our land if Pakistan became a reality. True to his word, he retired from service and returned home immediately after Pakistan was formed.[37]

It was not until March 1945 that Ghaffar Khan was released. By this time his brother was back as Premier, replacing Aurangzeb Khan, whose Muslim League ministry, installed in May 1943 when Badshah Khan and other KK leaders were in prison, lost the legislators' confidence in March 1945.

As a Pakistani scholar puts it, 'incompetence, factionalism and corruption' had hurt the Aurangzeb Khan ministry.[38] 'The name of the Muslim League administration is simply mud nowadays over the scandalous way in which they buy votes', Governor Cunningham had observed a year earlier.[39] Released in the summer of 1944, Gandhi supported Dr Khan Sahib's bid to return to office. Three Muslim League MLAs joined Dr Khan Sahib's backers in voting out the Aurangzeb Khan ministry.

*

The freed Ghaffar Khan saw an altered India. Most seriously for him, the Muslim League had made much headway, and a high-level conference held in Simla in the summer of 1945 disclosed that India's British rulers welcomed this change.

At this conference, which was preceded by the release of Gandhi and the Congress Working Committee, Gandhi, Azad, and Nehru accepted Viceroy Wavell's proposal of an interim council composed largely of nominees of the Congress and the League. But Jinnah rejected the proposal, insisting that the League alone could name Muslims to the suggested council. The Congress, he declared, was only a Hindu body. Present in Simla as the Frontier's Premier, Dr Khan Sahib asked, 'I am a Congressman. Am I a Hindu or a Muslim?'[40]

It was a question the British ignored. Though some British Governors advised Wavell, the Viceroy, to go ahead with Congress nominees and give Jinnah time to send his team, Wavell, supported by London, announced that his effort for a new council had failed, signalling that without Jinnah's assent the British would not transfer power to anyone in India.

But the world was changing too. Germany and Japan were about to surrender, and, two weeks after the Simla talks ended, British voters sent their victorious leader, Churchill, out of office. The new Labour government ordered fresh elections for a central Indian legislature and for the provinces.

Ghaffar Khan was not stirred when new elections were called in the Frontier. His KK associates had not coped brilliantly with the snares of office, and giving all his energies to help them return to power was hardly an exciting prospect. He would return to his constructive work and try to build a non-corrupt leadership among the KKs.

For part of the autumn in 1945 he went to Bombay to be with Gandhi. To Gandhi, who on his 1938 and 1939 visits had voiced doubts about the KKs' commitment to nonviolence, Badshah Khan was able to point out—with, we may assume, some pleasure— that whereas Quit India had seen a good deal of violence in Maharashtra, Bihar, and elsewhere, the stir had remained completely nonviolent in the Frontier. Interviewed by Haridev Sharma in Kabul in 1968, Badshah Khan would recall these conversations with Gandhi:

After Quit India and Gandhiji's release, I met him and said to him: 'We Pathans have all the instruments for violence. Indians don't keep those weapons. For a long time you were exhorting Indians to take to nonviolence. Our campaign (for nonviolence) is recent. Why then was violence in other parts of India greater than in the Frontier?' Gandhiji laughed and said: 'Look, nonviolence is not for cowards. It is for the brave. Those Pathans [are] brave. They refrained from violence and remained steadfast for nonviolence.'[41]

In public utterances in Bombay, Ghaffar Khan repeated his assessment that while the British 'could suppress violence ruthlessly', nonviolence 'stunned' them, and he noted also that 'in spite of their armed might', Germany and Japan had failed.[42]

What apparently changed Ghaffar Khan's decision in respect of the elections was the evidence of British support for the Muslim League. Westernized society ladies, girl students influenced by such ladies, and even, it would seem, some Englishwomen asked for votes for the League. 'When I saw Englishmen and Englishwomen actively participating in the election, I changed my mind, and for one month before the voting I plunged into the campaign,' he would later recall.[43]

About a fifth of the population was franchised for this election. Polling took place in the last week of January and the first two weeks of February 1946. Jinnah campaigned on behalf of the League and said, 'Every vote in favour of a Muslim League candidate means Pakistan. Every vote against a Muslim League candidate means Hindu Raj.'[44]

As Cunningham, the Governor, would privately concede, most Muslim officials in the NWFP harboured 'strong League sympathies'.[45] Even so, when votes were counted the Congress (or the KKs) had won thirty out of a total of fifty seats and the Muslim League had won seventeen. The Congress tally included nineteen Muslim seats (out of thirty-eight) and eleven out of twelve minority seats. One went to the Akali Dal. (In the NWFP and elsewhere, a system of weightage gave minorities a greater-than-proportionate share.) The Congress did not contest eleven Muslim seats in non-Pakhtun areas where it saw little prospect of winning, and the League emerged as the choice of urban and non-Pakhtun Muslims.

The Congress had won by stressing Pakhtun nationalism and social and economic issues, and because of Badshah Khan's ardent campaigning—'by utilizing the charisma of Badshah Khan', as opponents would afterwards charge.[46] On the other hand, election posters in Hazara, where non-Pakhtun Muslims were a majority, had proclaimed, 'This election is for Pakistan.'[47]

The Pakistan slogan did not move the Pathan. As Cunningham would say to Wavell, the Viceroy: 'The Pakistan cry has little reality to the average Pathan villager, to whom the suggestion of Hindu domination is only laughable.'[48] Cunningham's successor, Olaf Caroe, made another noteworthy remark. After meeting Dr Khan Sahib, who was re-elected as the head of the provincial government, Caroe wrote to Wavell on 9 March 1946: 'Dr Khan Sahib is as impressive as ever; in fact I think he is the most impressive Indian I have ever met.'[49]

The KKs were back in power in the Frontier, and for the subcontinent as a whole independence seemed near at hand. But clouds were gathering to challenge the sun that rose brightly over Utmanzai, Charsadda, and Peshawar in the early spring of 1946.

In his forties
(Photo: D.G. Tendulkar Collection, NMML, New Delhi)

'A small body of determined spirits . . . can alter the course of history.' Gandhi in the NWFP, 1938.
(Photo: D.G. Tendulkar Collection, NMML, New Delhi)

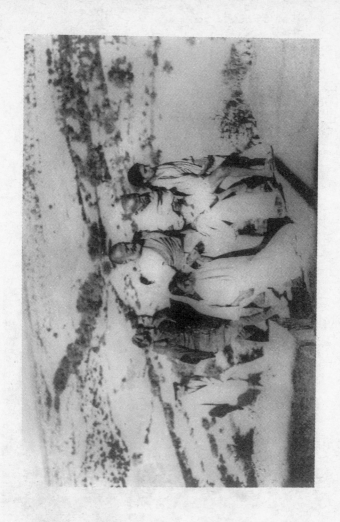

Gandhi's host, guide and interpreter in the Frontier. To
Ghaffar Khan's left, Prabhavati, wife of Jayaprakash
Narayan; to Gandhi's right, Sushila Nayar.
(Photo: D.G. Tendulkar Collection, NMML, New Delhi)

With Jawaharlal Nehru in 1946
(Photo: Mohd Yunus, NMML, New Delhi)

FIVE

Terminus Pakistan
1946–47

One man who looked expectantly at the clouds was Khan Abdul Qaiyum Khan of Peshawar city, at times called Qaiyum Khan 'Kashmiri' because of his origins in that province. A London-educated lawyer and an ally for years of the Khan brothers, Qaiyum Khan had only recently written a book called *Gold and Guns on the Pathan Frontier* in which, in a preface dated 31 March 1945, he highly praised the brothers, the Congress and Hindu–Muslim unity, and criticized the Muslim League. Later in 1945, however, he defected and joined the League.[1]

Like some other Muslims on the subcontinent, Qaiyum Khan sensed what was happening and switched his loyalties. The Pakhtuns as a whole had not done so. Even in the Punjab, despite the Muslim League's greater success there with Muslim voters, it was not the town-oriented League but the pro-farmer Unionist Party, led by Khizr Hyat Khan, that, in coalition with the Akalis and the Congress, found itself in office. And in Sindh, too, the League was having a hard time forming a government. Yet the assembly elections, central and provincial, had sent a message of polarization; except in the Pakhtun country, the League commanded a clear majority of the Muslim vote, while the Congress pulled the Hindu vote. Quickly in Muslim-majority Bengal, and before long in Muslim-majority Sindh, the League formed a government, and the Congress did likewise in most of the other provinces.

In a year and a half, Qaiyum Khan would prove correct in his calculation that the Punjab's Unionists and the Frontier's KKs too would have to acknowledge the rising tide of political Islam. But this was not yet the writing on the wall when, at the end of March 1946, Dr Khan Sahib was invited to New Delhi to meet three members, no less, of the British Cabinet and the Viceroy.

Evidently anxious to resolve the 'India' problem, Britain's new Labour government had flown Lord Pethick Lawrence, the Secretary of State for India, Sir Stafford Cripps, President of the Board of Trade, and Lord A.V. Alexander, First Lord of the Admiralty, to Delhi to talk with the subcontinent's political leaders. The three men plus the Viceroy, Lord Wavell, comprised Britain's Cabinet Mission that stayed in India three months, no less, and authored the seemingly promising and in the end unworkable Plans of 16 May and 16 June 1946.

Before going into these Plans we may look at some candid and doubtless biased pictures, drawn in British diaries, of the Khan brothers during the 1946 negotiations. Thus Wavell wrote about Dr Khan Sahib, who, on 1 April, was the first Indian politician to be interviewed by the Mission, that:

He had not obviously thought out the problems of Pakistan and refused to consider its possibility . . . Nor had he considered what Hindu domination at the centre might entail. He talked in fact entirely from the provincial angle, as if the Pathans were a separate nation living in Pathanistan.[2]

After starting in New Delhi, the talks shifted to the cooler air of Simla, where Badshah Khan was one of four Congress representatives, the other three being Abul Kalam Azad, whose term as the Congress president was about to end, Jawaharlal Nehru, who would take over from Azad, and Vallabhbhai Patel, the strongest figure within the party. Also associated with the Congress team, as an adviser, was Gandhi. The Muslim League group, led by Jinnah, included Abdur Rab Nishtar from the Frontier.

Whether or not enthusiastic about joining the Simla talks, Badshah Khan had not been eager for the KKs to form the Frontier ministry. Though the Muslim League had been defeated, the 'issues' of 'Islam versus Kafirs' and 'mosque versus temple' raised by the League had deeply troubled him, and he had also been 'disgusted' to see 'British authorities and their henchmen put all their weight on the side of the Muslim League'.[3] He did not expect the province's British officers to cooperate with a KK ministry.

His distrust was fully reciprocated by the British. Writing in his diary after meeting Badshah Khan in Simla, Wavell called him 'large, rugged, bearded, obviously hostile, silent, in rough khadi . . . , a stupid but obstinate man'.[4] Later recalling the failed Simla talks, Ghaffar Khan would say that at his instance Nishtar went to Jinnah to encourage a Congress–League accord but the League leader denied Nishtar any opportunity to get a word in.[5]

At Gandhi's request, Badshah Khan visited the slum where Simla's sweepers lived. When Ghaffar Khan reported that the quarters 'were not fit for animals, much less for human beings', Gandhi was filled 'with anger and grief'. On their return to Delhi, Gandhi and Badshah Khan stayed together at the Valmiki sweepers' colony on the edge of Reading Road, now Mandir Marg, and at evening prayer meetings in the colony Badshah Khan recited verses from the Qur'an. 'Prayer in whatever language or form', Ghaffar Khan said on one of these occasions, was 'prayer addressed to one and the same God.'[6]

On 23 May Badshah Khan said that 'neither religion nor anything else that is good can flourish in slavery', but he added that 'freedom can only flourish in India on a basis of amity and cooperation of all the different communities.'[7]

Alas, the Congress and the League did not display amity or cooperation when talking with the Cabinet Mission. The League's demand for a large Pakistan (inclusive, in the west, of all of the Punjab, Sindh, Baluchistan and the NWFP, and, in the east, of the whole of Bengal and all of Assam) was opposed by the Congress's demand for a single Indian Union (with substantial powers for all provinces, including the Muslim-majority ones). The Cabinet Mission responded with an ingenious, and apparently reasonable, three-tier solution of an Indian Union, consisting of Groups (one Hindu-dominant and two Muslim-dominant) of provinces, and Provinces. The Muslim Groups in this solution would coincide with the large Pakistan that Jinnah was asking for, yet a Union too was proposed.

If the Congress agreed to a Muslim Group in the west and another Muslim Group in the east, would Jinnah agree, he was asked in Simla, to a Union? Yes, said Jinnah, provided the Union was nominal and the Groups could quit it in a few years. If Jinnah agreed to a Union, would the Congress accept the Groups? Yes, said the Congress during the Simla talks, provided the Union was real—and provided a Province could opt out of a Group. The Congress was thinking primarily of the Frontier and Assam but any opting-out provision would apply to Sindh and Baluchistan as well.

The League hoped that the Muslim Groups would crack the Union eggshell and break out of it. The Congress desired that the Union and the Provinces, between them, would grind down the Groups. At this point the Cabinet Mission could have proposed a compromise: two solid Groups, together comprising a large Pakistan area, within a firm Indian Union. Yet neither the Congress nor the League was likely to accept such a solution. Since eminent Cabinet ministers do not spend weeks and months in a far-off country merely to announce the failure of their effort, the Mission instead designed an ambiguous 16 May Plan that the Congress could read one way, the League in an opposite way, and both still accept it. While in one place the 16 May text indicated that the Frontier *had* to join the Punjab-led Group, and Assam the Bengal-led Group, elsewhere the text stated that 'Provinces were free to form Groups', implying, as the Congress pointed out, that they were therefore also free *not* to enter a Group.

Under the League's interpretation (which the British eventually endorsed in December 1946, after killings had occurred in Calcutta, Bombay, East Bengal, and Bihar), the 'grouping' envisaged under the Plan would enable the Punjab, by virtue of its bulk in the western Muslim bloc, to dictate the Frontier's future, and similarly allow Muslim-majority Bengal to control Assam's future. Any plan that fettered the Frontier's freedom of action, or placed that freedom in the hands of the Punjab, was anathema to Badshah Khan, who therefore strongly opposed the 16 May Plan.

In his eyes, 'grouping' could prove, for the Frontier, 'a compulsion by the British government to join the Punjab'. Though some of his Pathan colleagues were 'willing to associate with Punjab on acceptable terms', he was clear, Badshah Khan wrote in *Pakhtun*, that the Pathans should be left alone to 'frame our destiny by ourselves'.[8]

Protecting Pakhtun identity was his primary consideration in objecting to any compulsory 'grouping', and he surely endorsed much in what was expressed at the time by Allah Nawaz Khan, the Speaker of the

Frontier provincial assembly. Employing, and suitably altering, the stylized language that Jinnah had previously used to justify the political separation of Muslims from Hindus, Nawaz Khan said:

> Pathans and Punjabis are two major nations by any definition or test of a nation and the idea and the very thought of grouping the NWFP with the Punjabis is revolting to the Pathan mind . . . We the Pathans are a body of people with our own distinctive culture, civilization, language, literature, art and architecture, names and nomenclature and sense of values and proportion . . . By all canons of international law a Pathan is quite separate from a Punjabi.[9]

*

To induce acceptance by the Congress and the League, the Mission relied on more than ambiguity. Each party accepting the 16 May Plan, the Mission declared on 16 June, would have the right to nominate ministers to an interim government of India.

Asserting that it heartily disapproved of the 16 May Plan, the League nevertheless proceeded, in writing, to accept it, and claimed that the Plan contained 'the foundations' of Pakistan. Spelling out its objections, the Congress also wrote that it 'accepted' the Plan, with, of course, its own interpretation of crucial sentences.

The 'acceptance' by the Congress was something that five of its leaders, Patel, Nehru, Azad, Rajendra

Prasad, and Rajagopalachari, had informally negotiated with the Cabinet Mission. Ghaffar Khan and Gandhi were excluded from the crucial talks of 22 June and 23 June when the deal was struck.[10] Patel, who was seventy-one, and Nehru, who was fifty-seven, had finally claimed their independence from Gandhi, who had conceded it. As for Ghaffar Khan, he did not seem to figure greatly in the urgent calculations of Nehru and Patel, who had emerged as the Congress's decision makers.

These 'acceptances' of the League and the Congress were in turn 'accepted', on behalf of the British government, by Wavell, the Viceroy. He asked Nehru, who by now was the Congress President, and Jinnah to help him form a new Executive Council. Since Nehru, leading the larger of the two parties, would be the Council's vice president—a de facto prime minister, the Congress said—Jinnah declined to serve himself, but he reserved the right to name others from the League.

He was seething, for he felt cheated. He had expected the Congress to reject the 16 May Plan and, as a result, to be invited to lead the interim government. Angry at what he saw as the Congress's insincere acceptance, he was angrier at the Viceroy's failure to reject it. And when, in July, Nehru thoughtlessly said that a new Constituent Assembly could modify the May 16 provisions, Jinnah exploded.

The League, he declared, would boycott the new government and launch Direct Action. This took place on 16 August, and at once sparked off the Great Calcutta Killing. On the opening day, many Hindus were killed in that city. In subsequent days, a larger number of Muslims were killed. Still, New Delhi saw, on 2 September, the installation of a Nehru-led ministry.

The Frontier Province did not quite share the jubilation observed in many parts of India at this inauguration of Indian self-rule. Since the League had kept out of the interim ministry, opponents of the Khan brothers called it a Hindu government and dismissed the non-League Muslims on Nehru's team as stooges. Badshah Khan and his brother were attacked as collaborators in a plan to Hinduize the subcontinent and, in particular, the Frontier.

The polarization of the subcontinent's communities and his exclusion, as well as Gandhi's, from critical talks profoundly concerned Badshah Khan. Now, in large letters, the writing on the wall conveyed ominous messages to him. On the subcontinent partition was possible, and in the Frontier Pakhtunness would be challenged by a fierce storm of endangered Islam.

Some remarks he made give us an idea of Badshah Khan's anxious spirit at this time. 'The time is critical', he said on 14 September in a village, north-west of Charsadda, that was not far from the lands of the Mohmand tribe.

> Our adversaries poison the people's minds by saying that the Hindu Raj has been established. I cannot counteract this propaganda by speech alone. I dwell on it in the *Pakhtun*. I request every village and home to subscribe to it and the Khudai Khidmatgars to read it out, if necessary.[11]

At times his tone towards the League seemed to soften, with sorrow superseding anger, and his words suggested a wish to woo them. He spoke of 'the Muslim League brethren', calling them 'sons of the soil', and added, 'The door is still kept open for the Muslim Leaguers to enter the government' in Delhi.[12]

*

The Pakhtun tribals were much on his mind—his instinct had told Ghaffar Khan that in a polarized situation the tribals would be a key element. 'I do not aspire to work only among the Pakhtuns of the Frontier province but also among the tribal brethren', he said in September.[13] But he could not go to the tribal areas. Neither could his brother. The British did not allow it.

In August, well before Nehru had taken office, the British had bombed a site in the Waziristan tribal territory, but League workers spread the word that Nehru, now heading the Delhi government, was responsible. Badshah Khan pointed out that he had publicly protested the Waziristan bombing as soon as he had heard of it, while 'the so-called torch-bearers of Islam, who are now profuse in their lip-sympathy for the tribesmen, did not even raise a finger while [the bombing] was on.'[14]

Nehru, too, had demanded an end to the bombing, which had stopped, but many tribal minds were poisoned by rumours and handbills linking the Congress government to the bombing, even though the allegation had been dismissed by an influential tribal leader, the fiercely anti-British Faqir of Ipi.[15] Badshah Khan alleged that the British allowed Leaguers 'to enter the tribal territory and hold meetings there, whereas the Khudai Khidmatgars were not permitted to enter that territory even to till their own lands'. Claiming that 'a dangerous situation is fast developing in the tribal areas'—a noteworthy assessment, made in 1946, of the potential for fanaticism and extremism in the tribal areas— Ghaffar Khan expressed the hope that Delhi's Ministry for External Affairs, now in Nehru's care, would change its outlook.[16]

Seeing in Nehru's new charge an unexpected opportunity for clearing the long-resented barrier at the tribal gate, Ghaffar Khan invited Nehru to visit the tribal areas. As Nehru's host, he, too, would enter tribal territory!

*

The prospect that excited Badshah Khan alarmed the fading Empire's still-vigilant guardians in Delhi and the Frontier. If allowed to go, Nehru would enter tribal territory not just as an individual but as the virtual head of the government of India. Worst of all, the Frontier Province's proudest rebel would go with him. For the Raj, the prospect upset more than feelings; it violated a long-obeyed sacred code.

Occupying the Empire's strategic frontier, the tribals were managed by the Frontier governor through their chiefs, whose autonomy within their domains did not bother the British. All that was required of them was peace towards the British and distance from the Empire's foes, whether Afghan, Russian, German—or Indian. To hold the chiefs to these two commitments, the Raj used cash and guns, or sometimes a defiant chief's son was won over by the British, as for example Bacha Gul, son of the Haji of Turangzai, and Fazal Din, son of Mullah Powinda, one of the staunchest allies of the Faqir of Ipi.

After the deaths of the Haji of Turangzai and Mullah Powinda, 'the one unpurchaseable mujahid left in the field', to use Wali Khan's phrase, was the Faqir of Ipi.[17] Though heartily disliking him, the British, too, found the Faqir of Ipi, in a Viceroy's words, 'not only implacable but also completely incorruptible'.[18]

Besides cash and guns, the British also used Islam. The Raj's records, including, for example, the diaries of George Cunningham, who occupied key positions in the Frontier, are frank about the paid employment of religious leaders from the Settled Districts for influencing the tribal chiefs, in the name of Islam, against Russia, Germany and supposedly 'Hindu' movements for Indian independence.[19]

Given the indoctrination over the years, a visit by Nehru to the tribal territory was likely to confuse and also perhaps provoke the chiefs. Wavell urged Nehru not to go. Caroe, the NWFP governor, spent three days in Delhi pleading with Nehru against the idea. If he went, Caroe warned Nehru, 'the flags of Islam would be unfurled'.[20] Gandhi, too, expressed reservations, as did Patel and Azad. But Nehru was not going to be budged. He had not become India's de facto prime minister in order to be barred by advisers, British or Indian, from visiting its frontier. On 16 October he flew to Peshawar.

A day earlier, the Muslim League had entered the interim government. The Congress had wanted it to do so. Through an intermediary (the Nawab of Bhopal), Gandhi and Nehru had talked with Jinnah about the League's participation. But what clinched its entry was a Wavell–Jinnah negotiation, not the Congress–Jinnah one.

Intriguingly, Jinnah's nominees included a Hindu 'untouchable' from Bengal, Jogendra Nath Mandal. Perhaps the League leader hoped for a Muslim-'untouchable' alliance in Bengal that might bring the whole of that province into the Pakistan that he and the League still sought. Speaking in Lahore on 20 October, Ghazanfar Ali Khan, another new minister from the League, declared: 'We are going into the Interim Government to get a foothold to fight for our cherished goal of Pakistan.'[21]

Nehru's visit to the tribal areas, made at Ghaffar Khan's suggestion, proved unsuccessful and revealed the hazards in violating a sacred code without careful preparation. Its timing, too, was open to question, for reports, at times exaggerated, of Hindu–Muslim riots in August and September in Calcutta and Bombay, where a number of Pathans were living, had poisoned the climate in the Frontier region. Also, immediately before Nehru's arrival, the Pir of Manki Sharif, a young but influential religious leader, toured the tribal territory and preached against the Nehru visit.[22]

On 16 October, when Nehru landed in Peshawar, some 5,000 Muslim League volunteers, wearing green uniforms and carrying long lances, spears and staves, lined the road from Peshawar airport as Nehru, accompanied by Dr Khan Sahib, the premier, was driven into the city. Leading the volunteers was Abdul Qaiyum Khan. Anti-Nehru slogans were raised, at times menacingly. At one point Dr Khan Sahib had to take out his revolver and threaten to shoot before the crowd gave way.[23]

Soon after welcoming Nehru to the premier's home, Badshah Khan declared at a press conference that the British had been behind the demonstrations: 'Since Pandit Nehru has the audacity to flout their wishes, they wished to teach him a lesson.' Ghaffar Khan also took the opportunity to say, 'What a tragedy it is that Mr. Jinnah could not settle with his Indian brothers but only with the Viceroy!'

This 16 October press conference revealed Badshah Khan's approach to the 'tribal' question. Reminding the journalists that the governor controlled the tribal areas through Political Agents (PAs) responsible only to him, Ghaffar Khan underscored the fact that 'even Dr Khan Sahib, the Prime Minister of the Frontier Province, cannot enter the tribal area without the previous permission of the Political Department.'

Asked if he favoured bringing the tribal areas under an Indian government, Badshah Khan replied: 'I would leave the choice entirely to the tribesmen . . . The tribesmen are the kith and kin of the Frontier people and should be won over by love and not by force. They must have a new deal.' He added:

I want to organize primary schools, civil dispensaries, centres for training technical hands for cottage industries among tribesmen . . . If the Political Department honestly cooperates with me, I can promise big results in five years' time. Love can succeed where bombs have failed. I admit that old wounds inflicted by British imperialism will take time to heal . . . I want to work for their economic prosperity.[24]

The next day, when, in company with his brother, Nehru and a British officer from Delhi, Badshah Khan flew over the tribal border and entered Waziristan for the first time, he called it 'the happiest moment of my life'. But at Miranshah in North Waziristan, where they landed, Waziri tribesmen told Nehru that they did not want 'any interference' or 'Hindu Raj'. After another hostile reception that day, in Razmak in South Waziristan, Nehru offered the view that the demonstrators were 'poor representatives of the people of the Frontier'. About 100 headmen were heatedly dismissed by Nehru, who then asked officers of the Political Department why they were afraid of 'these petty pensioners'.

Nehru's indignation was understandable but perhaps he should have been more patient with the proud Pathans. When a Mahsud chief told him, 'We are free people and don't want to lose our sovereignty', Nehru replied, 'I am amazed how you people who get government money and act as they like, talk of freedom. We are struggling for India's freedom. We want you also to be completely free of foreign rule.'[25] The Mahsuds were angered.[26]

From Miranshah the party flew to Tank and then to Jandola, where tribesmen received them warmly. Recalling the trip years later, Ghaffar Khan would attribute the Jandola welcome to the fact that the PA there, a Hindu, was immune to pressures from the League or the British. On the other hand, in the Khyber area, 'Afridis waved shoes at us' (in Jamrud) and 'people seated on the road began to throw stones at us' (in Landi Kotal) and the 'glass screens of our car were broken'. Only when guards accompanying the PA opened fire did the crowd become quiet.

Malakand was next on the schedule. In his later recollection, Badshah Khan said that he had doubts about going to Malakand, but Nehru was keen. Apparently Badshah Khan had asked Dr Khan Sahib for soldiers to accompany the party to Malakand; if they could not be assigned, he would take a KK patrol, Ghaffar Khan seems to have said. When on arrival at Risalpur, en route to Malakand, Badshah Khan saw no soldiers, he considered abandoning the rest of the journey. But a Pakhtun host could not thus let down a guest. Despite misgivings, he let the party proceed.

At Malakand, where they arrived earlier than expected, Badshah Khan was told by a local KK leader, Rahat Khan, that violence was likely. According to Badshah Khan's later recounting, Sheikh Mahbub Ali, the Malakand PA, was 'all along trying to please Dr. Khan Sahib, who could not resist flattery'. 'Are you not like a father to me? Am I not a Pathan?' Mahbub Ali said to the premier.

After a night spent at Malakand Fort, where they were seen off by some British officers, Mahbub Ali led the party out but soon separated himself from it. The car into which Nehru, the Khan brothers and a guard entered was soon attacked with stones. No soldiers or policemen had accompanied the car, and a truck stood across the road, blocking it. A stone hit Badshah Khan in the back and dazed him.

Once more Dr Khan Sahib rose to the occasion. Snatching the guard's revolver, he shouted, 'Move off, or I will shoot.' The crowd immediately dispersed. Dr Khan Sahib next ordered the truck driver to clear the road, and the truck driver obeyed. 'Thus we were saved', Badshah Khan would recall, indirectly acknowledging that his brother and the revolver had done the trick.

In his recollection Ghaffar Khan informs us that he had advised his brother that one truck carrying guards with lathis should precede their car and another truck carrying guards with any available guns should follow. If the first truck failed to pacify any violent crowd, there could be firing from the second truck.[27] Badshah Khan's nonviolence was thus clearly pragmatic and not limitless; he had no hesitation in asking for soldiers and guns or, later, in lauding his brother for threatening to use the revolver.

At Dargai, on the journey back from Malakand, a big crowd pelted stones. Although Badshah Khan managed to block a stone aimed at Nehru, Dr Khan Sahib was hit by 'an earthen pot filled with nightsoil'. 'With great difficulty we reached Peshawar and Dr. Khan Sahib was responsible for all this trouble', says Badshah

Khan, presumably because he did not arrange for
soldiers to accompany the party to Malakand. One has
to ask whether Badshah Khan is sufficiently charitable
in this later recollection, which, as we shall see, had
followed a period of political estrangement between
the brothers; and also whether Badshah Khan is
sufficiently self-critical, for it was he after all who had
invited Nehru to the tribal areas.

For the next day, 21 October, Badshah Khan had
arranged a public meeting in the afternoon at his
Sardaryab centre, which lay well within the 'settled'
territory of the Frontier province. He rejected, even
when his brother apparently wished to accept, an offer
from British officers to send soldiers to guard Nehru at
Sardaryab. To Badshah Khan it was outrageous for the
British to offer help when it was not needed after
withholding it where it mattered, in Waziristan and
Malakand, or, as he thought, after instigating trouble
there.

KKs lined both sides of the road from Peshawar to
Sardaryab. Behind the unarmed KKs, Badshah Khan
would afterwards recall, stood armed villagers, who,
following the Malakand incidents, had 'sympathy for
us' and were ready to 'meet violence with violence'. A
welcome address presented by the Pakhtuns to Nehru
and doubtless vetted by Badshah Khan spoke of 'the
Pakhtuns and the Indians' and said, 'As in the past, so at
present too, we share the difficulties and distresses of
India.' The address continued, 'The Central government
should keep in touch with the tribesmen through us . . .
The living conditions of the tribals are worse than ours.

Do not forget them.'

To an immense gathering, Nehru spoke of the 'free tribal people' but also of the incidents on the trip that had troubled him. He said he was glad he came and added:

> A few drops of blood of Badshah Khan and mine sprinkled on this holy land of yours will surely bear fruit . . . I want to convey through you to the tribesmen that I bear no grudge against them for all that has happened during these last few days.
>
> The KKs were never permitted to enter the tribal area, but the mischief-mongers could go there and tell the people that the Hindu Raj is being established. These ill-informed, uneducated people have been deceived.
>
> This is my first visit and I shall come again and again till the tribal wrangle is settled.[28]

Those final brave words could not be lived up to. After October 1946 Nehru would never again visit the Frontier, which a year later became part of Pakistan, and a student of the history of the period is bound to wonder, the 'no grudge' assertion notwithstanding, whether the October trip did not create a distance between Nehru and the Frontier region.

The Sardaryab meeting closed with a speech by Badshah Khan, who recalled the incident fifteen years earlier when he and Devadas Gandhi were saved 'on this very bridge over Sardaryab'. Ghaffar Khan added, 'None can destroy one whom God protects.' Asking why disturbances had occurred in Waziristan and Malakand, Ghaffar Khan answered his question by saying that since Nehru had defied the viceroy and the governor, 'a dirty trick was played on him to teach him a lesson'. Tribals were 'incited to throw stones at him. The Britishers do not want to be dethroned and want us to get exhausted by fighting with each other.'[29]

According to a later assessment by G.L. Mallam, a senior Frontier-based British civil servant, Nehru's visit to the tribal areas at a time when tribesmen were 'incensed by [reports of] the riots in India' was a blunder.[30] The League easily portrayed it as preparing the ground for extending into the Frontier the Hindu rule that had supposedly begun in Delhi on 2 September.

'From that moment (of Nehru's visit)', says Mallam, 'the common people of the Frontier began rapidly to switch their allegiance from Congress to the Muslim League, preferring for the time being the company of the hated [pro-British and pro-League] Khans to the worst of all evils—Hindu domination.'[31] It was an assessment that Abdul Qaiyum Khan had made within days of Nehru's visit. Writing to Jinnah of gifts to the League from that visit, Qaiyum Khan said: 'What we could not hope to achieve in several years, was in fact achieved within about a week.'[32]

But not without the Raj's help evidently. In 1994, the scholar Wiqar Ali Shah, who cites Mallam's assessment and Qaiyum Khan's letter to Jinnah, went to 'all those places which Nehru visited in October 1946', 'interviewed several persons some of whom were eye witnesses to the hostile demonstrations and some themselves took active part in them', and concluded that they indeed 'had the blessings of the officials'.[33] Similar admissions were recorded by the Swedish scholar, Erland Jansson. Thus Faridullah Shah, the assistant political officer in Khyber, told Jansson that Colonel Khursheed, the PA, had instructed him to 'do something' against the Nehru visit, for 'if the tribesmen should receive [Nehru] in a docile way, all Musalmans of this part of the country will go under the suzerainty of the Hindus'.[34]

We may briefly reflect here on the 'Hindu' charge levelled against the Khan brothers and the Khudai Khidmatgars by supporters of the League, sometimes with the blessings of the Raj. That, though treated with contempt, the charge, generally laced with abuse, was hurtful is suggested by a stinging retort that Wali Khan would later make. Claiming that Cunningham had advanced the line that it was *kufr* or anti-Islamic for the Khudai Khidmatgars to align with the Congress of the Hindus, who were described, in contrast to the British, as a people without a Book, Wali added that, going beyond this, some 'Muslim Leaguers . . . descended to the level of abusive language, . . . calling the Khudai Khidmatgars the natural offspring of Hindus.'

However, Wali went on, during the disturbances that were to mark the Frontier in 1947, it was the supporters of the League who had appropriated the properties of Hindus and Sikhs. Having laid claim to the estates and properties left behind by the Hindus, it was the Leaguer 'who alone had the right to their inheritance, and he alone was their offspring'.[35]

*

Qaiyum Khan strove to build on the League's unexpected gains. When, in November 1946, Badshah Khan thought of sending a peace deputation to the tribal areas, Qaiyum Khan called him 'anti-Muslim', accused him of wanting to prevent the tribesmen 'from rendering assistance to Indian Muslims in times of need' and declared that 'the Frontier Muslim League will take necessary steps to defeat his sinister move'.[36] Eleven months later, in October 1947, the kind of tribal support that Qaiyum Khan had in mind would be revealed as Afridis descended into the Vale of Kashmir and almost reached Srinagar.

Events, however, were helping Qaiyum Khan. After Muslims in Noakhali in East Bengal had avenged, in October 1946, Muslim deaths in Calcutta in August, some Hindu groups demonstrated their killing prowess in Bihar, where thousands of Muslims perished in October and November. Reports of the Bihar violence did little to strengthen Badshah Khan's position in the Frontier, and Muslim–Hindu relations in the province were damaged when, as London's *Daily Telegraph* said in a dispatch from Peshawar, '*agents provocateurs* from other provinces [stirred] Muslim feelings here by displaying the photographs of skulls and torn fragments of the Koran from Bihar.'[37]

Could the rock of Pakhtunness take on the wave of endangered Islam? This was the question that Badshah Khan now faced. He was fifty-six, and seasoned. He had seen many political tides. After a time they all ebbed out, but some rose higher, spread farther and stayed longer than others. No tide would turn rock to sand, but some tides could for a time overflow the rock. Was this that sort of tide?

We have little direct knowledge of the debates taking place inside Badshah Khan's mind in the winter of 1946-47 and the spring and summer that followed. He kept no journal and did not, it seems, communicate his inner thoughts in letters. Yet from what he did and where he chose to spend his time we may infer something of what he thought.

Much of his time between December 1946 and July 1947, including a three-and-a-half-month period between January and May, was spent outside the Frontier. In this fact we may detect a conclusion by Ghaffar Khan that successfully countering the League's propaganda in the Frontier during that frenzied time was not a promising proposition. Aware, too, that the future was being decided not in his beloved province but elsewhere on the subcontinent, he approached the wider arena.

There is a similarity between Badshah Khan's noticeable absences from the Frontier in 1946—47 and Gandhi's frequent absences, in the same period, from Delhi. Though the two attended some formal sessions in Delhi when the leaders of the Congress considered the Raj's proposals for the transfer of power, Badshah Khan and Gandhi also sought to influence the sources of polarization, the villages and streets in Bihar and Bengal where killings had occurred.

More than pure strategy caused this distance kept

by the two; Gandhi and Ghaffar Khan were also influenced by the fact that in 1946–47 some of their nearest colleagues, including Dr Khan Sahib, Nehru and Patel, seemed to draw away from them and closer to their British counterparts at the levers of power, to the Crippses, the Wavells, the Mountbattens, and the Caroes of the official world. From another angle we may say that where Dr Khan Sahib, Nehru and Patel tried, in association with the departing British, to draw the best out of a rapidly deteriorating situation, Badshah Khan and Gandhi sought— bravely, heroically, against long odds—to remedy the situation, while also offering comradeship, whenever possible, to Dr Khan Sahib, Nehru and Patel.

Entering India's Constituent Assembly as a Frontier delegate and thus becoming, for the first time in his life, a formal legislator, Badshah Khan admitted to that Assembly in December 1946 that 'many a time, while travelling on a train' he was asked by Muslims why he was 'not with them'. 'I am with the Muslims', Ghaffar Khan declared, 'but not with the Muslim League.' Alerting the Assembly to 'the communal bias' that was abroad in the land, he also reminded it, as he had reminded other audiences, that 'in the campaign of 1942, only our province fought nonviolently. We possess more weapons of violence and yet we adopted nonviolent methods.'[38]

*

In the opening quarter of 1947, however, fires of

religious violence erupted in the Frontier and the Punjab. There were riots in the districts of Hazara, Peshawar and Dera Ismail Khan in the Frontier and large-scale killings in Rawalpindi in the Punjab. Early in March, communal polarization and a strong campaign launched by the League forced out the Punjab's non-League coalition ministry headed by Khizr Hyat Khan, but in the Frontier Dr Khan Sahib manfully confronted the march of hate.

His grit had showed itself in the case of Basanti, a pregnant Sikh woman abducted in January 1947 from a village in Hazara district. Her husband and some other family members were killed. Basanti was declared a convert to Islam, renamed Aasia, and married to a Muslim, M. Zaman. Recovered by the provincial police, she was sent to Dr Khan Sahib's custody where, with her new husband and also her Sikh relatives present, she stated that she wanted to go back to her relatives and to Sikhism.

For the next seven to eight months, the restoration of Basanti to Islam was a central demand in what became the League's civil disobedience movement in the Frontier. Qaiyum Khan defied prohibitory orders and got himself arrested in a protest that accused Dr Khan Sahib of 'forcing the Muslim woman to reconvert to Sikhism'.[39]

When Dr Khan Sahib imposed fines on Hazara villages that had joined in violence against Hindus and Sikhs, the League, claiming that no fines had been imposed on Hindus in Bihar, charged him with 'repression'. The League found a valuable ally in the Pir of Manki Sharif, who commanded prestige among the Malakand tribals. On 19 February the League was able to mount a large rally in Mardan.

That day, several thousand miles to the west, Prime Minister Clement Attlee announced in London that the British would not stay in India beyond June 1948. Power would be handed over before then, either 'as a whole to some form of Central Government or in some areas to the existing provincial governments' or in another 'reasonable' way. To arrange the transfer of power, Attlee went on to say, Lord Louis Mountbatten, a dashing young admiral related to the King, would replace Wavell as viceroy.

If Attlee's announcement hinted at the possibility of partition, it spelt out in black and white the critical importance of 'existing provincial governments'. Dr Khan Sahib and his ministry would inherit the power of the Raj if the League and its allies failed the Frontier. They went to work at once. On 22 February a large protest meeting in Peshawar ended with an angry march to Dr Khan Sahib's house. 'Brave as a lion', as Governor Caroe commented, Dr Khan Sahib faced the crowd and declared that he would do his duty.

In this critical hour the premier received solid support from the KKs and from his cabinet colleagues, including the revenue minister, Qazi Ataullah, Ghaffar Khan's associate from 1921, and the education minister, Yahya Jan, a former principal who would shortly marry Mehr Taj, daughter of Ghaffar Khan and the late Nambata.

Police firing killed two Muslims in a Peshawar

procession in March; later that evening seventeen Hindus and Sikhs were stabbed in the city. Violence followed elsewhere in the province, especially in non-Pakhtun areas in Hazara and Dera Ismail Khan (DIK) districts. On 17 April, Mahsud tribesmen who had come into DIK bazaars for loot and plunder were fired upon; seventeen Mahsuds were killed on the spot by Dr Khan Sahib's police. By 25 April, ninety-three Hindus and twenty-eight Muslims had died in DIK.

In March and April peace committees were formed by KKs (and in some cases by Ahrars and Khaksars) all over the province, mainly to protect non-Muslims.[40] Charged with involvement in rioting, thousands of Leaguers were arrested.

Women members of the Muslim League, burka clad, took out several processions and also attacked government offices. Since the Pakhtun code forbade the use of physical force against women, the League's women campaigners were able to organize numerous meetings and processions. 'No woman agitator was arrested, physically assaulted or tortured by the Congress ministry.'[41] But the wave of threatened Islam had flooded the Frontier.

*

While Dr Khan Sahib grappled in the Frontier with riots and the League's challenge, the younger brother was in Bihar, working with Gandhi to restore a sense of security in that province. In a letter to Gandhi, Vallabhbhai Patel complained about Badshah Khan's location,[42] but then

Patel also expressed unhappiness that Gandhi was in Bihar.

It was a curious situation. While grumbling that Gandhi and Ghaffar Khan were not where they should be, Patel and Nehru (and the rest of the Congress Working Committee) had gone ahead and recommended, on 8 March, the partition of the Punjab. This decision, which was tantamount to conceding the partition of India, had followed the removal, in Lahore, of Khizr Hyat Khan's Unionist ministry and the installation of a League ministry headed by the Khan of Mamdot.[43] Once more a momentous step had been taken without consulting Gandhi or Ghaffar Khan, who learnt of it from the newspapers.

When Gandhi publicly expressed his unhappiness with the Punjab decision and later wrote to Patel and Nehru asking if they could explain it to him, Patel's reply was, 'It is difficult, in a letter, to explain the Punjab resolution about the Punjab', while Nehru said he was convinced they had done the right thing.[44] But Gandhi had allowed two weeks to pass before he wrote to Nehru and Patel; it was his choice to be in Bihar, far from his colleagues; and he had acquiesced in his exclusion from decision making in the Congress. Badshah Khan, similarly, had left it to his brother to manage the Frontier. The 'fault' did not lie with Nehru or Patel or Dr Khan Sahib. Nor did it lie with Gandhi or Ghaffar Khan. It lay, well, not in the stars, but in the hates, fears and piques of the subcontinent's inhabitants, Hindus, Muslims and Englishmen.

In Bihar, where Ghaffar Khan based himself from

January 1947, and where in the 1930s he had spent over two years in prison, he went to the villages where Muslim homes had been burnt or looted and sought help for the victims' relief from Bihar's Congress ministers and officials, finding the former more cooperative than the latter. At times he accompanied Muslims who had fled their homes back to their villages to look for valuables they had hidden before fleeing. And he encouraged Gandhi to come to Bihar from his mission in Noakhali in East Bengal, which had begun the previous November.

Badshah Khan and Gandhi spoke together to Bihari audiences, sometimes of tens of thousands. On 16 March, eight days after the Congress Working Committee's proposal to partition the Punjab, Ghaffar Khan said:

I find myself surrounded by darkness, which increases the more I think of the future of India. Indeed I see no light. India is on fire. If India is burnt down, all will lose, Hindus, Muslims, Sikhs and Christians. What can be achieved through love can never be achieved through hatred or force. The recent war in Europe showed what hatred can do.

The Muslim League wants Pakistan. They can have it only through love and willing consent. Pakistan established through force will prove a doubtful boon.[45]

On 31 March, Ghaffar Khan and Gandhi arrived in Delhi. After meeting delegates from Asia and the Middle East attending an Asian Relations Conference, the two met, on 1 April, Mountbatten, the new Viceroy, who by now had drawn up some versions of a plan to partition India. At this meeting, with Badshah Khan's full concurrence and support, Gandhi proposed his ingenious solution for avoiding partition and restoring peace: let the Nehru-led government be replaced with a new one headed by Jinnah. Gandhi added that as long as Mountbatten felt that Jinnah was acting in the national interest, he, Gandhi, would ensure that the Congress did not vote down a Jinnah government in the Central Assembly.

The story of the 'Jinnah card' that Gandhi played for India's unity is fairly well known and need not be told here in any detail. Suffice it to mention that Mountbatten thought, or feared, that the plan could work; that the Viceroy recorded the opinion of Azad that the scheme was 'feasible' and 'would be the quickest way to stop bloodshed';[46] that, following tireless exertions by Mountbatten and his staff, Nehru was persuaded to join an already opposed Patel to defeat the Gandhi plan;[47] and that finally the Congress Working Committee voted overwhelmingly against it. Despite what he had told Mountbatten, Azad joined Patel, Nehru, Rajagopalachari and Prasad in rejecting the proposal. It was never put to Jinnah.

To Mountbatten, Gandhi wrote: 'I am sorry to say that I failed to carry any of the Working Committee with me except Badshah Khan.'[48] Whether Jinnah would have agreed to the plan cannot of course be known with any certainty. Scholars have offered different guesses. That the League leader's acceptance was not wholly ruled out is suggested by what Jinnah had said about a similar proposal in August 1942:

> If they (the Congress) are sincere, I should welcome it. If the British Government accepts the solemn declaration of Mr. Gandhi and by an arrangement hands over the government of the country to the Muslim League, I am sure that . . . non-Muslims would be treated fairly, justly, nay generously . . . [49]

More directly relevant for our study is the evidence of Ghaffar Khan's collaboration with Gandhi in this intriguing initiative, which gives an idea of the unconventional thinking with which the two tried to confront the 'darkness' and the 'fire' acknowledged by Ghaffar Khan in his 16 March remarks in Bihar.

*

If partition was coming, as the Congress Working Committee's rejection (on 10 April) of the Gandhi plan indicated, what would happen to the Frontier province? Knowing that if his ministry survived Dr Khan Sahib might take over from the Raj, the League demanded his ouster and fresh elections in the Frontier.

Highlighted by an escalating civil disobedience campaign, this demand seemed reasonable to Mountbatten, who along with most of the Raj's functionaries thought it unnatural for a Muslim province to be linked to a 'Hindu' India. To Lord Ismay, who headed Mountbatten's staff, a Congress ministry running a Muslim-majority province was in itself a 'bastard situation'.[50] Reminders from the Khan brothers that the KK or Congress ministry had won power only a year earlier on the issue of Pakistan seemed to cut no ice.

The brothers' position was greatly weakened by the unwillingness of Congress leaders to make an issue of the Frontier. Though publicly opposing Jinnah's 'two-nation' theory ever since it was enunciated in 1940, many in the Congress privately subscribed to it. Like the Raj's officers, they too thought it natural for the Frontier to 'belong' under the unfolding Pakistan umbrella; the influential Sardar Patel, for one, had concluded that the NWFP 'would have to be written off'.[51]

In the previous year, when Gopinath Bardoloi, the Congress's chief minister of Assam, demanded a right to opt out of the eastern 'Muslim' grouping contemplated by the Cabinet Mission, the Working Committee had given Bardoloi full backing. Later in 1947, after partition was formally agreed to and the Punjab's boundaries were being demarcated, the representatives of the Congress would similarly, and successfully, fight for the allocation to East Punjab (and India) of a significant portion of Gurdaspur district, critical to India's link with the state of Jammu and Kashmir. In the future, Ghaffar Khan would always contrast the Congress's firmness in respect of Assam and Gurdaspur with what he saw as its lukewarm support to the Khan brothers' demand for the rights of the Pakhtuns.[52]

To return to April 1947. Mountbatten travelled that

month to Peshawar and talked with Governor Caroe, Dr Khan Sahib and other ministers, and their vehement opponents, Qaiyum Khan and the Pir of Manki Sharif, who, with other leaders of the League, had to be let out of detention by the provincial government for meeting the Viceroy. Qaiyum Khan and the Pir asked for new elections; Caroe supported their demand. Dr Khan Sahib recalled the verdict a year earlier and asked Mountbatten to do nothing that might 'destroy the Pathan nation'.[53]

This was the first reference to the only strategy now available to the Khan brothers: a fight for Pakhtun autonomy. Even as Mountbatten was rapidly developing his Frontier solution—a referendum to decide whether the people of the province wanted to join 'Hindu' India or 'Muslim' Pakistan—the Khan brothers fell back to Pakhtunness.

In the second week of May, after an absence of over three months, Badshah Khan returned to the Frontier. Here, faced with violent undertones in the League's campaign, his son Ghani, the talented maverick, had started Zalme Pakhtun, a new body, independent of the KKs, which freed its members to bear arms 'for the defence of nonviolent people'.[54] In a piece in *Pakhtun* (17 May 1947), Ghani poked fun at nonviolence and the spinning wheel and praised the pistol.[55]

'I still believe in nonviolence', Ghaffar Khan clarified on arrival in the Frontier. He was convinced, he added, that 'the country in general and the Frontier province in particular should stick to nonviolence', but he acknowledged that Ghani and some others had felt the need for an organization freed from the nonviolence rule.

In a speech in Shabqadar, not far from Charsadda, in mid-May, Ghaffar Khan criticized the call for new elections. Also, he took the governor to task for not preventing the killing of Hindus and Sikhs in the Frontier's districts. The British had ensured peace in the Frontier during the six years of the Second World War. 'Then they wanted peace, and there was peace.' But now, when 'hundreds of people had been butchered', British power in the Frontier not only 'looked on, unwilling to take [the] drastic measures which their ministers asked for to put down lawlessness', but it even 'pointed to lawlessness as a reason for the removal of those who had been returned to power by an overwhelming majority of voters and who still commanded a majority in the legislature'.[56]

'Lord Mountbatten emphatically told me', Badshah Khan added in Shabqadar, 'that he was going to be the last Viceroy and the Britishers were soon quitting India, and they would transfer power earlier than the time stipulated.' This was indeed the case. Mountbatten had advanced the deadline for British departure from June 1948 to August 1947.

The British were to leave in three months, the Congress seemed concerned only with Hindu-majority India, and hate and frenzy now marked his beloved Frontier. In Shabqadar, the words of Badshah Khan, whose usual style was to speak 'slowly, frankly, to the heart',[57] came from the depths of his own heart:

We are passing through critical times . . . Some people mislead you in the name of Islam. I feel it is my duty to warn you against future dangers so that I may justify myself before man and God on the Day of Judgment . . .

What gains will Islam and the Muslims reap from these riots and the slaughter of children, women and the aged? And how are the Pakhtuns going to be benefited? These happenings are against the tenets of the Holy Qur'an and the sayings of the Prophet. To lay hands on an innocent poor man goes also against Pakhtun tradition.

The other day an old Sikh pedlar was murdered on the road in spite of his willingness to embrace Islam. Is it done for the sake of Islam? I warn the League brethren that the fire they kindle will spread in wild blaze and consume everything in its way.[58]

In this utterance he also made a passionate appeal to the Frontier's Muslim Leaguers to sit with the KKs in 'a joint jirga' to look at the difficulties that lay ahead:

We can patch up our differences today if they meet us like brothers . . . I shall agree to any honourable settlement between ourselves. The Leaguers fear Hindu domination, while we fear British domination. Let us meet together and convince each other.

But the League in the Frontier had scented victory and was in no mood to sit down with the KKs. At the end of May, Badshah Khan returned to Delhi, where

Mountbatten was giving finishing touches to his Partition Plan. Unveiled on 2 June but known in essence several days earlier, the plan provided for the division of India as a whole and of the provinces of the Punjab and Bengal. India and Pakistan would become independent dominions within the British Commonwealth. Princely states were left free to join India or Pakistan or, perhaps, even claim independence. And in two far-apart areas, the NWFP and the Muslim-majority district of Sylhet in Assam, the people would choose between India and Pakistan.

The Congress Working Committee considered the plan during sessions held on 31 May, 1 June, and 2 June. On 17 May Nehru had written to Mountbatten agreeing to the key proposals, adding that Patel too went along with them, but the Working Committee's ratification was necessary. Four persons attending the sessions expressed disagreement: Ghaffar Khan, Gandhi (a special invitee), and the socialists Jayaprakash Narayan and Rammanohar Lohia. The rest, a great majority, favoured ratification. Lohia has given an account of a brief intervention by Ghaffar Khan:

> He spoke a bare two sentences. He expressed his sorrow over the fact that his colleagues had accepted the scheme of partition. As a small mercy, he wanted them to find out if the proposed plebiscite in the North West Frontier could include the alternative of independence alongside the choice of India or Pakistan. He spoke not a word more . . . [59]

This the Working Committee was not willing to do. Though supported by Gandhi, Ghaffar Khan's plea was passed over. The truth was that as early as the third week of April, Nehru had conveyed to Mountbatten his acceptance of the viceroy's referendum scheme.[60] Nehru admitted this in a letter he wrote on 8 June to a dissatisfied Gandhi, who wanted an attempt by the Congress to alter the terms of the referendum in line with Badshah Khan's proposal:

> The British Government and the Viceroy are definitely committed to the referendum, and some of us are more or less committed. The question of the referendum is therefore a settled one, and it is not clear how we can get out of it. For the Viceroy it is still more difficult. Any change in the plan may even lead to conflict on a big scale.[61]

If he reopened the Frontier question with Mountbatten, Nehru was implying, every other question, including the division of the Punjab and Bengal and the future of the princely states could come up for reconsideration. In not wanting to jeopardize the agreement the Congress had reached with the British and the League, Nehru represented the sentiment of every senior Congress leader. Having finally settled numerous points of contention with the Raj and the League, Nehru, Patel, Azad, Prasad, Rajagopalachari, and the rest were about to take over the running of three-fourths of India.

Should they risk upsetting everything for the sake of a distant corner that lay beyond the new boundaries they had accepted, even if that corner contained friends who had stood with the Congress through thick and thin? Patel was prepared, if it came to that, to write off the Frontier province, and we cannot escape the conclusion that so was Jawaharlal. Though he claimed in his letter to Gandhi that 'We have a good chance of winning [a Frontier referendum]', citing a remark by Mountbatten that the Frontier's British officials saw Congress's chances as fifty-fifty,[62] we must wonder whether Nehru really believed that.

Unmistakably from March, and ominously from the previous autumn, Ghaffar Khan had seen the betrayal coming. Yet when, with the ratification by the Working Committee, it actually came, he was stunned. Getting up from the session with an effort, he left the room, sat down on the steps outside, supporting his head with his hands, and muttered, 'Toba, toba!'[63]

In Delhi he was again staying, along with Gandhi, in the Valmiki sweepers' colony. On some nights he pressed Gandhi's arms and legs to ease the older man's passage into sleep. Some of the remarks the two made, recorded by Gandhi's grand-niece, Manu, give an idea of what Badshah Khan was going through.

Ghaffar Khan to Manu, May 5 or 6: Before long we shall become aliens in Hindustan. The end of our long fight will be to pass under the domination of Pakistan – away from Bapu, away from India, away from all of you. Who knows what the future holds for us?[64]

Gandhi to Manu, May 6 or 7: Verily Badshah Khan

is a fakir. Independence will come but the brave
Pathan will lose his. They are faced with a grim
prospect. But Badshah is a man of God.[65]

Gandhi to Manu, early on June 1: I cannot bear to
see Badshah Khan's grief. His inner agony wrings
my heart. But if I give way to tears, it would be
cowardly, and stalwart Pathan though he is, he
would break down.[66]

Eighteen years later, while an exile in Kabul, Ghaffar
Khan recalled the Delhi deliberations of 1947.
According to this recollection, Ghaffar Khan told the
Working Committee:

We Pakhtuns stood by you and had undergone great
sacrifices for attaining freedom, but you have now
deserted us and thrown us to the wolves. We shall
not agree to hold referendum because we had
decisively won the election on the issue of Hindustan
versus Pakistan . . . Now as India has disowned us,
let the referendum be on Pakhtunistan or Pakistan.[67]

Badshah Khan would say that he 'bitterly complained'
to Gandhi, and add:

With an aching heart, Gandhiji replied, he was sure
that if the Frontier Province were not given a square
deal or if the Khudai Khidmatgars were oppressed,
India would feel in honour bound to come to their
aid, and he for one would not hesitate to advise
Indian government to treat it as casus belli. Gandhiji

had later repeated that statement to my son. When Ghani asked him what would happen to his nonviolence in that event, Gandhiji told him not to worry about his nonviolence. 'I am nonviolent, the Government is not.'[68]

Three years after he dictated these recollections, Badshah Khan was interviewed in Kabul by Haridev Sharma. Asked by Sharma why, in his view, Nehru accepted the Partition Plan, Badshah Khan offered two explanations: 'the influence of Lord and Lady Mountbatten' and 'more than that, keenness to receive power'.[69] As for the Working Committee's ratification, Ghaffar Khan told Sharma:

> It was a formality. The decision had already been taken. On the referendum, Gandhiji supported me. Rajaji at this point said, 'The situation has changed, decisions have been made.'
>
> Azad, who was sitting next to me, said, 'You should now join the League.' I was shocked that they thought that we would sacrifice our principles for the sake of office. Patel, angry with Gandhiji, would say, 'What Pakistan, a castle of sand!' Despite Jinnah's invitations to me, we did not leave Congress.[70]

Sharma asked Ghaffar Khan why Gandhi acquiesced in the partition after having opposed it strongly. Badshah Khan replied: 'If you appraise the situation at the time, you will find that the whole country was filled with violence, everywhere there was hatred and talk of destruction. More than that, his closest associates left him. What could he do in those circumstances?'[71]

*

Numbed as he was, Ghaffar Khan quickly thought out his response to the betrayal. One, there was no question of his taking part in an 'India or Pakistan' referendum, due to take place in the middle of July. It would at once be turned into a choice between Muslim Pakistan and Hindu India. Apart from the fact that the KKs could never hope to win on behalf of Hindu India, a contest in the political climate of 1947 would lead to terrible bloodshed. Pakhtun killing Pakhtun was not a prospect he could stomach.

Two, the Congress having let them down, the KKs would before long have to break with the Congress and, indeed, with India. As he would later say, 'Hindustan had already deserted us and had handed us over to the enemies, hence it was against the Pakhtun pride and character to thrust ourselves on Hindustan.'[72]

Three, in its competition with the League for the Pathan mind, the KKs would, on the one hand, stress Pakhtun autonomy and, on the other, oppose the League's acceptance of dominion status for Pakistan. Finally, given Jinnah's dominant position in the Pakistan then coming into being, Ghaffar Khan concluded that he should be willing to explore the attitude of the League leader.

The Congress Working Committee wanted the Pathans to fight the referendum with all their might and win it for India. From their New Delhi sitting rooms, the leaders of the Congress visualized the gallant Khan brothers once again tramping the Frontier's hills and valleys and obtaining the Pathans' vote for India, even as they had won the 1946 elections. These Congress leaders had little idea of the impact on the Pathans of subsequent killings in Bengal, Bihar and Bombay, or of the frenzy created in the Frontier itself.

But Badshah Khan knew better. Gandhi at once saw his point of view and agreed with it. He had always recognized that the Pathans loved and followed Badshah Khan because he symbolized Pakhtunness and a caring Islam, not because they necessarily felt an unbreakable bond with India.

Before returning to the Frontier, Ghaffar Khan authorized Gandhi to approach Jinnah via Mountbatten. On 6 June, accordingly, Gandhi wrote to Mountbatten requesting him to speak in the following terms to Jinnah:

> Lest the referendum should lead to bloodshed and blood feuds between brother and brother Pathan, now that you have got your Pakistan, would it not be wise for you to go to the NWFP and speak to the ministry and others there? You could explain what Pakistan, hitherto a vague expression, really is, and present your case in an attractive manner, and woo them to become a province of Pakistan, with perfect freedom to frame their own provincial constitution.

> If you are successful in your persuasion, the proposed referendum and all that it involves would

be avoided. If you felt disposed to adopt this suggestion, I could I think give a positive assurance that the Khan brothers and their followers would meet you as friends and give you a positive hearing.[73]

In this letter to Mountbatten, Gandhi added, 'Abdul Ghaffar was so anxious about the permanent blood feuds that would result from the referendum that he would go to almost any length, consistent with honour, to avoid it.'[74]

Mountbatten passed on Gandhi's thoughts to Jinnah. Plainly, Gandhi was aiming to strengthen the hands of his Pakhtun friends in any negotiations they might have with Jinnah. Even if the terms of the referendum could not be altered, he wanted Jinnah confronted with the question of Pakhtun autonomy. The Pathan was entitled to know, he said in another letter to Mountbatten, whether or not 'his entity will be fully protected' in Pakistan. To Nehru, Gandhi wrote: 'Would it be wrong if you insisted that referendum would be wrong without the presentation of the picture of Pakistan?'[75]

Back by this time in the Frontier, Badshah Khan found that most of his KK colleagues agreed with him. 'I have consulted all my important workers', he wrote to Gandhi on 8 June, 'and we are all of the considered opinion that we cannot agree to the holding of the referendum [as spelt out in the Mountbatten Plan]. Moreover, the conditions prevailing in the province are such that the holding of the referendum will lead to serious violence . . . We would like to have a free Pathan state within India.'[76]

Three days later, on 11 June, 'a joint meeting of the Provincial Congress Committee, the Congress Parliamentary Party and the Salars of the Khudai Khidmatgars was held for four hours.' All parts of the province were represented. 'The consensus of opinion was that we should not take part in the referendum. All desired that the issue be amended on the basis of Pakistan or a free Pathan state.'[77]

A week later Badshah Khan was in Delhi again, hoping to see whether Mountbatten and/or Jinnah would budge. On the morning of 18 June, Badshah Khan and Gandhi talked together with Mountbatten at the Viceroy's house, where Ghaffar Khan bumped into Jinnah, who too was having a meeting with the Viceroy. Later that evening, Badshah Khan called on Jinnah in his home on Aurangzeb Road.

Recalling this interview in 1965, Badshah Khan said that he told Jinnah that if three conditions were met the Pathans would happily join Pakistan. One, the terms had to be honourable. Two, the Pathans of the Settled Districts and the tribal areas should have the right to opt out of Pakistan if the latter, after independence, stayed as a British dominion. Three, all matters concerning tribal people should be settled by the Pathans without the interference or domination of non-Pathans. According to the 1965 recollection, the talks were friendly and lasted over an hour; Jinnah saw Badshah Khan off to his car; but the attempt at a compromise failed.[78]

While Ghaffar Khan was meeting Jinnah, Gandhi spoke at his prayer meeting. Saying that Badshah Khan was 'straining every nerve' to avoid bloodshed, Gandhi asked the congregation to 'pray with him' for the success of Ghaffar Khan's mission to Jinnah.

'Pathanistan', Gandhi significantly added, was 'a movement that had come to stay.' It was 'meant to conserve Pathan life and culture'. Let both the Congress and the Muslim League honour the Pathan sentiment and let the Pathans have their own constitution for internal affairs and administration. The movement would promote Pathan solidarity, avoid internal conflict, retain Pakhtun culture and the Pakhto language. 'If they could do that, they would be better able unitedly to federate with Pakistan or the Union of India.'[79]

We do not have a record of what Ghaffar Khan told Gandhi after returning from Jinnah's house, yet we know that Gandhi was 'greatly disturbed over the outcome of the interview', as a result losing most of his sleep that night, and also that he marvelled once more at Ghaffar Khan's poise. To his grand-niece Manu, Gandhi said in the early hours of 19 June:

> No, I can't sleep. The thought of him has robbed me of my sleep . . . I cannot cease thinking of Badshah Khan. He is a prodigy. I am seeing more and more of his deeply spiritual nature daily. He has patience, faith and nonviolence joined in true humility. Countless Pathans have enshrined him in their hearts as their uncrowned king. For such a person there can be no defeat. I am sure he will not shrink from any sacrifice or suffering, but will die serving the Pathans with his last breath. He lives

only for that. He is a man of penance, also of illumination, with love for all and hatred towards none.[80]

The future would validate both the appraisement and the prediction. That morning, meanwhile, Badshah Khan was excoriated in *Dawn*, the Delhi-based newspaper founded by Jinnah, which alleged, among other things, that the approach to Jinnah followed a refusal by the Congress to provide financial help to 'Ghaffar Khan and his henchmen'. Badshah Khan wrote to Jinnah:

> I have been pained to read the *Dawn*'s report. There are some statements in it that are completely untrue . . . I paid a visit to you so that, if possible, we might find a way out, peaceful and honourable to all concerned. Unfortunately, we could not agree. But in any event the tone and manner as well as the contents of *Dawn* are not such as to lead to a friendly approach or to a settlement.[81]

Jinnah, on his part, attacked Badshah Khan and Gandhi for mentioning Pathanistan, though he also seemed to hint at some autonomy for the Frontier as a unit of Pakistan.

*

Pathanistan was a concept over which Ghaffar Khan was obliged to maintain some ambiguity. He would lose all bargaining (and enthusing) power if every reference to Pathanistan or Pakhtunistan or, in Pakhto, *Pakhtunkhwa* was followed by an explicit disclaimer of sovereignty. Equally, he could not campaign for a sovereign Pakhtunistan without inviting British displeasure, the wrath of the Muslim League and its supporters, and the disapproval of most of his friends in India, who feared nothing more than post-independence fragmentation or disintegration. So he spoke of a free Pathan entity, sometimes adding that it could be part of a wider federation.

Another sensitive question quickly came to the fore. With the Empire withdrawing, the Afghan government sought to reopen the question of the Durand Line, drawn up in 1893 as Afghanistan's border with British India, arguing that an imperial construct was no longer binding. Even if he harboured some sympathy for Kabul's position, Badshah Khan could not quite support it, for Pakhtun unity, which he desired, was different from an expansion of Afghanistan.

Nonetheless, he and his brother were accused by some Muslim League elements of colluding with Afghanistan and of sending an emissary to Kabul. Since the rulers designate of the subcontinent were more than willing, whether in India or Pakistan, to inherit the borders of the Raj, a clarification was sought from Dr Khan Sahib by Nehru, who as the Member for External Affairs in the Viceroy's Executive Council had received the communication from Afghanistan. Dr Khan Sahib wrote back:

We assure you that we have never thought of joining Afghanistan . . . We know nothing of a Congress emissary approaching the Afghan Government.[82]

His teamwork with Ghaffar Khan continuing, Gandhi said in New Delhi on 30 June that

Badshah Khan and his coworkers do not relish being asked to choose between Hindustan or Pakistan . . . Even before the Congress ministry came into being,[83] Badshah Khan had on the brain Pathan independence in internal matters. He does not want to create an additional state. It is difficult for me to understand the objection to this yearning after Pathan autonomy, unless the object is to humiliate the Pathans and to tame them into subjection.

The more serious charge is that the Badshah is playing into the hands of Afghanistan. I consider him to be incapable of any underhand dealing. He would not allow the Frontier Province to be absorbed by Afghanistan.

More intriguing, in these public post-prayer remarks, was the following comment by Gandhi:

As [Badshah Khan's] friend and because I am his friend, I must admit one failing of his. He is highly suspicious especially of the British profession and intentions. I would urge on all to overlook this failing, which is by no means peculiar to him.[84]

For whose ears did Gandhi say this? In all probability, he was aiming his remarks at the departing British officials, who still had cards left to play, including those over the Frontier.

*

On 21 June, a joint meeting of the Frontier Province Congress Committee (FPCC), the Congress Parliamentary Party, the Khudai Khidmatgars and the Zalme Pakhtun, chaired by Khan Amir Mohammed Khan, unanimously resolved that 'a free Pathan state of all the Pakhtuns' be established. 'The constitution of the state', the resolution added, 'will be framed on the basis of Islamic conceptions of democracy, equality and social justice. The meeting appeals to all the Pathans to unite for the attainment of this cherished goal and not to submit to any non-Pakhtun domination.'[85] Badshah Khan sent a copy of the resolution to Jinnah.

Three days later, in Peshawar, Ghaffar Khan issued a statement asking the KKs and their supporters 'not to participate in the referendum and to keep away from it peacefully'. He added:

> Our struggle was against the British rule and domination, and in this we allied ourselves with the Indian National Congress . . . Our struggle all along has been for the freedom of India and more especially of the Pathans.
>
> The June 3 announcement limits our choice to

two alternatives (India or Pakistan), neither of which we are prepared to accept. We cannot vote as we want to vote, for a free Pathan state . . .

Religious passions of the unsophisticated Pathans also are being aroused by describing the contest . . . as one between kafirs and Islam.

Perhaps Mr Jinnah thought that I had seen him because of our weakness; I approached him as a Muslim for maintaining the unity amongst the Muslims. It is not out of our weakness that I approached him but out of strength of our cause and because of our earnest desire to have peace in the Frontier as well as freedom.[86]

At a meeting on 27 June he said:

We have decided to establish Pathanistan, an independent state of all the Pathans. There will be no king and the land will be ruled by the entire Pathan nation jointly. [Since we fought the British alongside the Congress,] we were called Hindus and Hindu agents, but when we have refused to join Hindustan, we are [being] forced to fight the referendum on the issue of Pakistan versus Hindustan.[87]

In the summer of 1947 the end of the Second World War was two years in the past and the Cold War was still in its womb. But Badshah Khan, who never forgot the Great Game that Britain and Russia had fought on Pakhtun lands from the time of his ancestors, saw meaning in a visit that General Bernard Montgomery made to India. He commented:

> The seeds of the third world war have already been sown . . . For that emergency the Britishers want to make the Frontier Province a military base against Russia. In that connection the arrival of General Montgomery into India and his meetings with Mr. Jinnah are indeed most significant.[88]

Badshah Khan's feelings regarding the referendum were described in another letter that Gandhi addressed, on 29 June, to Mountbatten:

> Badshah Khan writes to me to say that . . . the referendum would go on without any interference by his followers, the latter abstaining from voting either way. He fully realizes that in this case the Frontier would probably go to Pakistan.
>
> He wants me also to draw your attention to the fact that the Punjab Muslims, men and women, are being freely introduced in the Frontier Province to affect the referendum and that notable non-Frontier Muslims too have been sent to the Frontier Province for the same purpose. This increases the risk of bloodshed and worse.
>
> He also says that the non-Muslim refugees numbering many thousands will have no chance of taking part in the referendum and they are threatened with dire penalty should they dare to exercise their votes.[89]

After the start of the referendum, which would take two weeks in all, Ghaffar Khan said, in a letter to Gandhi, that in places ballots were being stuffed ('eighty to ninety percent votes have been polled, a thing unheard of in any election'), and added:

> We have been working under very difficult and trying circumstances but have adhered to nonviolence in thought, word and deed . . . [even though] the Muslim Leaguers backed by officials are out to create disturbances.
>
> Another matter which is causing serious concern to us is the presence in our province of a large number of Punjabis who openly incite people to violence . . . They have also gone to the length of suggesting in public meetings that the top leaders of the Red Shirts should be done away with. They also proclaim openly that after Pakistan has been established, there will be a trial on the lines of the Nuremberg trial and all of them who are called as traitors will be killed.[90]

Partly because of a demand from Badshah Khan, Governor Caroe was asked to proceed on leave, and Mountbatten placed the referendum in the charge of General Sir Rob Lockhart, until then the chief of the Southern Command. Announced on 20 July, the voting figures were 2,89,244 for Pakistan and 2,874 for India. The votes of about 50 per cent of the number on the rolls had been cast.

For three days at the end of July Badshah Khan was again in Delhi. He had long talks with Gandhi, who said to him, 'Make Pakistan really *pak* (pure).'[91] The two would not meet again, and for the next twenty-two years Ghaffar Khan would not visit India.

SIX

Biting Loyalty
1947–88

On 14 August 1947, the Pakistani flag flew atop government buildings in Peshawar, and the Khan brothers did not protest. They did not protest when, a week later, the Khan Sahib ministry was dismissed and Qaiyum Khan was installed as the Frontier's chief minister. The Assembly did not meet until the spring of 1948, by when seven MLAs had crossed over to the League, giving Qaiyum Khan a majority.

Early in September 1947 the brothers and a large number of their colleagues met in Sardaryab, looked at the subcontinent's altered map, and took some hard decisions. Pakistan was their own country; they would safeguard its interests and not create difficulties for its government, which was operating from Karachi with Jinnah as the governor general and Liaqat Ali Khan as the premier. Despite Qaiyum Khan's role, they would not create difficulties for his Frontier ministry either.

Also, they formally severed the KKs' ties with the Congress; instead of the Congress tricolour, they would now march under a new all-red flag.

Badshah Khan and his brother had no hesitation in seeing themselves and the KKs as contributors to Pakistan's independence, and the League as its beneficiary. After all, unlike most members of the League, the KKs had embraced death and jail to send the British home. We can assume, too, that the Khan brothers had noted the somewhat surprising contents of a speech that Jinnah made on 11 August, three days before the creation of Pakistan, to the Constituent Assembly:

> If you change your past and work together in a spirit that everyone of you, no matter what community he belongs to, no matter what his colour, caste, or creed, is first, second and last a citizen of this state, with equal rights, privileges and obligations, there will be no end of the progress you will make . . .
>
> I cannot emphasize it too much. We should begin to work in this spirit and in course of time all those angularities of the majority and minority communities, the Hindu community and the Muslim community—because even as regards Muslims you have Pathans, Punjabis, Shias, Sunnis, and so on, and among the Hindus you have Brahmins, Vishnavas, Khatris, also Bengalis, Madrasis and so on—will vanish.[1]

Yet the most significant resolution passed by the Sardaryab gathering, which included the KKs' provincial committee, the legislature party, the Zalme Pakhtun and some tribal representatives, was the one asking for Pakhtunistan. The new entity would 'comprise the present six Settled Districts of the NWFP and all such other contiguous areas inhabited by the Pakhtuns which may wish to join the new state of their own free will' and 'enter into agreement on defence, external affairs, and communications with Pakistan'.[2]

When, in November, word of the sharp attacks that the Pakhtunistan resolution invited reached Gandhi, he wrote to Ghaffar Khan welcoming him to India to work 'with me or otherwise', the last phrase hinting at the possibility of Gandhi's removal from the scene. The other alternative, Gandhi added, was for Badshah Khan 'to remain where he was and let the Pakistan authorities do their worst'. 'Don't worry', Badshah Khan replied, 'just pray for us.'

On 30 January 1948, it was a small band of Hindus in India that did their worst, killing Gandhi for being, in their eyes, too friendly to Muslims. Ghaffar Khan had begun eating the evening meal with his son Wali in the latter's home, Shahi Bagh, in the village of Muhammad Naray, when they heard the news on the radio. They could not eat any more. After some minutes they stepped out and held a condolence meeting, where Ghaffar Khan spoke of Gandhi as 'the only ray of light to help us through these darkest days'.[3] Wali, who had married a cousin in 1944, was now more of a political ally to his father than his older brother Ghani, whose artistic interests, left-wing views, and carefree lifestyle had combined to weaken his chances in any political succession to Badshah Khan.

By this time the Great Punjab Killings of August and September 1947, and the great migrations associated with those killings, had occurred. As Wali Khan would later put it, 'the singing and dancing and illuminations to celebrate independence' had been accompanied by 'the leaping flames, the overflowing streams of blood and the screams of resounding anguish'.[4] Mercifully the Frontier was spared large-scale communal riots in August and September, thanks in part to the role the KKs played. 'Despite their desertion by the [All-India Congress], the Khudai Khidmatgars still held strength in the province and . . . protected the lives and property of the non-Muslims in the NWFP.'[5]

By this time, also, Qaiyum Khan 'Kashmiri' had facilitated the incursion into Kashmir of some 5,000 armed tribals, mostly Afridis, in nearly 300 lorries, which also carried surplus arms and ammunition. Sir George Cunningham, who after independence again became, at Jinnah's invitation, the NWFP governor, noted that his chief minister, Qaiyum Khan, 'was encouraging the tribesmen to go into Kashmir and even collecting . . . militia transport for a tribal invasion'.[6] This exercise, which began on 21 October 1947, aimed at pre-empting a union of Muslim-majority Kashmir with India. However, it resulted in the accession to India by the Hindu Maharaja of Kashmir, in the airlift to Kashmir of Indian troops, and in an India–Pakistan war that would divide Kashmir into two halves.

Another Pakistani move was perhaps wiser;

certainly it won tribal goodwill. In December 1947, the large Pakistani garrisons in the tribal territory forts of Razmak and Wana were withdrawn.

His membership of the Constituent Assembly transferred to its Pakistani portion, which also served as Pakistan's first Parliament, Badshah Khan attended, on 23 February 1948, its session in Karachi and took the oath of allegiance to the new country and its flag. Jinnah, who was the president of the Assembly as well as the head of state and the Muslim League chief, invited Ghaffar Khan for tea. On this occasion he seems to have embraced Ghaffar Khan, remarking, 'Today I feel that my dream of Pakistan is realized.'

Jinnah was acknowledging the significance of Ghaffar Khan's allegiance to Pakistan. The next day the two had a long talk over lunch, Jinnah assuring Badshah Khan that as a constitutional governor general he was not for or against any political party, and Badshah Khan inviting Jinnah to visit the Frontier and get to know the KKs. Jinnah said he would come. Evincing support for Badshah Khan's efforts to encourage cottage industries, Jinnah offered a large number of spinning wheels for the Frontier. The question of Kashmir, too, was discussed, and Ghaffar Khan 'offered his services' to Jinnah towards its settlement.[7]

On 5 March 1948, Ghaffar Khan spoke for the first time to the Pakistan Parliament. Speaking in Urdu, he admitted that he had opposed the division of the subcontinent, pointed out that Partition had led to great massacres, but added, 'Now that the division has been done, the dispute is over.' Complaining that British officers continued to occupy many key positions in Pakistan, and arguing that the Muslim League's 'work is now over with the achievement of Pakistan', he asked for new political parties organized on economic lines.

But Pakhtunistan was the principal theme of this speech. Liaqat Ali Khan, the premier, and two senior leaders from the Punjab, Firoz Khan Noon and Ghazanfar Ali Khan, demanded clarification, with Noon alleging, 'You will join Afghanistan!' and Ghazanfar deploring 'provincialism'. Retorting that Sindhis, too, were being accused of provincialism, Ghaffar Khan asked, 'Who taught provincialism but the Punjabis?' He added:

The people inhabiting this province are called Sindhis and the name of their country is Sindh. Similarly the Punjab or Bengal is the land of the Punjabis or Bengalis. In the same way, there is the NWFP. We are one people and ours is a land within Pakistan; we also want that the mere mention of the name of the country should convey that it is the land of the Pathans. Is that a sin under the tenets of Islam?

The people of India used to call us Pathans, and we are called Afghans by the Persians. Our real name is Pakhtuns, and we want to see all the Pathans on this side of the Durand Line united together in Pakhtunistan . . . If you argue that Pakistan would be weakened by it, then I would say that Pakistan would become stronger . . . Government is run on good faith and not on mistrust.[8]

Feelers regarding places for his associates in governmental and diplomatic posts left Ghaffar Khan cold. Along with G.M. Syed of Sindh, who saw threats to Sindhi identity, Badshah Khan started the Jamiat-ul-Awam, or the Peoples' Party in March. In April, when he returned from Karachi to the Frontier, Ghaffar Khan found that *Pakhtun* was gagged, the other newspapers pressurized to deny space to the KKs, and many KKs arrested. Qaiyum Khan's police even appeared to obstruct Badshah Khan's social contacts.

Yet the Karachi talk with Jinnah had given him some hope. When Jinnah visited the Frontier in the middle of April, the KKs sent the governor general a resolution of support, and Ghaffar Khan urged Jinnah to meet the KKs. On the ground that he was not having any non-official meetings, Jinnah declined. However, at a Peshawar reception given by Sir Ambrose Dundas, who, Cunningham being ill, was acting as governor, Badshah Khan and the governor general talked with each other.

Jinnah asked Badshah Khan to join the Muslim League. Ghaffar Khan said he found it hard to join a body whose members had only recently looted the properties of Hindus and Sikhs. 'Surely there were exceptions—some who did not loot', Jinnah said. 'Yes', Badshah Khan agreed, 'those who did not get an opportunity.'

Our account of this conversation is taken from Badshah Khan's 1965 recollections. Ghaffar Khan added that in April 1948 he found Jinnah's ears poisoned against him by Qaiyum Khan and also by the British officers, led by Dundas, who continued to man the Frontier's top posts.

The final move, Ghaffar Khan would recall, was planned with consummate cunning. Jinnah was to address a public meeting. Abdul Qaiyum Khan planted his agents at strategic points, with instructions to get up during Jinnah's speech, create disturbance, and then walk out . . . Whenever any such individual or group got up, Qaiyum Khan would shout, 'You, Khudai Khidmatgar badmash, why don't you desist?' The trick worked. Jinnah was convinced that the Khudai Khidmatgars were a dangerous lot and out to kill him.[9]

In 1956, when he was brought before the High Court of West Pakistan, Ghaffar Khan would refer to the belief that 'at the time of his departure from the Frontier Province, the Qaid-e-Azam [had given] full powers to Abdul Qaiyum Khan and Dundas to crush the Khudai Khidmatgars'.[10]

*

The discovery that Jinnah's support would not be forthcoming was sobering but not surprising. Hostile to Pakhtunistan, the Pakistani establishment had also been suspicious towards the Peoples' Party, which was expressly non-communal and socialist. The new party's aims also included 'the stabilization and security of Pakistan', 'full and unimpaired autonomy for all', and 'cultural relations with the Indian Union'.

Ghaffar Khan did not make himself more acceptable when, in a press statement in May 1948, he contrasted the League's monopoly in Pakistan's politics with the complexion of the Indian cabinet, which included recent foes of the Congress like Syama Prasad Mookerjee of the Hindu Mahasabha and Bhim Rao Ambedkar of the Scheduled Castes Federation, even though, as Badshah Khan pointed out, these two leaders 'had not merged their organizations in the Congress Party in power'.[11]

In ensuing weeks he was more candid. Worse, he sought to reach his Pakhtuns in the mass. His chief companion on these tours in May and June 1948 of the districts of Peshawar and Mardan was a KK colleague and former Frontier minister, Qazi Ataullah Khan. Addressing a huge gathering in Mardan, Ghaffar Khan said:

> I have witnessed the show of the Pakistan Constituent Assembly. There is absolutely no difference between the Pakistan leaders and the old British bureaucracy. [It is argued in defence] that the new state is yet in its infancy. I invite them to look at India where the leaders have safely piloted the ship of state despite extremely stormy weather, and have even framed their draft constitution . . .

Pointing out that many of Pakistan's leaders were 'refugees who [did] not originally belong to Pakistan', he also said that 'as Governor General, Qaid-e-Azam Jinnah is not a representative of the Muslim nation. He was appointed by the British King.' Then came the ethnic call:

> My Pathan brothers, you are fully entitled to a one-fourth share in Pakistan . . . Unite and act with

determination, and thus demolish the sandy walls which the leaders of Pakistan have built around you . . . We will not rest content until we succeed in establishing Pakhtunistan – rule of the Pakhtuns, by the Pakhtuns, and for the Pakhtuns.[12]

It was too much for the new state. On 15 June, before he could take his message to the Pathans of the Frontier's southern districts, he and his son Wali were arrested near Bahadur Khel in Kohat. Qaiyum Khan told a press conference that but for a delay in obtaining Jinnah's signature, Badshah Khan would have been arrested before his speeches in Peshawar and Mardan.

Charged with 'sedition' and 'intended collaboration with the hostile Faqir of Ipi', Badshah Khan said he was not guilty. But he refused to offer a defence. Ten months after the departure of the British, Badshah Khan was sent to Montgomery Jail in West Punjab for three years' rigorous imprisonment.

Qaiyum Khan had armed himself with powers to outlaw all organizations 'objectionable to peace and security'. About a thousand KKs found themselves in jails, including many who courted arrest, ignoring Badshah Khan's advice that they should stay out of prison. On 12 August the Babra massacre occurred, when the police fired at hundreds of men and women assembling at the mosque in Babra village, south of Charsadda.

Their aim was to pray for arrested relatives and friends. Hanging from the necks of many of the women were miniature copies of the Qur'an, some of which the bullets pierced. Official figures mentioned fifteen dead and fifty injured, but KK sources maintained that 150 had been killed and 400 wounded. It seems that the police addressed the Pathans gathered in Babra as 'Hindus' and dubbed the mosque a Hindu mosque. After the massacre there was a manhunt of KKs in which the military joined. Dr Khan Sahib and Ghani, who had eluded arrest, were also caught and jailed, and in September the KK organization was proscribed and the Sardaryab centre attached.

That month, September 1948, also saw the death by illness, at the age of seventy-two, of Jinnah.

*

Did the suppression take Badshah Khan by surprise? Had he thoughtlessly silenced himself? Or did he consciously prefer being put away to a meek submission to Qaiyum Khan's rule? The latter explanation may be closer to the truth. Ghaffar Khan seems to have sensed that if he did not articulate the Pakhtunistan call now, he might not get another chance to do so. Qaiyum Khan, and probably Jinnah as well, seem to have calculated along similar lines. If they did not stop Badshah Khan and the KKs now, it would become far more difficult later.

Subduing the KKs in the Settled Districts was not hard for Pakistani authorities but the tribal territory was another matter. In Waziristan the Faqir of Ipi, always able, it seemed, to enter and exit caves and thus elude British troops, bristled at the continuance of British officers in Pakistan. In 1950 the Pakistan air force resorted to bombing several Pakhtun villages. That year a Pakhtun Provisional Parliament was created in the tribal territory, with one branch in Tirah and another in Waziristan and with the Ipi Faqir as its president, and the flag of an independent Pakhtunistan was hoisted.

But though Afghans displayed sympathy and, in a speech to the Afghan legislature in Kabul, the King spoke of 'the freedom-loving aspirations of the trans-Durand Afghans',[13] the emotional project of an independent Pakhtunistan was not fated to succeed. There seems to be no evidence that Badshah Khan subscribed to it. Neither the early 1950s nor the decades to follow offered a favourable climate for creating new states. Imperial maps had become nationalist maps, large new nations were more than willing to use overwhelming force to preserve inherited borders, and the world as a whole was not disposed to challenge them.

Solitary confinement in the summer heat and winter cold of Montgomery was trying. Ghaffar Khan weakened and had to be taken at times to hospital. Claiming to speak on behalf of Premier Liaqat Ali, the jail superintendent asked if Badshah Khan was interested in joining the League government and received the predictable answer. When the three years' sentence expired, Ghaffar Khan was detained afresh, for six months, under an 1818 Regulation. When the six months ended he was again detained for a further six months. The process was relentlessly repeated.

The British had never shut him up, at one stretch, for this long. Once during this period (in April 1952) it looked as if he would die of illness but he was saved by surgery in Lahore's Mayo Hospital. On this occasion thousands prayed for him in Mecca, and messages were received from India's Prime Minister, Nehru, and the King of Afghanistan.

Asked once how he faced the possibility of dying, Ghaffar Khan seems to have replied: 'If I die, I will be with God; if I live, God will be with me.' Twice in 1951 and again in 1953 Nehru publicly voiced concern at Ghaffar Khan's continuing detention and deteriorating health, inviting accusations from Pakistani authorities of interference in their internal affairs.

In 1952 the *Pakistan Times* of Lahore ran an account of Ghaffar Khan's condition in Montgomery Jail supplied by Mohammad Yahya, a Pakhtun, who had been allowed to interview Badshah Khan in the presence of jail officials and a police officer from the CID. Since the others did not follow Pakhtu, the prisoner and Yahya were told to speak only in Urdu. The interview revealed one of Ghaffar Khan's problems: because a new set of teeth ordered for him did not fit, he was eating without any teeth. He had been alone in a cell for much of the time but had cooked for, and nursed, a fellow prisoner called Syed Ashiq Shah.[14]

*

Even as mornings took long to arrive in Montgomery Jail, and new moons took infinitely longer, time was claiming lives or careers. In September 1951 Premier Liaqat Ali Khan was assassinated in Rawalpindi, a crime that was never resolved. In April 1953 the Governor

General of Pakistan, Ghulam Mohammad, who had emerged from the civil service, dismissed the Prime Minister, Khwaja Nazimuddin, a scion of the Nawabs of Dhaka, who was replaced by another Bengali, the diplomat Mohammed Ali Bogra.

The League's central leaders were at one another's throats but the high-level conflicts reflected serious problems on the ground. Pakistan's two wings were growing apart, and the Muslim League was rapidly losing ground in East Bengal. In the Frontier, Qaiyum Khan, 'unable to brook any opposition',[15] had become unpopular.

Visiting Ghaffar Khan in jail in 1953, Sardar Bahadur Khan, Pakistan's Communications Minister and a brother of General Ayub Khan, the army chief, said that though the government was not in favour of his continued incarceration it was afraid that he would never forgive or forget what he and his colleagues had suffered. This was the first indication of a possible change in Karachi's attitude, and also, perhaps, of a realization that the Khan brothers might be needed in Pakistan's altering scenario. Badshah Khan replied that as a votary of nonviolence he could not harbour any feeling of retaliation or revenge but releasing him was an issue for the government, not for him.[16]

On 5 January 1954, Sardar Bahadur Khan accompanied Badshah Khan as he emerged from Rawalpindi Jail, where he had earlier been brought from Montgomery. The release, after five-and-a-half years in prison, was partial and conditional: he would have to stay in the Rawalpindi Circuit House, he could not visit the Frontier, and even in the Punjab, or elsewhere in Pakistan, his movements would be regulated by the government.

Dr Khan Sahib and several other prominent KK leaders and Abdus Samad Khan, the leader of the Pakhtuns of Baluchistan, were also released because, it was said, 'of the healthy atmosphere prevailing in the Frontier Province'.[17] By this time May Khan had died after spending over three decades on the subcontinent during which she had taken care of her husband, their children, and the children of Ghaffar Khan, twice seen her husband steer the Frontier as its Premier, and lost their son Jan. Dr Khan Sahib had her buried in the grounds of a house he had built in Utmanzai.

There was speculation that Badshah Khan's release was linked to the Kashmir question. Earlier, when a prominent Punjabi politician, the Nawab of Mamdot, visited Ghaffar Khan in Montgomery Jail, and the journalist Hamid Nizami of *Nawa-i-Waqt* was also present, Badshah Khan had put forward 'some proposals' on Kashmir.[18] Asked on his release whether he would exert his influence in Pakistan's favour, Ghaffar Khan replied that if he urged Kashmiris to fight for joining Pakistan, they might ask him: 'Who are you and what about yourself? Do you want to take us into detention?' He added that in the six years since he had offered his services to the late Mr Jinnah, 'the Kashmir dispute had become much more complicated'.[19]

In fact, the releases had less to do with Kashmir than with the need of Pakistani politicians to find allies with grass-roots support. Apart from trends in East

Bengal, resentment at the Muslim League's 'outsider' leaders, i.e. those who had migrated from India, was growing in the Punjab, Sindh, and the Frontier. In this situation the Khan brothers, sons of the Pakhtun soil, their popularity enhanced by imprisonment, held great promise: they could help realign Pakistani politics.

Appealing to numerous politicians, within or outside the League, who were dissatisfied with their slices of power, the possibility of new alignments was also grasped by the Khan brothers, who however reacted differently to it. Prison walls did not, in the case of Badshah Khan, destroy his dream of Pakhtun unity. Patiently if never easily endured, prison's hurtful hours seemed merely to add to his stock of faith. With the older brother it was different. Unable in jail to use his political or medical skills, he saw every minute ticking by as another wasted grain of life. In jail Dr Khan Sahib made his strategic choice: he would be open to a role in any new political coalition.

But we need not conclude that Badshah Khan, by contrast, was a mere idealist. As his daughter Mehr Taj would later put it, his was 'a deep mind'.[20] As canny as he was committed, he saw that his Pakhtuns would be suspicious of a merely top-level compromise with Pakistani politicians. Conceding Ghaffar Khan's distinctive political style, the scholar Erland Jansson, author of the careful 1981 study, *India, Pakistan or Pakhtunistan?*, noted nonetheless that Badshah Khan's 'political writings and activities have shown remarkable consistency over the years and his perspicacity has often been striking'.[21]

Ghaffar Khan was more intensely aware than his brother of the strength of Pakhtunness. True, there was pain in the world existing between the Khyber and the Indus, while a promise of gain beckoned from across the big river, yet a sense of belonging went with the pain, whereas in an alliance beyond the Indus lay the possibility of being abandoned, as both brothers had found in 1947.

*

Eight months after their release an increasingly sick Ghulam Mohammad declared an emergency and dismissed the cabinet, installing in its place a semi-dictatorial executive. Though Premier Bogra chaired this executive, power now lay with the Governor General and two of his colleagues, the Interior Minister, Iskander Mirza, the Bombay-born politico-military officer of Bengali and Iranian origins who had served for decades in the Frontier, and Ayub Khan, the new Defence Minister, whose family had roots in the Frontier's Hazara district and in the Punjab's Campbellpur area.

Mirza, who knew well the Khan brothers, especially the older one, from his Frontier days, had been uneasy about their long detention. Now, in October 1954, he 'strongly urged the inclusion of Dr Khan Sahib in the new cabinet, as this would reassure the Pakhtuns'.[22] Ghulam Mohammad extended an invitation, and Dr Khan Sahib, old foe of the Muslim League and recent prisoner, convicted of sedition, accepted it. He had consulted Ghaffar Khan, who advised him to reject the offer. However, in the belief that he might 'induce others to serve Pakistan selflessly', Dr Khan Sahib joined the cabinet, saying, 'In case of failure I can resign.'[23]

The younger brother, meanwhile, had been allowed to travel from Rawalpindi to Karachi for another session of the Constituent Assembly. From Karachi station he 'walked along the railway track up to Khan Sahib's bungalow'. That evening, when the older brother reached home, accompanied by a journalist, Hiro Shroff, they found Ghaffar Khan, 'with his light bundle of bed-sheet and clothes, sitting on the steps' of Dr Khan Sahib's bungalow. He had refrained from entering the house because 'the rightful occupant', the older brother, was not in. According to Shroff, when the brothers met each other, 'the two did not hug but merely exchanged greetings'.[24] Decorum and hospitality did not necessarily spell warmth.

After interviewing Badshah Khan in Karachi, James W. Spain, an American writer, referred to Ghaffar Khan's 'prominent Pathan nose', 'glistening dark eyes', 'simple long garment of homespun, something like an old-fashioned night-shirt'—and, six years in jail notwithstanding—his strong grip.[25] Reminding the Constituent Assembly of his imprisonment, Ghaffar Khan said on 20 March 1954:

During all this period of my incarceration you did not even ask the Government as to what crime I had committed . . . I had to go to prison many a time in the days of the Britishers. Although we were at loggerheads with them, yet their treatment of us in jail was gentlemanly . . . But the treatment which was meted out to me in this Islamic state of ours was such that I do not even like to mention it to you . . .

Six years ago I announced on the floor of this House that Pakistan is our country, and its solidarity and protection is our duty . . . I repeat those words of mine even today. If we had not forced the Britishers to quit, how could Pakistan have come into existence? How can we betray a country for the freedom of which we have suffered so much?

Then he referred to the League's big defeat in East Bengal, which had just occurred, to Pakhtunistan, to the KKs, and to his beliefs:

For the solidarity of Pakistan it is necessary that the various sections of its people should mutually trust one another and respect one another's rights, interests and distinctive features. You will perhaps recall that six years ago I had said in this connection that after the establishment of Pakistan, the country had no need for the Muslim League. The recent elections in Bengal have proved this contention . . .

The English had destroyed our unity by cutting us, the Pakhtuns, into several parts in order to weaken us. For the solidarity of Pakistan, it is necessary to restore that unity by bringing together all those areas in which the inhabitants are racially and culturally homogeneous into one unit of Pakhtunistan.

I am still virtually a prisoner, for except in the Punjab I am not allowed to move into any other part of Pakistan. My Khudai Khidmatgar Party is under a ban; our national paper, the *Pakhtun*, was made to cease publication the day Pakistan came into being; and our two-storeyed training centre (*in Sardaryab*) has already been razed to the ground.

You know that I have always been an adherent of nonviolence. I regard nonviolence as love and violence as hate. I have ever been a law-abiding citizen, and so I want that our country, Pakistan, too should be a peace-loving country.[26]

Three weeks later, after killings in East Bengal in riots against non-Bengalis, Ghaffar Khan's words in the Constituent Assembly again showed that his loyalty to Pakistan had a cutting edge:

[The riots in East Pakistan] are the direct outcome of the policy that you had been following in that part of the country for the last seven years. You gagged public opinion and imprisoned people without trial . . . You governed the province in an arbitrary manner [and] whose goodwill you took for granted . . .

You suppress the legitimate aspirations of the people in general and play off one section against another, and when matters come to a head, a scapegoat is readily seized and declared responsible for all the troubles.[27]

*

The anti-League ministry in Dhaka was dismissed following the riots, and for some months prior to his joining the Pakistani cabinet Mirza functioned as East Bengal's hard-line Governor. The League's decimation in East Bengal, and the upsurge there of a separatist Bengali sentiment, contributed to the birth of the One Unit scheme for West Pakistan. This scheme envisaged a merger of the Punjab, Sindh, the NWFP and Balochistan that would, among other things, shore up the western wing in its equation with East Bengal, which contained more than half the Pakistani population.

Conceived as part of a package giving East Bengal what West Pakistani politicians had hitherto opposed, namely autonomy, and West Pakistan what Bengalis had hitherto opposed, namely parity with the more populous eastern wing, the One Unit scheme was advocated by prominent Punjabis including Chaudhri Mohammed Ali, Mumtaz Daultana, and Nawab Gurmani, by Governor General Ghulam Mohammad, and by Mirza and Ayub Khan.

Significantly, One Unit also secured the backing of Dr Khan Sahib, who seems to have felt that a unified West Pakistan could lower the profile of the Punjab, to the Frontier's advantage, especially if, as now seemed possible, he found a major role himself in the West Pakistan government. Other supporters, however, saw One Unit as a means of eliminating separatist tendencies in the Frontier, Sindh and Baluchistan.

Over One Unit, implemented in 1955 with the

agreement of the legislatures of the Punjab, Sindh and the NWFP, the brothers were totally divided. Dr Khan Sahib became the active proponent of One Unit and the younger brother its ardent foe. Still confined to the Rawalpindi Circuit House, though allowed to attend a session of the Constituent Assembly in the hill town of Murree, Badshah Khan asked, in March 1955, for a popular vote on One Unit and said that autonomy, not One Unit, would contain provincialism.

*

About the days in Murree, Hamida Khuhro has written: 'Even the towering khaddar clad figure of Khan Abdul Ghaffar Khan, just released from jail, was seen strolling down the Mall.'[28] While in Murree, Badshah Khan visited the Jesus and Mary Convent, where his granddaughters (Ghani's daughters) were boarders (and where his daughter Mehr Taj had once studied), and thanked the nuns for their dedication.[29] But we can be certain that the granddaughters, whose father too had just spent five years in prison, as had their uncle Wali, were the reason for visiting the convent. Ghaffar Khan was separated for long periods from his family, and austerely resolved to live for the Pakhtun people, yet his heart hungered for the company of his children and grandchildren.

Along with one of the twins she was carrying, Wali's wife had died in 1949. The surviving twin, Asfandyar, would in time become a prominent politician. In November 1954, while Badshah Khan was barred from the Frontier province, Wali was married to Naseem, daughter of Amir Mohammed Khan, an old associate of his father's. Attended by Badshah Khan, the wedding took place just east of the Indus in Attock. We saw earlier that Mehr Taj had married the educator–politician, Yahya Jan. Her brother Ali (Lali) married Qazi Ataullah's daughter, cementing a friendship between the families that had begun in Rev. Wigram's school, where Ataullah's father was a teacher, and Jabbar and Ghaffar were students. Also imprisoned from 1948, Ataullah had however died while in detention.

Comments on Badshah Khan's attitude to his family were provided to the author in the summer of 2003 by Mehr Taj and her son Salim, by Wali Khan's son Asfandyar, and by Ali Khan's sons, Zulfiqar and Nasir. Mehr Taj remarked that her father was on the whole 'cold' towards her, adding, 'It was Dr Khan Sahib and Memsahib (May Khan) who brought me up.' However, Mehr Taj went on, 'when I matriculated, Father gave me a wrist watch.' Asked if she had ever enquired of her father what her mother, Nambata, Badshah Khan's second wife, was like, Mehr Taj said there was no question of her doing so. Asfandyar Khan gave a similar reply when asked if he had ever asked his grandfather about his grandmother, Mehr Qandh. 'Even now, though times have changed, such questions are rarely asked', Asfandyar said.

According to Asfandyar, his grandfather had firmly disciplined his emotions. Rarely displaying great affection towards his children, he almost never allowed himself to break down. 'The only time I saw him close to breaking down', said Asfandyar, 'was when (in 1958) he was burying Bibi's father.' The reference was to Amir Mohamad Khan, the father of Wali Khan's second wife, Naseem, who, following the death of the first wife, had raised Wali's children. Yet Salim, Zulfiqar, and Nasir spoke of their grandfather's 'warmth' and 'affection'. The grandchildren clearly 'saw' more of Badshah Khan's affection than his own children did, though Mehr Taj too said that 'when in the mood'—she repeated the phrase twice—'Father would laugh a lot and tell us stories.'

'Do you remember any of the stories?' 'Well, he spoke of this Pathan servant who accompanied him once to Bombay and said to him, "There seems to be the same moon in Bombay as in Charsadda", and added, "And the donkeys of Bombay also seem to speak Pakhto." Then Father laughed and laughed.' Another story of Badshah Khan's laughter was related by Mehr Taj's son, Salim. After watching his grandfather struggle in vain against a persistent fly, Salim, it seems, caught the fly in his hand and rattled it inside his fist. 'What are you doing?' Badshah Khan asked. 'I am trying to confuse the fly', Salim replied, whereupon the grandfather 'laughed and laughed'.

Allowing himself the right to laugh, Badshah Khan had however iron-bolted the doorway to tears; he had to have a strong stomach and a strong heart to carry the burdens of all his Pakhtuns.

*

To return to our narrative: In July 1955, after an unpopular Qaiyum Khan had finally resigned as the Frontier Chief Minister, Badshah Khan was at last allowed to re-enter the Frontier. One of his first calls was to the village of Babra, to pray for those gunned down in 1948. The Pakhtuns could not contain their joy, and on this occasion Ghaffar Khan could not contain his tears.[30]

Hoping to win Ghaffar Khan's backing for One Unit, his older brother and Iskander Mirza talked at length with him in Peshawar. When the week-long effort failed, Mirza said at a press conference that the Khudai Khidmatgars had 'endangered peace and order at the inception of the state and may do it again' and the government would prevent their revival. Badshah Khan's reply was to ask again for a popular vote on One Unit, apart from clarifying that 'provincialism was outside his creed and he looked upon the Punjabis as his brethren'.[31]

If Dr Khan Sahib and the Pakistani establishment were now on the same side, Ghaffar Khan, too, found himself in unaccustomed company. The Pir of Manki Sharif, who in 1947 had joined the League in demanding the ouster of the Khan Sahib ministry and, before that, had encouraged demonstrations against Nehru's visit to the tribal areas, was, in 1955, as opposed as Ghaffar Khan to One Unit. Tramping the country together, the two addressed scores of meetings. The Pakhtuns responded with fervour, thousands offering to court imprisonment. The Pakhtuns' love for Ghaffar Khan had not ebbed.

Suspecting that One Unit would make it easier for the Punjab to control 'the electricity of the Frontier

Province, the mineral wealth of Baluchistan and the lands of Sindh',[32] Ghaffar Khan had additional grounds for his opposition. His vision was for the NWFP and the tribal areas to unify into a Pakhtunistan, which One Unit threatened to supersede. Also, One Unit was to him a top-down scheme that gave little consideration to the interests or wishes of the Pakhtuns, or, for that matter, of the Punjabis.

*

Formed in the summer of 1955, a new Constituent Assembly endorsed One Unit, and in October Dr Khan Sahib, who successfully persuaded many Pakhtun politicians to try it out, was sworn in as West Pakistan's Chief Minister. Continuing, on his part, a campaign of opposition, Badshah Khan travelled to Baluchistan, Sindh, the Punjab and Bengal. On one occasion he said:

> My elder brother is the Prime Minister of West Pakistan, and among the Pakhtuns the elder brother is given the position of the father. But then I have dared to disagree with him on the issue of One Unit because I see great harm in it for my people.[33]

By this time Pakistan's volatile politics had ended the careers of Governor General Ghulam Mohammad and Premier Mohammed Ali Bogra, who both resigned in August 1955. Iskander Mirza became Acting Governor General, then Governor General, and then, in March 1956, following the acceptance at last of a Constitution

for Pakistan, the new republic's first President. Dr Khan
Sahib was one of those who had proposed Mirza for the
Presidency. Recalling Mirza's earlier career in the
Frontier, Dr Khan Sahib also managed to convey to the
national assembly his pride in the 'non-cooperation' and
'civil disobedience' movements 'in the cause of freedom',
though he did not explicitly refer to the Congress or to
the Khudai Khidmatgars.[34]

The Muslim League was now weakening in West
Pakistan as well, and the national assembly saw
realignments in quick succession. After taking over as
head of state in August 1955, Mirza worked with four
prime ministers in a little over three years: Chaudhri
Mohammad Ali of the Muslim League, a former
bureaucrat hailing from East Punjab, who followed
Bogra; East Bengal's Hassan Shahid Suhrawardy, who
had left the Muslim League and overcome it in his
province and was Premier from September 1956 to
October 1957; Ismail Chundrigar, with links to Bombay
and the Muslim League, whose premiership survived a
mere two months; and Malik Firoz Khan Noon of the
Punjab, formerly of the League and later of the new
Republican Party, who was prime minister from
December 1957 to October 1958.

One of the founders of the Republican Party was
Dr Khan Sahib, or, rather, it was the issue of Dr Khan
Sahib's continuance, on Pakistan becoming a republic,
as the West Pakistan chief minister that triggered the
new party's formation. While President Mirza and Prime
Minister Chaudhri Mohammad Ali wanted Dr Khan
Sahib to stay on as chief minister, many in the Muslim

League 'still regarded Dr Khan Sahib as their enemy',[35] and a revolt was organized by Mian Mumtaz Daultana. Those 'who felt that the bond given by Chaudhri Mohammad Ali should be honoured', and Dr Khan Sahib endorsed, broke off and formed the Republican Party.[36] In April 1956 Dr Khan Sahib was confirmed as chief minister by a one-vote margin.

*

On 16 June 1956, when he was in Shahi Bagh, Ghaffar Khan was arrested again and taken to Haripur Jail. Charged with 'inciting hatred against the Government', he was tried in September by Justice Shabir Ahmed of the West Pakistan High Court in Lahore.

The inner struggles, and inner victories, of persons like Badshah Khan who kept no diary or wrote few private letters are sometimes revealed in a public speech or a courtroom statement. The nineteen-page statement in Urdu that Ghaffar Khan submitted to the court is a powerful and in places introspective summary of his life thus far: his boyhood, the cancelled journey to England, the origins of the Khudai Khidmatgar movement, his fight, alongside the Congress and Gandhi, for independence, his stand on Pakistan, his effort, following Pakistan's creation, with Jinnah, his 1948–54 imprisonment, and his differences with his brother over One Unit. Said Badshah Khan:

My Lord, had I desired to create hatred against the government, there was sufficient material for a

revolt in the oppression to which my people have
been subjected. But I, on the contrary, have always
preached the doctrine of nonviolence and have even
declared that we have forgiven those who have done
injustice to us or insulted us . . .

We consider the Punjabis, Bengalis, Sindhis and
Baluchis to be our Muslim and Pakistani brethren.
I do not hate even those who are responsible for
the destruction of the autonomy of the Frontier
province. Personally I have no reason to hate the
Punjabis, nor do I hate them.[37]

After lengthy proceedings, on 24 January 1957,
Justice Shabir Ahmed sentenced Badshah Khan to
imprisonment until the rising of the court and a fine of
Rs 14,000. When the accused said he would not pay the
fine, Justice Ahmed ordered its realization from Ghaffar
Khan's property.

His brother was the West Pakistan chief minister
when the judgement was given, but not for much longer.
In the summer of 1957 Dr Khan Sahib lost his majority.
By this time the Punjab's politicians had lost their faith
in One Unit, in part because One Unit had given a
Pakhtun some authority over the Punjab.

In the wilderness once again, this time after a spell
of nearly three years in ministerial office in independent
Pakistan, old Dr Khan Sahib was surely intrigued when,
in July 1957, an announcement came from Dhaka that
his younger brother had combined with G.M. Syed of
Sindh, Maulana Bhashani of East Bengal, and Mian
Iftikharuddin of the Punjab (once the head of the Punjab

Congress Committee) to form a new party, the National
Awami Party.

In less than a year, however, on 9 May 1958, Dr
Khan Sahib was knifed to death in the house in Lahore
of his eldest son, Sadullah Khan, an engineer working
for the government. The assassin, apparently a speaker
of Punjabi or Seraiki, found Dr Khan Sahib in the
veranda, stabbed him near the groin, and ran. He was
chased by the seventy-six-year-old victim, by two
Alsatians in the house, and by a driver, and was caught,
but old Dr Khan Sahib, struck in a vital artery, bled to
his death. Although after a trial the assassin was hanged,
his motive and possible links to any others were never
clearly brought out.

Dr Khan Sahib was buried, in obedience to his
instructions, alongside May Khan in his Utmanzai house.
Surviving him by four years, his first wife, Khurshid,
would find her resting place in the family graveyard in
Utmanzai.

Declaring that he would 'watch and see what the
police and the Government were doing with the
[murder's] investigation', Badshah Khan said that 'he felt
that Dr Khan Sahib had been done to death by those
people for whom he had forsaken his own people'.
Adding that the murder had 'accentuated a feeling of
hatred between the Pathans and the Punjabis', he urged
the Pathans and the Punjabis to find 'an effective remedy'
for the 'growing distrust and hatred'.[38] Two months
later, Badshah Khan was arrested in Quetta, where he
had gone to speak against One Unit, taken to Peshawar,
and released there.

Others, meanwhile, and notably President Mirza and the chief of the army, General Ayub Khan, were contemplating 'an effective remedy' of another kind. To them the assassination of Dr Khan Sahib confirmed the sickness of Pakistani politics, which had also been proclaimed by daily squabbles over portfolios in Firoz Khan Noon's cabinet. On 7 October, President Mirza abrogated the Constitution, dismissed the central and provincial governments, dissolved the national and provincial assemblies, abolished all political parties, proclaimed martial law, and named Ayub Khan as Chief Martial Law Administrator (CMLA).

It did not take Ayub Khan long to send two generals to the President's House, obtain the resignation of Mirza, who went into exile in London, and replace Mirza as President.

On 11 October, Badshah Khan was arrested in the home of his son Ghani in Muhammad Naray village. Maulana Bhashani of East Bengal and Abdus Samad Khan of Balochistan were also arrested, as were hundreds of others. To be jailed was not exactly new for Ghaffar Khan, yet being imprisoned by an army regime was an experience for which neither the British nor Qaiyum Khan had prepared him. He was kept in Haripur Jail in Ayub Khan's Hazara district. The seclusion was stricter than before. He was allowed fewer interviews. Guards and warders were rude to him.

Six months later, on 4 April 1959, an official press note said that Badshah Khan, now sixty-nine, was being released from detention 'somewhere in Pakistan on consideration of his old age and indifferent health'. The note added that the government hoped that he would 'no longer indulge in activities prejudicial to the solidarity and security of Pakistan'.[39]

The released Ghaffar Khan went to Utmanzai, where he received a notice from a tribunal appointed to purge unwanted politicians from public life. The notice asked him to show why, having been detained often for subversive activities, he should not be disqualified from holding any elective office. Since he could not dispute the 'charge' of previous detention, Ghaffar Khan was declared barred from office for seven years.

For two long years he exercised patience. In 1960 he heard of the death of a fellow Pakhtun who had waged a long war against intruders, the Faqir of Ipi. The London *Times* called the old enemy of Empire 'a man of principle'.[40] Never captured by his British or, later, Pakistani pursuers, the Faqir had moved from cave to cave in the tribal territory even as Ghaffar Khan had moved from prison to prison. Unlike Badshah Khan, the Faqir used guns. Unlike Badshah Khan, the Faqir did not mix with a wider world. Yet there was something common in their constancy for the Pakhtun dream.

In March 1961, Badshah Khan started stirring out. His strategy, in this time of military rule, was to speak in mosques, to speak indirectly, to cite from the Holy Book. In Bannu he said:

In the Qur'an God has mentioned that He does not punish people because of their lack of faith. If that were not so, America, Soviet Russia and Europe would have been destroyed long ago. They are rising higher and higher.

God destroys those who are tyrannical, who are disunited and who are ungrateful to Him. God was so kind to you that He relieved you from the yoke of slavery of the British. When we were striving to throw out British rule, our present lords did not even think that was possible . . . They thought we were striking against a mountain . . . But God relieved us from the rule of the biggest power in the world.[41]

Ayub Khan did not wait for more than a month. On 12 April 1961, Ghaffar Khan was arrested in Dera Ismail Khan for 'indulging in anti-State activities'. From Rawalpindi, designated by the General as Pakistan's new capital, Ayub Khan, safe in his army rule from correction or contradiction, declared:

Abdul Ghaffar Khan wanted the Frontier area to become a part of India. Having failed in that venture, he demanded a separate province in Pakistan, where he wanted to be the king. Later, he wanted to make this Frontier region a part of Afghanistan.[42]

Kept first in Paniala, Badshah Khan was later removed to Hyderabad Jail in Sindh. Every six months his detention was extended. At the end of 1962, Amnesty International named Ghaffar Khan 'Prisoner of the Year' and demanded his release.

In May 1963, Wali Khan, increasingly a political leader himself of the Pakhtuns, declared that some 3,000 followers of his father were rotting in detention camps and that properties worth over forty-two crores of rupees had been confiscated.

Often ill, at times refusing to eat, and always unbending, Ghaffar Khan was moved first to Lahore Jail, then to Multan, and back to Lahore. After visiting him in Lahore Jail in December 1963, Wali Khan complained to Pakistan's Home Minister that his father was kept in solitary confinement and forced to cook his own meals. Shifted once more, this time back to Haripur, Ghaffar Khan fell alarmingly ill.

Not wanting him to die in prison, the regime let him out on 30 January 1964, but kept him under house arrest. He was not allowed to meet the villagers or make statements. At the end of May he heard that Nehru had died in Delhi. In a telegram to Nehru's daughter Indira, Ghaffar Khan called Nehru 'one of the greatest sons of the soil, who put into practice Gandhiji's ideals of love and peace on earth'.[43]

Four months later, Pakistan's military government allowed Ghaffar Khan's family to take him to the UK for treatment, enabling him to make in 1964 a journey that, but for his mother's objection, would have been made fifty-five years earlier. In England he was surprised at the care he received from the former Frontier Governor, Sir Olaf Caroe. Taking Badshah Khan to his home and enabling him to rest there, Caroe treated his former foe 'with great courtesy and genuine admiration'.[44] At a London meeting, Ghaffar Khan made remarks that suggested that Caroe's concern had made an impact:

> It is good that I came to your country, because in the past I did not have a good opinion about you. The Britons whom I met in India were different. Thank God I came here. The misunderstanding about you has vanished.[45]

Wanting to visit California for the winter that lay ahead, he applied for a US visa but soon tired of his visits to the American consulate, where he felt he was examined 'like a schoolboy'. He would probably not have got an American visa in any case; the Pakistani authorities had communicated their objections to Washington. The Pakistan embassy in London told him of three countries he could visit—Iran, Lebanon, and Egypt. But India and Afghanistan were out.

At the end of 1964 Ghaffar Khan went to Cairo, and thence, disregarding Pakistani objections, to Kabul. At Kabul airport he found the Afghan prime minister, other members of the cabinet, and thousands of Afghans. Slogans about 'Fakhr-e-Afghan' and Pakhtunistan were raised. Kabul's relations with Pakistan were at a low point, and Badshah Khan was received as a hero.

*

The Afghan government put him up as a state guest in a gracious house in Dar-ul-Aman, five miles from Kabul. The city's best doctors treated him. For the first time in years, every physical need of his was fully met. And he was free, free to meet anyone, say anything. Though prison had damaged his constitution—his heart was weak, he felt numb in his legs, his appetite was poor, and he suffered from lack of sleep at night—Kabul restored him to some sense of wellness, which was heightened whenever one of his sons joined him.

He got up early in the morning at 4.30, took a cup of light tea at 6.00, and at 7.30 had a breakfast of a couple of eggs and a slice or two of toasted bread washed down with tea. For lunch and dinner he had a plate of boiled vegetables, nan, yoghurt, and some fruit. Before retiring he had a cup of milk. Morning and evening he walked. From 9.00 to midday, and again from 3.30 till late in the evening, he was surrounded by visitors—members of the government, students, tribal chiefs, or divines. Some of these details were noted down by Pyarelal, Gandhi's secretary and biographer, who travelled to Kabul in 1965 to meet Badshah Khan.

Pyarelal found that Badshah Khan was out of the house a lot and at times far out of Kabul, including in Herat, near the Iranian border. Unlike in the NWFP, the Pakhtuns of Afghanistan, he felt, 'had grown up in independence' and were 'spontaneous'. The Afghans were fighters, he told Pyarelal, and had discipline; all that was needed was to give them a nonviolent turn.

Their response to him was wholehearted. They vied with one another to entertain him and even to catch a glimpse of him. Some spread the word that touching Badshah Khan or kissing his hand brought merit. He protested sharply, criticized 'this false teaching' and said that his sole wish was 'to serve you, to teach you to become Khudai Khidmatgars', but the aura refused to vanish.[46]

In Kabul Ghaffar Khan was an exile who at times felt at home, and here he found it possible, at last, to look back upon his life and record some of its moments. He had not written in prison. Apart from the explanation earlier offered, recalling the past in a British or Pakistani jail might have seemed a confession of defeat. Or maybe he expected prison authorities to confiscate and destroy anything he wrote.

But in Kabul, where he could relax and feel safe, he dictated the story of a life of seventy-five years to Kanwar Bhan Narang, a Hindu who had served in the Frontier legislature as a Khudai Khidmatgar. Narang took down Badshah Khan's Pakhto, and a woman named Helen H. Bouman translated it into English. That helper of the wronged of the subcontinent, Mridula Sarabhai, turned up from India and encouraged Badshah Khan in the project. In his autobiography Badshah Khan would say that Mridula had long been like a daughter to him and acknowledge her 'great sympathy for the victimized'.[47]

From Kabul, and earlier from London, Ghaffar Khan wrote letters that could not have been sent from the Frontier.

To Pyarelal, from England: Perhaps you have forgotten us but we have not forgotten you. Man in his happiness forgets his friends but those who are in distress cannot. In our adversity we think of you. If Mahatmaji had been alive he would certainly have remembered us and come to our help. It is our misfortune that he is no more and the rest have forgotten us . . . Remember me in your prayers and pray for me that God may restore me to health.[48]

From Kabul he wrote again to Pyarelal:

Nothing worse can befall us . . . We are still dubbed 'Hindus' . . . What saddens me is that while we shrank from no sacrifice for the sake of India's independence, the Congress, on attaining it, forsook us . . . This was unbecoming of the Congress.[49]

Learning of the letters to Pyarelal, Vinoba Bhave, who had been one of Gandhi's closest colleagues, wrote to Badshah Khan admitting that 'in our freedom fight a great injustice had been done to you and you have been practically let down by your friends'. Added Bhave: 'Maybe, after putting you to so much trial, God intends to use you as an instrument in solving world problems!'[50] Sent in May 1965, Badshah Khan's reply to Vinoba reveals the blows his faith had received:

I was deeply touched by your affectionate letter . . . to a person who is fighting a losing battle not only with his adversaries but with his own rank and file who have become so desperately disgusted with the tyrannical government of Pakistan. They are losing confidence in the creed of nonviolence . . . Their argument is that with the Britishers nonviolence could have its efficacy, but not with Pakistanis . . .

In the last eighteen years, since Pakistan came into being, I have been behind bars for fifteen years—mostly in solitary confinement, with taunts and insults from those who were my wardens. All those who were Khudai Khidmatgars have gone through similar treatment, rather worse than mine. Their property is confiscated and their children and family are now destitute . . .

There is none to report these brutalities to the outside world . . . The Government and people of Pakistan label us Hindus whenever we open our mouth or move in the public . . .

My comrades in India who are now in Government cannot realize my difficulties . . . I am now a man of a different world to them . . . I do not know what their conscience says . . . Sorry to have bothered you.[51]

In July 1965 Pyarelal visited Kabul, stayed with Badshah Khan in the house placed at his disposal, talked with him at leisure, and brought his report to India:

For all his seventy-five years he seemed, indeed, extraordinarily fit. He walked with a firm, steady step. Speech, eyesight and hearing were unimpaired and memory fairly sharp. The countenance bore marks of intense suffering but the eyes beamed deep compassion, and an air of kindliness surrounded him.

In a reference to 'the neglect by us' from which Ghaffar Khan and his people had suffered, Pyarelal added:

Even more striking was the complete absence of rancour or bitterness on his part [towards] . . . his friends, Congress colleagues and the people of India.

Thanks to Pyarelal, we have a glimpse of Badshah Khan's social life in Kabul. On the way to a dinner in a Pathan home, Badshah Khan asked Pyarelal not to expect anything more than masoor ki dhal and nan. What they got was a banquet, music and Pashto songs. 'After the [other] guests had gone, the womenfolk [of the host] had a meeting with Khan Saheb.'

The next evening Badshah Khan and Pyarelal were asked to dinner by the Indian ambassador, General Thapar. 'After dinner the ladies had [Badshah Khan] all to themselves and kept him engaged till late. It was past midnight when he retired. When I pointed this out to [Badshah Khan], he said, "Yes, but it was a most pleasant evening."' [52]

At another dinner out, where Ghani Khan accompanied his father and Pyarelal, little children climbed onto Badshah Khan's lap and rested their heads on his knees. There were twenty-eight persons in the room. The conversation was in Pashto but Pyarelal could make out that it was about 'the little things of life, Pakhtunwali, and the origins and characteristics of the Pathans'. Here we may mark the ease with which the 'little things of life' and Pathan characteristics slide into one another, revealing the great self-awareness of the Pathans, and their continuing interest in their story. Later Ghani told Pyarelal that 'Father delivered himself of the whole of Encyclopedia Afghanica.'[53]

These welcome vignettes, revealing a love of life in this austere, always-ready-for-prison figure, are rare not because the scenes they disclose were rare but because the accessible 'record' of his life is largely silent about them. Most accounts of his life, including the autobiography, exclude such scenes, and few letters (to or from relatives or friends) describing them seem to be available.

But the vignettes enable us to see a warmth that was as central to Ghaffar Khan's life as his faith. All who came close to him—including his family and men like Gandhi, Nehru, Desai and Pyarelal—at once noticed it, and many a photograph has caught it. No wonder Nehru spoke of a character 'soft with the gentleness of one who loves his kind exceedingly', even as it displayed 'the hardness of the man of faith believing in his mission'.[54]

At times, of course, a thread of bitterness crossed the warmth of this man blessed with almost uninterrupted suffering. So another Indian who visited Badshah Khan in 1965 and stayed with him, Haribhau Joshi, found his host's 'voice hard and indignant at times'. Joshi thought that Badshah Khan was 'half his previous size, dried up and wrinkled, looks and laughs like a child, and his eyes suggest pain and anxiety'.[55]

We may note here that a Pakhto song written by Ghani Khan, '*Ay zama watana*' ('O homeland mine'), would become Afghanistan's national anthem. Political differences coexisted alongside Ghani's fondness for his father. More to the left than Wali or his father, he would claim, in a 1990 interview, that he had 'had a fight with Father. I did not agree with his programme. I am a bit of a socialist.'[56]

*

'The Pakistani ambassador has been trying to lure him', Pyarelal noted in Kabul. 'But', added Pyarelal, 'he is not going back to Pakistan where he is convinced only lingering death in prison awaits him.' Badshah Khan hoped for assistance from the Afghans. Recalling the support that he and other Pathans had given to Nadir Khan in 1929, he said to Pyarelal, 'We went to their aid when they were in distress. We expect them to come to ours, now that we are in distress.'

But Kabul was less interested in autonomy for the Pathans of Pakistan than in a revision, in its favour, of the Durand Line. Moreover, its support for Badshah Khan had always to be balanced against the risk of antagonizing the government of Pakistan. His political goal seeming remote, Badshah Khan once more pursued social aims. He sought new Khudai Khidmatgars, even among the big khans. 'I don't want the big Khans to become small', he told Pyarelal. 'I want the small Pakhtuns to become Khans.' One of Badshah Khan's hosts at a Kabul dinner where Pyarelal accompanied Ghaffar Khan was 'an Afridi chief, commanding a following of 26,000 men in arms'.

Despite its ambivalence, Kabul observed

Pakhtunistan Day every year on 31 August. On three successive Pakhtunistan Days—in 1965, 1966 and 1967—Badshah Khan spoke to large rallies in Kabul. Pyarelal heard Ghaffar Khan's speech at the first of these rallies, and all three speeches can be found in the autobiography edited by Narang.

In these Kabul speeches, Ghaffar Khan is a proud Pakhtun who recalls Sher Shah and Abdali, reminds the Afghans that 'at first you were the slaves of Iran',[57] and cries out, 'O Pathans, when will you wake up?'[58] But, aware of the other races of Afghanistan, he also says, 'Anyone who lives in Afghanistan is a Pakhtun. Those amongst you who are trying to tell you that Hazaris, Pakhtuns and Tajiks are different people are not your friends but your enemies.'[59]

He sees 'other nations reaching out to the skies' but laments that 'we (Pakhtuns) cannot even walk upon the earth', a curse invited, he thinks, by love of money and lack of brotherhood.[60] And in these public speeches he speaks again of his private wound at the Hindu tag fastened on him by some of his foes, and of his refusal to be cowed down by the charge of apostasy:

> Well, take a look at me and see if I have become a Hindu. Who has the right to sit in judgment and pronounce me a Hindu? It was the British who called me a Hindu and since then nobody has been able to make me a Muslim again.[61]
> The Prophet said, belief in God [means] to love one's own fellowmen . . . My people are drowning before my eyes and to save them I shall grasp any

helping hand, be it the hand of a Hindu or an infidel.[62]

I was called Hindu by those who used to pick crumbs from British tables.[63]

A picture of Badshah Khan's Kabul years has also been provided by Sher Zaman Taizi, a Pathan who worked in the Pakistan Embassy in Kabul for a Pakistan intelligence agency, followed Badshah Khan's doings, and often met him. Aware of the nature of Taizi's job, Badshah Khan was nonetheless glad to find a channel, in case of need, to Pakistani authorities.

Taizi says in 'Bacha Khan in Afghanistan'[64] that while Ghaffar Khan demanded an autonomous status for Pakhtuns, 'in not a single speech did he express any desire for a separate and independent state', a judgement confirmed by a sentence in Badshah Khan's 1967 Pakhtunistan Day speech, reproduced by Narang: 'We want a name, a room in the same house, but we want to be masters of the room.'[65]

Earlier we saw that on Pakistani soil, too, Badshah Khan had complained that unlike Punjabis, Bengalis, Sindhis or Balochis, Pathans did not find *their* name in the title of their province. Persisting with the imperial name for a former empire's frontier province was nothing but anti-Pathan discrimination. But if Pakhtuns could be masters in a room called *Pakhtunkhwa* or Pakhtunistan, they would not object to Bengalis, Punjabis, Sindhis, Balochis and others occupying other rooms in the Pakistani house.

That the Pakhtunistan sought by Badshah Khan had

a connection to Pakistan was also the assessment of, for instance, Hassan Suhrawardy, a central figure in Pakistani politics in the 1950s and close to the Khan brothers. Writing warmly of Badshah Khan in his memoirs, Suhrawardy would contend that 'the autonomous province of Pakhtunistan which he visualized was to remain an integral part of Pakistan'.[66]

Shortly after Pyarelal's visit, Kamalnayan Bajaj and his sister Madalasa, whose father Jamnalal had offered hospitality to Badshah Khan and his family in Wardha in the 1930s, arrived in Kabul. Badshah Khan took the siblings to Bamiyan and showed them the great Buddha statues. 'Look how deep has been the influence of Buddha in these parts . . . We were all Buddhists once', Badshah Khan said to Madalasa.[67]

Kamalnayan, as candid as the man he had come to visit, asked Badshah Khan whether his 'creed of love embraces Pakistan also?' 'Yes', Ghaffar Khan replied. 'I have no quarrel with the people of Pakistan. My heart aches for them . . . My quarrel is with the rulers. I pray for the rulers also.'[68] Earlier, Pyarelal had sought, in Gandhi's name, Ghaffar Khan's assistance over the India/ Pakistan, Pakistan/Afghanistan and Kashmir problems,[69] and marvelled at the

> unconquerable spirit of this man of God who having watched from behind prison bars with a bleeding heart the things had given his life to broken, had now, in the evening of his life, set about, undeterred by overwhelming odds arrayed against him, to build them up again with outworn tools.[70]

Yet Pyarelal also recorded Badshah Khan's human confession when Pyarelal took his leave in Kabul: 'I feel lonely.'[71]

*

Late in 1967, Tendulkar's biography of Badshah Khan was published in India. In a foreword, Jawaharlal's daughter, Indira Gandhi, who by now was India's Prime Minister, spoke of being 'overcome by a feeling of shame' at the story of the abandonment of Badshah Khan. Two years later, at the invitation of Indira and also of her future foe, the socialist leader Jayaprakash Narayan, Badshah Khan arrived in India.

It was the Gandhi centenary in 1969, an ideal time, it was thought, for an encounter between independent India and Badshah Khan, who travelled on his Pakistani passport. This had expired, but the Pakistan embassy in Kabul stamped an extension. By now popular demonstrations in Pakistan had forced Ayub to resign, and to Badshah Khan's delight Ayub's successor, General Yahya Khan, had announced the annulment of One Unit. According to Taizi, 'Bacha Khan was so pleased over the disintegration of One Unit that he sought special permission to broadcast a message over Radio Kabul and offer his gratitude to President Yahya Khan.'

Taizi claims that he arranged an undisclosed meeting between Badshah Khan and the Pakistani ambassador, Hakeem Ahsan, in the home of an official of the Afghan tourism department, Mohammad Ali Lawangin Momand of Kama, and that at this meeting Ahsan conveyed a message from Yahya: would Badshah Khan be good enough not to criticize Pakistan in India? It seems that Badshah Khan 'responded with a smile'.[72] However, some in Pakistan objected to his visiting India, and at least one newspaper, *Jang*, demanded that Badshah Khan's passport be revoked.

Landing in New Delhi in time for Gandhi's birth anniversary in October 1969, Badshah Khan returned to Kabul four months later, shortly after the anniversary of Gandhi's death. In India Badshah Khan was an unusual state guest who carried his bundle of belongings and washed his clothes himself. Affectionate in every personal relationship, he was blunt in every public utterance and also in some private conversations.

Stirred by a reminder of less petty times, many Indians asked Badshah Khan to make India his home. Shaken by the reality of Indian public life in 1969, Badshah Khan asked to be excused. On 7 October he said, 'Even if I live in India for a hundred years, it will have no impact. No one cares here for the country or the people.'[73]

Disappointed that India was importing food and taking aid even from Japan, he said: 'You talk a lot but don't know how to work. It seems as if you think that to clap, give or hear speeches and get photographed is work. After being free for 20 years you beg from small countries but you don't remember your poor.'[74]

In India he did not hesitate either to ask for democracy in Pakistan, or to declare that he was a citizen of Pakistan. As for the demands of the Pathans, Ghaffar

Khan said that his first preference was for Pakhtun autonomy within Pakistan.

Whether by accident or by design, the Gandhi centenary saw communal riots in different parts of India, including in Gandhi's Ahmedabad. For three days, in Delhi, Ghaffar Khan fasted for peace. Then he went to Ahmedabad, where he expressed disappointment (on 18 October) that 'Hindus work only in Hindu areas.' 'Get close to the Muslims', he implored. 'Don't think of them as outsiders.'

After meeting and hearing him in Wardha in November 1969, this author wrote in the Bombay weekly, *Himmat* (14 November):

Indians have thronged open spaces, maidans and station platforms at all hours of night and day to look at him and hear him. Badshah Khan listens to those talking with him, his eyes fixed on them as they talk. In Wardha, when a tray of tea was brought to him just after a barber had cut his hair, Badshah Khan prepared a cup and asked that it be given to the barber . . . In a speech in Wardha he said, 'Last night I heard on the radio that I had left Ahmedabad, that great welcomes were given to me on my journey, and that people garlanded me on my arrival in Wardha. But the radio did not say what I said!'

On 24 November, addressing a joint session of both houses of Parliament, Ghaffar Khan was franker still: 'Your revenue is from taxes and duties on liquor. You are forgetting Gandhi the way you forgot the Buddha.'

He mentioned the cities disfigured by recent riots—
Ahmedabad, Jabalpur, Ranchi, Rourkela, Jamshedpur,
Indore, and Malegaon—and said he was horrified that
no one had been punished for rioting or killing. 'Your
laws are only for show', he added. A few days earlier,
receiving the Nehru Award for International
Understanding from President V. V. Giri, he related what
a Muslim girl had told him in Gujarat: 'Muslims were
being asked by Hindu communalists to leave the county
or live like untouchables.'[75]

To India's Muslims, he recommended non-retaliation,
in the name of the Qur'an: 'If you plant a slap after
having been provoked by a slap, then what is the
difference between the followers of the Qur'an and the
evildoer?'[76]

When he met Indira he seems to have said, 'Your
father and Patel, behind Gandhiji's back, threw me and
my Pakhtuns to the wolves.'[77] To Indira's credit, she
did not hold such bluntness against Badshah Khan, and
instructed a succession of ambassadors to Kabul and
Pakistan to attend to Badshah Khan's needs. In 1969
and later, Indira, who was more emotional than she let
on, seemed to see Badshah Khan 'as the sole remnant of
the band that had brought freedom to India and thus
the Premiership of India to her'.[78]

Congress leaders had left their guide and betrayed
him over Partition, Badshah Khan told Indian audiences.
Gandhi, he added, 'helped us in every difficulty and
ordeal. He replaced fear with courage in Indians and
gave nonviolence to the whole world. By forgetting him
we hurt ourselves, not him.' Before leaving India in

February 1970, Ghaffar Khan thanked everyone, including the government, for the hospitality he had received and added, 'I am no friend if I offer false praise.'

But he had also said, 'I have considered myself a part of you and you a part of me.' After interviewing him, Dom Moraes wrote of 'this tall old wizard, this Pathan chieftain with the Cassandra tone' and also of 'the great gentleness that cloaks him like a crusader's chain-mail' and of 'a peaceful and utterly truthful aura' he conveyed.[79]

During these four months Indians and their government had given him honours and also funds. Returning to Kabul, Badshah Khan deposited eight million rupees in the National Bank of Afghanistan, and also bequeathed two-and-a-half acres of his Frontier land. He wished to create a trust and use the money and the land for a resumption of *Pakhtun*, the development of the Pashto language, and the welfare of the Pakhtun nation. But this dream, too, was destined to be shattered. 'The Trust could not be set up', says Taizi, 'mainly due to the uncertain political situation in Pakistan . . . After the fall (in 1992) of Dr. Najibullah, the money also perished.'[80]

*

Something nice, however, happened in Afghanistan in, it would seem, the late 1960s or early in 1970. The authorities there gave him a house in Jalalabad, a small brick house with two floors. It was not prepossessing; the workmanship and material that had gone into it was

average, the floor was of cement, and it had charpoys
rather than beds. But it was a house that sometimes felt
like home, and it had a garden. Badshah Khan, who slept
in the veranda on the upper floor, even in winter, seemed
fairly happy there.[81]

One of those visiting him in Afghanistan was the
writer Ved Mehta. To him Badshah Khan was as blunt as
he had been in India:

> In India Gandhism is dead. Gandhi is completely
> forgotten. It's the story of Buddha all over again . . .
> Your government does all the things that Gandhi
> opposed the British for doing . . . Gandhism has
> more life among us Pathans than among you.[82]

When a cyclone hit East Pakistan in 1970, the worst
in decades, Badshah Khan gave a cheque of $5,000. This
was cashed in dollars and changed into Pakistani rupees
in Kabul's Shahzada bazaar, and Rs 55,000 were deposited
in the Pakistan embassy, which issued a receipt for that
sum. But when a Pakistani newspaper reported that
Badshah Khan had donated Rs 25,000, he demanded a
refund of Rs 30,000. It is not known whether he
obtained it.[83]

More than a cyclone had smashed East Bengal. The
refusal of Pakistan's leaders to accept the overwhelming
victory of Sheikh Mujib-ur-Rahman's Awami League had
set the stage for secession and bloodshed. Badshah Khan,
who had felt close to Bengal ever since his work among
its peasants in 1934, thought he should do something.
According to Taizi, 'Bacha Khan offered his services for

mediation. He proposed to the Embassy that he would go back to Pakistan to lead a Jirgah of a few elders from Punjab, Sindh, NWFP and Balochistan to meet Mujib-ur-Rahman and settle the dispute through negotiations.' The embassy conveyed Badshah Khan's offer to the foreign office but there was no response. It would appear that Zulfiqar Ali Bhutto, now West Pakistan's most influential politician, was opposed to the move.[84]

A gory struggle ensued and an independent Bangladesh emerged in 1971–72. Yahya Khan resigned, Bhutto became the ruler of a truncated Pakistan, and the National Awami Party founded by Badshah Khan and led since 1967 by his son Wali Khan won a share of power in the NWFP and Balochistan. Taizi claims that some tribal jirgahs called on Badshah Khan in Kabul, and also on King Zahir Shah, saying they were prepared to fight for an independent Pakhtunistan if supplied with arms. According to Taizi, neither Badshah Khan nor Zahir Shah encouraged them.[85]

On 24 December 1972, after an eight-year exile, Badshah Khan returned to the Frontier. Bhutto had not wanted him back but the new governor of the NWFP, Arbab Sikandar Khan, was insistent on the return of one who was still the Frontier's best-loved figure. Badshah Khan, now eighty-two, nursed some hope and gladness while returning, for military rule and One Unit had both ended in Pakistan.

Yet he would receive four major blows before the end of the 1970s. First, Zulfiqar Ali Bhutto disillusioned him. Among other things, Bhutto dismissed the elected government of Balochistan and compelled the resignation of the Frontier government. Thereafter both father and son spent long spells in detention. Second, in the name of republicanism, Zahir Shah was ousted from his Kabul throne by a cousin, Daud Khan. No Pakhtun was keener on egalitarianism than Ghaffar Khan, yet he had also, right from 1919, invested effort and faith in the Kabul throne, which he saw as a symbol of Pakhtun dignity. To him the removal of Zahir Shah was a mistake.[86] Third, power in Pakistan was seized in 1977 by another military ruler, this time a Punjabi military officer, General Zia-ul-Haq. Finally, Afghanistan saw great violence in 1978–79, including the killing of Daud Khan (1978), of the man replacing Daud Khan, Nur Mohammad Taraki (1979), killings under the rule of Hafizullah Amin and then of Amin (1979), and, at the end of 1979, an invasion by the Soviet Union of an Afghanistan it had come to increasingly control.

In Bhutto's Pakistan, democracy was hardly comprehensive. In 1975 the NAP was outlawed and Badshah Khan and his son Wali Khan were both arrested. Subsequently released 'on account of his age', Badshah Khan was re-arrested and barred from leaving his village. Earlier, Bhutto had crafted constitutional changes that made Islam Pakistan's state religion and stipulated that only a Muslim could be the nation's president or prime minister.

The populism that dictated these steps also led Bhutto to support a declaration from the National Assembly that Ahmadis (or Ahmadiyas or Qadianis), members of a sect denounced by orthodox ulama as heretical, were non-Muslims. The moves could only have troubled Badshah Khan, who throughout his life had been at odds with men who advertised their Islam and used it for politics rather than for justice or service. He and Wali Khan spent the mid-1970s—the Zulfiqar Bhutto years in Pakistan—in disappointment, in detention, or under house arrest.

The Zia takeover of 1977 was no improvement, however, and Badshah Khan was glad in April 1978 to move out of Pakistan again and into his Jalalabad home. Perhaps he hoped, among other things, to activate the trust fund. Alas, Afghanistan too would prove to be a trial. Within weeks of Badshah Khan's arrival in Afghanistan, Daud Khan was killed in a coup masterminded by Hafizullah Amin, who allowed Nur Mohammad Taraki to become prime minister.

*

In 1978 and 1979, S.K. Singh, India's ambassador to Afghanistan, often called on Badshah Khan, regarding him as a grandfatherly figure, the only one alive among the leaders who had obtained India's independence. Singh sensed 'an ocean of affection' from Ghaffar Khan, but he also noticed, on the one hand, a 'highly pragmatic' element and, on the other, a strand of 'extreme dryness', which Singh linked to Badshah Khan's austerity.

On occasion 'irritable' and 'complaining', Badshah Khan would however 'straighten me up, embrace me and kiss me on the head' every time Singh tried, while taking leave, 'to bend down so as to touch his knee'.[87] An aspect of his austerity was a continuing determination, if travelling, to carry his bundle of belongings in his own hand. Helpers or friends offering to carry the bundle, or to pack it in a suitcase, could be brusquely told off, Singh noticed.

Badshah Khan was approaching his nineties, and talk often turned to the past. Recalling these sessions later, Singh said that Badshah Khan spoke of Dr Khan Sahib with 'normal fraternal affection' and positively, to Singh's surprise, of Jinnah and Caroe.[88]

But the present, whether in Pakistan or Afghanistan, was worrying. Badshah Khan saw through Zia's Islamism, which was far more glaring than that of Bhutto (who was hanged in 1979). '*Bandookwale namaazi ho gaye hain*', Ghaffar Khan noted: 'The men with guns have become the prayer experts.'[89]

It is not quite clear whether Badshah Khan was in Jalalabad or with his family near Utmanzai when, in 1979, Taraki was assassinated and massacres occurred under the rule of Amin. The atrocities of Amin, a Pashtun educated at Columbia University, upset Badshah Khan so much that he welcomed the Soviet intervention of December 1979 that 'got rid of the tyrant Amin', as he would later acknowledge to another Indian ambassador to Kabul, J.N. Dixit.[90] As Afghanistan's new chief executive, the incoming Russians installed Babrak Karmal, son of a Farsi-speaking Tajik father and a Pakhtun mother.

His medical problems took Badshah Khan in 1980 to Delhi and, in the autumn of that year, to Moscow. The Moscow visit and his stay in a Soviet-occupied Afghanistan troubled Badshah Khan's admirers among the Afghan refugees who had poured in immense numbers into Peshawar. However, by the end of 1981, when for health reasons he visited Delhi again, Ghaffar Khan had become sharply opposed to the Soviet presence in Afghanistan.

His ability to remember the layout of a place was noticed when he visited Patna to obtain medical help from Dr Mukhopadhyaya. 'Badshah Khan knew the streets of Patna better than I did', the doctor later told the Indian politician, Bansi Lal, who had recommended Dr Mukhopadhyaya to Ghaffar Khan.[91]

To Dixit, newly named ambassador to Kabul, who called on him in Delhi, Badshah Khan said: 'Afghans, Pashtoons will never accept Communism or Russia. They will just die. Those who can will leave the country.'[92] 'The Communists', Ghaffar Khan went on, 'are not only destroying people but trees in Afghanistan. The revolution has become oppression.'[93]

Badshah Khan said similar things to the Soviet ambassador in India, Yuli M. Vorontsov, and also to Prime Minister Indira Gandhi. He urged Indira to arrange for him to meet the Soviet ruler, Leonid Brezhnev. He would ask Brezhnev, Badshah Khan said, to withdraw his troops from Afghanistan. Indira was most reluctant to make the attempt. She did not think the Soviets would appreciate such a request from her. Moreover, as she told Dixit, she thought that 'in the short term, the Russian presence in Afghanistan is not against India's interests.'[94]

Having made his request, Badshah Khan returned to Jalalabad, where he suffered a hip fracture. Dixit noted that the plane that brought Badshah Khan on a stretcher from Jalalabad to Kabul in early March 1982 'also brought gun-toting youngsters and a dead body', evidence of the escalating conflict in Afghanistan between the mujahedin and the Soviets. To Dixit, the ninety-two-year-old man with a broken hip 'did not seem much the worse for wear'. His 'voice was vigorous, eyes sparkling and [he revealed] a tone of stubbornness'.

On 6 March, calling on Badshah Khan at Kabul's military hospital, Dixit said he was bringing Indira Gandhi's wishes for an early recovery. 'His response', Dixit recorded in his diary, 'was shukria, but you and your PM are doing the Afghans in. You have no raham (pity) etc.' Then Badshah Khan asked the ambassador to take down, in long hand, his reply to Indira's message, which he dictated in Hindustani. The reply was this:

I was sorry to read your statement that Russia cannot leave Afghanistan before establishing a stable rule there. I had explained in detail to you that all the Afghans are against the Communists. I also said to you that Communism can never be established in Afghanistan. If the war continues, the people of Afghanistan will be destroyed. As Nehru's daughter and one who lived in Gandhiji's company, you are like a daughter to me. Children, women and men are dying in Afghanistan. Is there no pity in your heart? . . . You can do a lot. I asked you to help me meet Brezhnev. I asked Karmal too but he is afraid. You should do something about this.[95]

Afraid that Badshah Khan might die in Kabul, thereby giving the mujahedin a propaganda weapon, Karmal pressed India to accept the old man for treatment. Indira was willing to oblige Karmal, but 'the highly pragmatic' Badshah Khan named his price: a meeting with Brezhnev. To Dixit he said: 'Send this message to Indira, and tell her I will only come if she gets me to meet Brezhnev.'[96]

After making several attempts to persuade Badshah Khan to go to India, Dixit got this answer: 'I don't want to go to Delhi. I will go to Moscow and if that is not possible I will stay back in Kabul. I don't want to live any more. I won't go to India.'[97] 'I must tell [Brezhnev]', Badshah Khan added, 'Show raham towards Afghans.' If he does not listen to me then I will have to think of other means to resolve the miseries of my people— Afghans and Pakhtuns both.'[98]

Indira yielded. She passed on Badshah Khan's message to Ambassador Vorontsov and to the visiting Soviet Vice President, Vasiliy V. Kuznetsov. Also, when the Afghan foreign minister, Shah Mohammad Dost, visited India and called on Indira, she said to him: 'What are you planning to do about organizing withdrawal of Russian forces from Afghanistan?'[99] We know that Indira harboured some caution about Soviet forces remaining permanently in India's neighbourhood, but it also seems that Badshah Khan's firm line had contributed to the question she put to Dost.[100]

In his Afghan diary, later published as a book, Dixit implied vanity in Badshah Khan's keenness to meet

Brezhnev and said: 'It is a merry go-round of ambitions and anxieties; even great men find it difficult to realize that a time comes to tell them that history has passed them by.'[101]

While acknowledging Badshah Khan's humanness, we must ask whether the diplomat's comment was not influenced by his failure to accomplish the task that both Indira and Karmal had assigned to him, which was to land Badshah Khan in Delhi. And we can only speculate about Badshah Khan's goal in his ninety-third year. A better deal for the Pakhtuns? A high profile for himself? The latter for the former? What is certain is that in his nineties Badshah Khan was very clear on the only card he possessed, which was his readiness to die, that he knew how and when to play it, and that in his diplomatic tussles with Dixit, Indira Gandhi and Babrak Karmal, he was not the loser.

When, on 14 March 1982, Dixit again called on Badshah Khan, he found the old man 'remarkably alert'. He told Dixit: 'Are you sure you want to talk? This room might be bugged by the Russians and the Afghans.' 'He is recovering', Dixit noted, adding, 'The bones have set and he can walk with crutches.'[102]

'That nation is great which rests its head upon death as a pillow.' So Gandhi had written, way back in 1909, in *Hind Swaraj*. From his twenties to his nineties, in prison or outside, in illness or in health, whether in British India, Pakistan, or Afghanistan, Ghaffar Khan had always rested his head on the pillow of death. He obtained power as a result, which he used not for personal or family wealth but for the sake of the Pakhtuns, to whom also, as we have seen time and again, he spoke with biting frankness.

Unsurprisingly, the Soviets did not arrange for Badshah Khan to call on Brezhnev; the Soviet leader died in November that year.

The afflicted old man in his nineties lying in the Soviet-style Kabul hospital was vulnerable, Dixit thought, to assaults of suspicion and possessiveness. Once he said to Dixit, when the nurse was not in the room, 'Don't bring too many oranges at once. She removes some of them.'[103] Sensing also a coldness in the hospital's care, Ghaffar Khan longed for the warm touch of a long-deceased and at times estranged brother, and a remark he made to Dixit revealed the craving for human affection he had always had, which made solitariness hard for him to endure, and which was probably a motor for the affection he himself ceaselessly offered to others:

> My brother, who was a doctor, told me that if a doctor really loves his patient, he can remedy all illnesses by just placing his hand on the patient's chest. The doctors here do not love me.[104]

But Dixit also relates that in his encounters he found Badshah Khan 'affectionate, on occasion giving me a box of fruit, and asking me to be sure that my wife also took some'.[105]

*

Singh, in the late 1970s, and Dixit, in the early 1980s, both heard Badshah Khan say that he was working on a new autobiography. According to Dixit, Wali Khan and Ajmal Khan Khattak seemed to be taking down the old man's dictation during their visits to Afghanistan; and Taizi mentions a third person, Fazal Rahim Saqi, as having been invited by Badshah Khan to help 'compile his autobiography', evidently in the late 1970s. Also referring to a new autobiography, Girdhari Lal Puri, a former Frontier MLA, writes that Badshah Khan told him in Delhi in the summer of 1980 that he had 'completed the draft'.[106]

But the fate of any Ghaffar Khan autobiography updated until 1980 is not clear. A Badshah Khan autobiography in Pakhto was indeed published in Kabul in the 1970s, but this was an expanded version of the autobiography published in India in the 1960s and could not have included Badshah Khan's thoughts after the Soviet invasion of Afghanistan.

The mystery seems larger. In an interview in May 2003 in the town of Akora Khattak in the Frontier province, Badshah Khan's colleague, Ajmal Khan Khattak, said to this author that in the late 1970s in Kabul, in Khattak's presence, Badshah Khan had given to someone called Sadaqat a volume of handwritten diary entries, and asked Sadaqat to have the material sent out safely and published. Later, Khattak added, Sadaqat denied ever having received the volume.

Why, if the texts existed, they were not preserved or published is an unanswered question. In any case this author has not come across any text from a Badshah

Khan autobiography written in the late 1970s or the 1980s, or from the set of journal entries referred to by Khattak. If either text exists, it might throw additional light on Ghaffar Khan's views on Pakistan under Bhutto and Zia, on Afghanistan during the Soviet occupation, on the future of the Pathans, and also, who knows, on his own long life.

Ajmal Khan Khattak also told this author that he had been present, some time in the 1970s or early 1980s, when Badshah Khan, standing on the ground of his Jalalabad home, declared that he wanted to see in that space a university for orphaned and destitute Pakhtun girls—and that he wanted to be buried there.

*

From the late 1970s onward he seemed to move almost at will between Pakistan and Afghanistan; for himself at any rate the Durand Line had ceased to exist. In the Frontier province he stayed with his sons or daughter or, briefly, in a small house that he had had built for himself. In the summer of 1983, when he was in Pakistan, statements that he and Wali Khan made seemed to link the Soviet entry into Afghanistan to the facilities in the NWFP and Balochistan that Zia's Pakistan was giving to the USA. Father and son and many other opposition leaders were arrested. A house of the irrigation department in Khesghi, about eleven miles from Muhammad Naray, was turned into a sub-jail, and the ninety-three-year-old Badshah Khan was detained in it.

But neither jail nor Pakistan kept him continuously for long. In April 1984 he was back in Jalalabad and Kabul, suffering from acute arthritic pain, a fracture in his left leg, and a bad lung that made breathing hard. Calling on him in hospital, Dixit however thought he was 'politically alive and sharp'.[107] In May 1984 Badshah Khan returned to Peshawar, but July saw him back in Afghanistan. From Kabul he went to Prague for treatment for a month but told Dixit afterwards that he felt no better.

At some point in 1984, while he was staying in 'Gulrang', the home in Muhammad Naray of his son Lali, Badshah Khan was asked by his grandson, Salim Jan—son of Mehr Taj and Yahya Jan—how he had managed to persevere over the long, difficult decades.

'What else can I do', the ninety-four-year-old replied, his hand tapping his chest, 'if Allah has placed this feeling for my people inside here?' Recalling the conversation in the summer of 2003, Salim Jan choked. Another grandson, Nasir, son of Lali Khan, who often performed the tasks, when Badshah Khan was ill, of washing his grandfather and changing his clothes, smilingly recalled the chores in 2003, adding that he felt the old man's warmth and affection.

If now the final leg of his journey had indeed commenced, Badshah Khan would insist on some unscheduled stopovers. One was in Bombay, where Badshah Khan attended, in 1985, the centenary of the Indian National Congress. In 1987 he was again in India, where the nation's highest award, the Bharat Ratna, was bestowed on him. Among the many offering their respects while he was in India was this author, who went up to the bed in Bombay's Raj Bhavan where Badshah Khan was sitting up; he was given a kiss on the forehead.

By this time the Soviets had made a decision to withdraw from Afghanistan. Though the formal Geneva accord for Soviet withdrawal would only be signed in April 1988, the decision to leave was made in 1986. Badshah Khan shared the relief and the joy. In the summer of 1987 he suffered a stroke. Thereafter he spent several spells in Peshawar's Lady Reading Hospital, the last confinements of an oft-imprisoned man. Finally the pillow refused to let go of the weary head resting on it. At 6.55 a.m. on the morning of 20 January 1988, Abdul Ghaffar Khan breathed his last.

Long-defied death was never wholly dismissed by Badshah Khan—apart from the declaration described by Khattak, he had asked his family to bury him in the garden of his Jalalabad home in the heart of the Pakhtun country. The wish was granted. Though the Afghan struggle was not yet over, the Kabul government and the mujahedin both announced a ceasefire for the event.

Tens of thousands of the Frontier's mourning Pakhtuns accompanied the coffin and crossed the Durand Line. Pakistan's military ruler, Zia-ul Haq (who would be killed in a plane crash later in the year), and India's prime minister, Rajiv Gandhi (also destined for a violent death), were present for the last rites. Korejo, Badshah Khan's Pakistani critic, would write that 'the funeral procession from Utmanzai to Jalalabad was an event with few parallels in history. The caravan of cars, buses, trucks and other vehicles carrying his followers, friends and admirers was endless. A sea of humanity greeted them in Jalalabad. This was, so to say, a caravan of peace.'[108] Viewing this pageant across the Khyber Pass alongside the processions down the ages of Alexander, Tamerlane, Ghazni, Ghori, Babur, and Abdali, Korejo thought that Badshah Khan's did not suffer in comparison.

SEVEN

Badshah Khan and Our Times

Born ten years before the end of one century and dying twelve years before the end of another, Ghaffar Khan of the Pakhtun country, loved by his people, was, we saw, a man with an acidic, defiant sense of humour and of spoken and unspoken sorrows who hated loneliness but bore it with fortitude for interminable spells; who satisfied his longing for human affection by pouring it out; whose love of life enhanced the power issuing from his readiness to die; whose all-too-human old-age infirmities never snapped the courtesy he had stitched into his character; who harboured suspicions, usually directed at British foes and often if not always justified, but was willing to be challenged on them; and who in his difficulties turned to his God.

Before reflecting on what Badshah Khan may say to us at the start of the twenty-first century, we should recognize an inadequacy in the story told in the preceding pages.

Many accounts helped compose it: the autobiographical narrative he fortunately left behind; numerous pen sketches drawn over a long period by skilful observers and interviewers including Gandhi and Nehru and several journalists; the biographies written by Desai, Pyarelal, Tendulkar and Easwaran; the writings of his sons—Ghani Khan's essay on the Pakhtuns and recollections of times with his father, and Wali Khan's tracts; Caroe's study of the Pathans; some valuable analyses of the movements that Badshah Khan was involved with, including those by Banerjee, Jansson, Korejo and Wiqar Ali; Taizi's informative memoir about Ghaffar Khan's years in Afghanistan; items, spanning seven decades, from the press of India and Pakistan; interviews with colleagues, descendants and others who interacted with Ghaffar Khan; and more.

These add up to a priceless collection of sources. Yet they are short on glimpses of his inner life or his family life, crippled as the latter was by struggle and imprisonment. The precise texture of his relationships with the two young women who, one after the other, married him, but died early, with his sisters, with his parents, with his sons and daughter, with his brother, with his nephews and nieces, with his grandchildren; an impression, let alone an understanding, of the wives and sisters; the hopes and fears, year by year, inside his own mind—to such questions only partial answers are provided in the foregoing pages. This means that imagination, goaded by the vignettes we saw, has to supply what diaries, private letters or more detailed accounts by near and dear ones might have provided. If such papers exist, a future writer with access to them will be able to complete the story.

Perhaps the account offered in these pages will spark off in some a desire for further research, including on, for instance, the remarkable life of Dr Khan Sahib, whose role contrasted with Ghaffar Khan's but also complemented it, and on the relationship between the brothers.

Ghaffar Khan's life will remain connected to the Charsadda/Peshawar valley, surrounded by the rivers Indus, Swat and Kabul and overlooked by the Malakand mountains, where he was raised, to which he was deeply devoted, from which he was again and again removed, often coercively, and where, in the villages of Muhammad Naray and Utmanzai, his descendants, and those of his brother and sisters, continue to live.

In and around Utmanzai and Muhammad Naray, a visitor is likely to encounter canals in full flow, piles of newly-harvested sugar beet, fields of sugar cane and tobacco, gardens of roses and other flowers, sounds, from an improvised classroom, of children of Afghan refugees, and knots of Pakhtun peasants and their children. Close by is the bustle of Peshawar city. In different homes in Muhammad Naray, Utmanzai and Peshawar may be found Badshah Khan's son Wali Khan and daughter Mehr Taj, their children and grandchildren, a grandson of Ghani Khan, sons of Ali or 'Lali' Khan, as well as sons of all three of Dr Khan Sahib's sons, Sadullah Khan, Ubeidullah Khan and Hidayatullah Khan.

Ghaffar Khan's grave is in Jalalabad, across the Khyber. Dr Khan Sahib and May Khan lie near each other in a corner of Utmanzai, some distance away from the family graveyard in the village. Here is buried Mehr Qandh, the mother of Ghani and Wali. Here, too, is Khurshid, Dr Khan Sahib's first wife. The grave of Nambata, Ghaffar Khan's second wife and the mother of Mehr Taj and 'Lali', lies somewhere in Jerusalem. Also resting in the family graveyard in Utmanzai are Behram Khan and his wife, at least one of their two daughters, Ghani Khan and his wife Roshan, and some at least of the sons and daughters-in-law of Dr Khan Sahib.

*

Writing seven years before Badshah Khan's death, the Swedish scholar Jansson identified four 'messages' from his life: intense Pakhtun nationalism, moral and social reform, nonviolence, and Islam.[1] As to what Ghaffar Khan may mean to us today, let us attempt to appraise him as a Pakhtun, as a subcontinental figure, as a Muslim, and, finally, as a voice in today's world.

Born the younger son of a khan in a feudal society where 'impoverished tenants provided menial services and manpower to magnify the status of their Khan', Ghaffar Khan appeared to raise ordinary Pakhtuns 'from ignominious depths of ignorance and obscurity to heights of enlightenment and glory'.[2] According to Taizi, who served a Pakistani government that was suspicious of our subject, it was Ghaffar Khan's 'stamina, struggles, patience, devotion and determined tolerance in the face of suffering that lifted Pakhtuns from the lowest level of serfdom to the high status of nationhood'.[3]

We saw that his feeling for the Pakhtuns, probably the biggest passion of his life, emanated from almost every word, gesture and breath of his. For this love, sustained for a century, he was willing to walk miles, to give up the privilege and comfort of a khan's life and the joys of family life, to be locked up in small cells, to be fettered, to grind corn on heavy chakkis, to eat horrible food, to be slandered, and more. If ever a man lived, sacrificed, suffered and died for his people, Ghaffar Khan was such a man.

Had not his Muslim tradition, to which he was both instinctively and thoughtfully loyal, forbade the appellation, Badshah Khan might have been called a prophet for his people. He cannot be called that, but through his austerity, bearing, unwavering commitment and unsparing frankness he brought to his times a hint of the prophets of yore.

Loving his Pakhtuns, he also saw them clearly, in their strength and in their weakness, and spent all of himself in striving to free them of *badal* or revenge. With many Pakhtuns he succeeded, at least for some time; the subcontinent, the Raj, Afghanistan and the world acknowledged that thanks to him a number of Pakhtuns had moved from a love of the rifle to a commitment to nonviolence.

Officers of the British Raj thought that nonviolence would be 'almost unintelligible on the Frontier where most men carry firearms and the maintenance of the blood-feud is still regarded as a sacred duty'.[4] Yet Halide Edib, the Turkish writer, found on her visit to the

Frontier in the 1930s 'a new interpretation of force'. She characterized this demonstration of nonviolent force, 'coming from strong and fearless men', as 'very unexpected'.[5] It was Ghaffar Khan's creative leadership, and his success in linking nonviolence to Islam, that had achieved it.

Like any 'buffer' people elsewhere in the world, caught between bigger neighbours, the Pakhtuns have always been obliged to adjust to changing events. In shifting sands they were grateful to be led by a man who adhered to his principles. Even when they did not heed Ghaffar Khan, and persisted with their mutual jealousies and self-seeking, they loved him as they had not, for decades, loved another Pakhtun. Every new incarceration or exile that he suffered only increased this love, which at his death took the unforgettable form of a pageant across the Khyber. Free behind bars, and a general without a gun, he was also, in some ways, a king who did not need a throne.

The Pakhtuns' admiration for him was stronger than their compliance. Although the Khudai Khidmatgars have been called 'arguably the best organized' rural force involved in the freedom struggle 'in the entire subcontinent',[6] they did not remain as selfless in politics, or as dedicated in social service, or as strong in numbers, as Ghaffar Khan desired. His admonitions on their shortcomings shamed them but did not change them.

Did the magnet that drew Badshah Khan to his Pakhtuns keep him away from other sections of humanity? Was he a nationalist rather than a universalist?

We should note, before attempting to answer this question, that Badshah Khan's story reminds us of the importance, in almost every conflict, of ethnicity. Even where religion, or Islam in particular, appears to be the central question, closer study may reveal that ethnicity is not less crucial.

We noticed that Badshah Khan's references to the Pakhtuns' neighbours—Punjabis in Pakistan, Tajiks in Afghanistan, and Iranians—were not always magnanimous. But apart from the fact that defending the dignity of the Pakhtuns, a central goal for him, involved tensions and at times conflicts with Punjabis (and, in Afghanistan, with Tajiks), we should also note that reflection always prompted him to deplore, and also, as far as he was concerned, to disavow, any ill will towards the Pakhtuns' ethnic neighbours.

He did not call Punjabis or Tajiks 'my people' but he did see them as equals and sometimes as brothers. Also, as Jansson points out, he used the term Pakhtun 'in a very wide sense, comprising all those living in Pakhtun society or even in the NWFP'.[7] All the same, we should acknowledge, as no doubt he would have done, that at the beginning of the twenty-first century the need for reconciliation across ethnic (or national) divides is at least as critical as the need for nonviolence in struggles for justice.

The Badshah Khan story will not hurt the goal of reconciliation, and it may help the cause of democracy. Our survey confirms the assessment of the Pakhtun scholar, Ahmad Sha Mohabbat, that 'despite his strong nationalism and anti-British sentiments, Ghaffar Khan at no time advocated the sort of nationalism from which stems the degenerate creed of authoritarian totalitarianism or the cult of national self-worship' and that he offered 'a humanitarian nationalism'.[8]

As for the subcontinent, his story highlighted some stubborn contradictions within the independence movement. If it showed what one person can do to confront heavy odds, it also confirmed the tragic potential for betrayal in nationalist endeavours.

Equally, the story provided evidence of Ghaffar Khan's loyalty to the peoples of India, Pakistan and Bangladesh. We saw that this loyalty always bore the sharp edge of honesty and refused to condone injustice. He and his brother saved Hindu and Sikh lives in the Frontier; he brought succour and relief to Muslim victims in Bihar; he confronted Jinnah in Pakistan and, twenty years later, India's Parliament with uncomfortable facts of attacks on minorities.

His fight for the rights of the threatened, the weak and the poor, his sympathy for peoples across the subcontinent's borders, his scepticism about the effectiveness of guns and bombs, and his frankness towards both rulers and citizens make him an inspiring model. He and his older friend, Gandhi, present themselves to posterity, as they did to their contemporaries, as brothers in arms, wielding the weapons of conscience and courage.

His Islam seemed to be of the most natural kind. When, on his end-1934 arrest in Wardha, which occurred within days of a rare family reunion, he told Jamnalal Bajaj, 'What pleases God pleases me', and left smilingly with his captors, he gave expression to Islam's fundamental tenet of submission to God's will. If acceptance of God's will is a matter of the heart rather than of the lips, then Badshah Khan's inner obedience over a long and hard lifetime makes him a true and exemplary Muslim.

We saw also that he was a courageous Muslim, unafraid to believe his own honest interpretation of scripture, and unafraid to question voices from Muslim platforms that he felt were using religion for politics or commerce. Such voices criticized him several times during his long life, including when he and his older brother Jabbar went to Rev. Wigram's school, when he started his own schools, when, alongside Hindus, Sikhs and Christians, he joined the fight for India's freedom, when he and his brother sent their children to the West for education, when he opposed India's division along religious lines, when he defended Hindus and Sikhs in the Frontier province, when he visited India in 1969–70, and when he opposed the Zia regime in Pakistan.

Some of the criticisms, we saw, were extreme and offensive. Unfazed, Badshah Khan was content to have his Muslimness confirmed in his own heart, in his prayers, in his practices, and in the Holy Book he treasured. Again and again he insisted that the Prophet's chief demand of a Muslim was the service of fellow human beings.

His Islam impelled Badshah Khan not towards power but towards social and humanitarian purposes, seeking to relieve poverty and to fight oppression and injustice. It also prodded him to work for the education

of women and for their involvement in efforts for justice.
His prison-going and political campaigns limited Ghaffar
Khan's exertions for women's empowerment, but his
honesty before the Frontier's women—'Today we are
the followers of custom and we oppress you'[9]—was
exceptional.

We may assert that Ghaffar Khan's story, which is
that of a Muslim and of a universal voice, speaks usefully
to the twenty-first century. Its claim to a Muslim
platform is certainly not weaker than that of Osama bin
Laden or Mullah Omar. The open and accessible life of
Badshah Khan, who was rooted in the Peshawar valley,
with links to Jalalabad and Kabul, is a contrast to the
concealed and mysterious figure of Kandahar's Mullah
Omar.

This 'Peacemaker from the Pashtun Past' sought to
replace revenge with justice and reconciliation. This son
of a feudal khan wanted the meanest Pakhtun to come
into his own. For all his austerity and simplicity, he
embraced the modern world and acknowledged the
progress that Europe and America had made in some
crucial areas. And unlike Mullah Omar, who recruited
armed followers from the cities, Ghaffar Khan enlisted
unarmed recruits from the countryside and hoped to
supersede the culture of the gun.

Yet we also found that Ghaffar Khan's nonviolence,
which was shaped by two longings—to rid the Pakhtuns
of *badal* and save them from the destruction that violence
would invite from the British—was pragmatic and not
limitless. One of those motivated by Ghaffar Khan's
realistic nonviolence was the Palestinian-born academic

and activist, Mubarak Awad. Noting that Ghaffar Khan
'practised Islam and nonviolence and showed that it was
not only for the weak',[10] Awad started a network called
Nonviolence International to promote social change and
international peace.

In the wake of 9/11, the 2003 attack on Iraq, and
continuing violence in Israel-Palestine and in Kashmir,
others, too, have recalled Badshah Khan. Thus Dilip
Simeon writes in New Delhi's *Outlook* magazine
('Fareedian Slips', 23 June 2003) of 'Gandhi and Ghaffar
Khan who did not need to bomb people to teach them
liberal democracy or civic restraint'. Viewing struggles
for human and democratic rights, Harold Gould, the
American scholar, contrasts nonviolent strategies that
'brought down empires' in South Asia with the 'walking
bombs' in the Middle East and Kashmir 'whose self-
detonations invite devastating retaliatory assaults on
their innocent fellow citizens'. Ghaffar Khan's life has a
role in the 'radical rethinking by radical Islamists' that
Gould and other voices, Muslim and non-Muslim, ask
for.[11]

We saw that Ghaffar Khan the Muslim thought that
'prayer in whatever language or form was addressed to
one and the same God'. His daily life demonstrated this
belief in the unity of humanity. We noticed the joy with
which he showed the Buddha statues of Bamiyan to
Kamalnayan Bajaj and Madalasa Agrawal, statues that
the Taliban would later destroy. Comfortable with his
Hindu friends, comrades and colleagues, Badshah Khan,
we saw, also loved Westerners and Christians like the
Wigram brothers and was even able to forgive a white

political foe who had blocked some of his plans, Olaf Caroe.

In 1946, alluding to the potential for fanaticism in the Frontier region, he warned that 'a dangerous situation is fast developing in the tribal areas', and a year later he said, 'I feel it is my duty to warn you against future dangers so that I may justify myself before man and God on the Day of Judgment.'[12] This was a quintessentially Muslim thought from one whose directness invited charges of apostasy from those made uncomfortable by it.

The naturalness of his Islam, his directness, his rejection of violence and revenge, and his readiness to cooperate with non-Muslims add up to a valuable legacy for our angry times. This legacy may be of help to Muslims and non-Muslims today in the task of overcoming divides between Islam and the West (and modernity), between Afghanistan and the subcontinent, between Islam and the subcontinent's Hindus, Sikhs and other non-Muslims. His bridge-building life is a refutation of the clash-of-civilizations theory.

But he was also a rock. No force or threat could shake his stand for Pakhtun dignity, which at bottom was a stand for the freedom and dignity of every human being. The Pakhtuns between the Hindu Kush and the Indus were his first love but also his links to humankind, and we can, if we wish, hear him, even if we are west of that mountain range or east of that river.

Notes

The Setting

1. Translated by Olaf Caroe, the verse is quoted in Olaf Caroe, *Wells of Power: The Oilfields of South-western Asia: A regional and global study*, London: Macmillan, 1951, p. 17.
2. Quoted in D.G. Tendulkar, *Abdul Ghaffar Khan: Faith is a Battle*, Bombay: Popular Prakashan, 1967, pp. 529-30.
3. Statement of 12 April 1961 in Dera Ismail Khan, quoted in Tendulkar, p. 518.
4. From James W. Spain, *The Way of the Pathans,* London: R. Hale, 1962, in Tendulkar, pp. 480-81.

Chapter One

1. D.G. Tendulkar, *Abdul Ghaffar Khan: Faith is a Battle*, Bombay: Popular Prakashan, 1967, p. 5.
2. Mohamed Amin, Duncan Willetts and Graham Hancock, *Journey through Pakistan*, Nairobi: Camerapix, 1982, p. 54.
3. Reproduced from Ghaffar Khan, *My Life and Struggle*, published by Orient Paperbacks, New Delhi, 1969, p. 16.

4. Amin, Willetts and Hancock, *Journey through Pakistan*, pp. 53-54.

5. Ibid., p. 61.

6. From the back cover of Charles Miller, *Khyber: British India's North-West Frontier: The Story of an Imperial Migraine*, New York: Macmillan, 1977.

7. Sher Zaman Taizi in *Badshah Khan in Afghanistan: A Memoir*, www.asianreflection.com/khanafghanistan.shtml, June 2002.

8. Geoffrey Moorhouse, *To the Frontier: A Journey to the Khyber Pass*, London: Phoenix, 1998, p. 236.

9. Ibid., p. 224.

10. Olaf Caroe, *The Pathans: 550 B.C.–A.D. 1957*, Karachi: Oxford University Press, 1976 (first published by London: Macmillan, 1958), p. 57.

11. Ibid., p. 63.

12. Al-Biruni quoted in Caroe, *The Pathans*, p. 109.

13. Caroe, *The Pathans*, pp. 112-13.

14. Ibid., p. 122.

15. Ibid., p. 133.

16. Ibid., p. 148.

17. Ibid., pp. 201, 203 and 230.

18. Ibid., p. 245.

19. Ibid., p. 230.

20. Ibid., p. 242.

21. Ibid., p. 257.

22. J.S. Grewal, *The New Cambridge History of India: The Sikhs of the Punjab*, New Delhi: Orient Longman, 1990, p. 91.

23. In a 1959 biography of Ahmad Shah, the Sikh historian, Ganda Singh, acknowledging that 'Sikhs and Afghans have met in the battlefield with swords drawn in relentless

hostility', adds: 'I have been brought up in prejudices against [Ahmad Shah] and heard of him as a robber chief who swooped down upon India for plunder . . . But the more I read of him, the more impressed I became with the traits of his greatness.' Ganda Singh, *Ahmad Shah Durrani: Father of Modern Afghanistan*, Bombay: Asia Publishing House, 1959, p. vii.

24. Caroe, *The Pathans*, pp. 297-98.

25. Ibid., p. 305.

26. Colin Davies, quoted in Tendulkar, p. 9.

27. Louis Dupree, *Afghanistan*, Princeton, NJ: Princeton University Press, 1973, p. xvii.

28. From Sir Winston Churchill, *My Early Life*, quoted by Erland Jansson, *India, Pakistan or Pakhtunistan?: The Nationalist Movements in the North-West Frontier Province, 1937–47*, Uppsala, Sweden: University of Uppsala, 1981.

29. See, for example, Mukulika Banerjee, *The Pathan Unarmed: Opposition and Memory in the North-West Frontier*, New Delhi: Oxford University Press, 2001, p. 15.

30. Tendulkar, *Abdul Ghaffar Khan*, p. 55.

31. Moorhouse, *To the Frontier*, pp. 222-23.

32. Abdul Ghani Khan, *The Pathans: A Sketch*, Islamabad: Pushto Adabi Society, 1990, p. 8.

Chapter Two

1. Haridev Sharma, Oral History Transcript [henceforth referred to as *OHT*], Interview with Badshah Khan, Kabul, July 10, 1968, Nehru Museum and Memorial Library, New Delhi, p. 15.

2. D.G. Tendulkar, *Abdul Ghaffar Khan: Faith is a Battle*,

Bombay: Popular Prakashan, 1967, p. 14.

3. Or, according to a minority view in the family, Abdul Sattar. The given name was seldom used, however, and he is known to history as Dr Khan Sahib.

4. Ghani Khan (1914–96), older son of Ghaffar Khan, to Omar Khan (no relation) in an interview in Mohammad Naray village, Charsadda district, in 1990. www. harappa.com/sounds/ghani035.html

5. Ghaffar Khan, *My Life and Struggle*, Delhi: Hind Pocket Books, 1969, p. 14, and Tendulkar, p. 18.

6. Tendulkar, pp. 13-14.

7. Sharif Khan, great-grandson of Dr Khan Sahib, to author, 18 March 2003.

8. Haridev Sharma, *OHT*, p. 15, and Tendulkar, p. 14.

9. Sharma, *OHT*, p. 15.

10. Names supplied to the author by Dr Khan Sahib's grandson Anwar Khan and Badshah Khan's grandson Asfandyar Khan.

11. Tendulkar, p. 18.

12. Tendulkar, p. 19.

13. Mahadev Desai, *Two Servants of God*, New Delhi: Hindustan Times Press, 1935, p. 17.

14. Tendulkar, p. 21.

15. Omar Khan interview.

16. Tendulkar, p. 98.

17. Name supplied to the author in May 2003 by her grandson Asfandyar Khan, by her stepdaughter Mehr Taj, and by Mehr Taj's son Salim Khan.

18. Abdul Ghani Khan, *The Pathans: A Sketch*, Islamabad: Pushto Adabi Society, 1990, p. 45.

19. Ghani Khan in Omar Khan interview.

20. Tendulkar, p. 24.
21. To Girdhari Lal Puri in New Delhi on 28 December 1981. G.L. Puri, *Khan Abdul Ghaffar Khan: A True Servant of Humanity*, New Delhi: Congress Centenary Celebrations Committee, 1985, p. xviii.
22. Rafiq Mukhlis, *Badshah Khan*, Delhi: Maktaba Jamia, 1952, p. 39.
23. Ghani Khan, *The Pathans*, pp. 45-46.
24. Sharma, *OHT*, p. 17.
25. Tendulkar, pp. 27-28.

Chapter Three

1. D.G. Tendulkar, *Abdul Ghaffar Khan: Faith is a Battle*, Bombay: Popular Prakashan, 1967, pp. 29-30.
2. Name supplied to author in May 2003 by her daughter Mehr Taj.
3. Tendulkar, p. 31.
4. Copyright Oxford University Press, Pakistan, 1993. Reprinted with the permission of Oxford University Press from their publication entitled *The Frontier Gandhi: His Place in History* by M.S. Korejo, p. 15.
5. Tendulkar, p. 38.
6. Tendulkar, p. 39.
7. See Eknath Easwaran, *Badshah Khan: A Man to Match His Mountains*, New Delhi: Penguin Books India, 2001, p. 85, p. 242. Originally published as *Nonviolent Soldier of Islam* by Eknath Easwaran, founder of the Blue Mountain Center of Meditation, copyright 1999; reprinted by permission of Nilgiri Press, P.O. Box 256, Tomales, Ca 94971, www.nilgiri.org.
8. Remarks in November 1939, Tendulkar, p. 283.

9. Statement of 18 December 1981, to Girdhari Lal Puri. See G.L. Puri, *Khan Abdul Ghaffar Khan: A True Servant of Humanity*, New Delhi: Congress Centenary Celebrations Committee, 1985, p. xviii.

10. Tendulkar, p. 38.

11. Ghani Khan to Omar Khan (no relation) in interview in Muhammad Naray village, Charsadda district, in 1990. www.harappa.com/sounds/ghani035.html

12. Anwar Khan, grandson of Dr Khan Sahib, to author in May 2003 in Muhammad Naray.

13. Tendulkar, p. 39.

14. Ibid., p. 40.

15. Ibid., pp. 41-42.

16. Ibid., p. 42.

17. Ibid., p. 43.

18. Ibid., pp. 43-44.

19. Ibid., p. 45.

20. Ibid., p. 45.

21. Mahadev Desai, *Two Servants of God*, New Delhi: Hindustan Times Press, 1935, p. 23.

22. Tendulkar, p. 45.

23. Omar Khan interview.

24. Tendulkar, p. 46.

25. Desai, pp. 40-41.

26. Sharma, *OHT*, pp. 15-16.

27. Tendulkar, pp. 52-53.

28. Omar Khan interview.

29. Ibid., p. 56.

30. Ibid., p. 58.

31. Ibid., p. 59.

32. Ibid., p. 59.

33. Korejo, p. 17.
34. Omar Khan interview.
35. Fazal-ur-Rahim Marwat, 'Ghani Khan', in www. geocitiies.com/khyber007/ghani2/html
36. Tendulkar, p. 78.
37. Remarks in Bardoli in early June 1931, Tendulkar, p. 93.
38. Tendulkar, p. 94.
39. In April 1931 in Bombay, Tendulkar, p. 85.
40. In June 1931 in Bardoli, Tendulkar, p. 94.
41. Tendulkar, p. 95.
42. Ibid., p. 105.
43. Ibid., p. 108.
44. Ibid., pp. 116-17.
45. Ibid., p. 117.
46. Ibid., p. 131.
47. Ibid., p. 132.
48. Ibid., p. 161.
49. Ibid., p. 146.
50. Ibid., p. 146.
51. Ibid., p. 130.
52. Ibid., pp. 101-02.
53. Ibid., p. 135.
54. Ibid., p. 155.
55. Deputy Commissioner of Hazaribagh to Chief Secretary of Bihar, Tendulkar, p. 155.
56. Tendulkar, p. 155.
57. Ibid., p. 160.
58. Mehr Taj to author, Peshawar, May 2003.
59. Remark made in Abbottabad to Pritam Pal Singh. Related to author by Singh.
60. Tendulkar, p. 162.

61. Ibid., p. 162.
62. Ibid., p. 161.
63. Ibid., p. 171.
64. Ibid., p. 170.
65. Ibid., p. 174.
66. To Mira Behn, 24 September 1934, Tendulkar, p. 171.
67. Desai, pp. 61-62.
68. Quoted in Tendulkar, p. 175.
69. Desai, pp. 61-62.
70. Ibid., p. 62.
71. Ibid., p. 72.
72. Tendulkar, p. 187.
73. Police report of statement in ibid., pp. 186-92.
74. Omar Khan interview.
75. Desai, p. 106.
76. Dated 26 February 1935, Tendulkar, p. 208.
77. See ibid., pp.168-70.
78. Ibid., p. 209.
79. Ibid., p. 212.
80. Ibid., p. 125.
81. Ibid., p. 213.
82. Ibid., p. 215.
83. Brigadier Pritam Pal Singh (retd.), nephew of Parmanand, to author in an interview in Pune, 6 June 2003.
84. Tendulkar, p. 220.

Chapter Four

1. D.G. Tendulkar, *Abdul Ghaffar Khan: Faith is a Battle*, Bombay: Popular Prakashan, 1967, p. 222.
2. Ibid., p. 231.
3. Ibid., p. 233.
4. Ibid., p. 230.

5. Ibid., p. 232.

6. Ibid., pp. 246-47.

7. Ibid., p. 235.

8. Ibid., pp. 267-68.

9. Ibid., p. 267.

10. Ibid., p. 240.

11. Ibid., p. 270.

12. On 31 October 1938, Tendulkar, p. 273.

13. Ibid., pp. 264-65.

14. Ibid., p. 291.

15. From *Harijan,* 11 November 1938, in ibid., p. 285.

16. Tendulkar, p. 244.

17. Ibid., p. 259.

18. Ibid., p. 275.

19. Ibid., p. 237.

20. Ibid., p. 237.

21. Ibid., p. 273.

22. Ibid., pp. 245-46.

23. Ibid., p. 251.

24. Ibid., p. 244.

25. Ibid., pp. 253-54.

26. Ibid., p. 285.

27. Ibid., p. 238.

28. Pritam Pal Singh to author, Pune, 6 June 2003.

29. Tendulkar, p. 300.

30. Statement of 16 July 1940, in *Collected Works of Mahatma Gandhi*, Vol. 72, pp. 277-78. See also Tendulkar, p. 327.

31. Tendulkar, pp. 327-28.

32. See Erland Jansson, *India, Pakistan or Pakhtunistan?: The Nationalist Movements in the NWFP, 1937–47,* Uppsala, Sweden: University of Uppsala, 1981.

33. Tendulkar, p. 353.

34. Ibid., p. 366.

35. Ibid., p. 355.

36. Ibid., p. 356.

37. Ibid., p. 358.

38. Copyright Oxford University Press, Pakistan, 1999. Reprinted with the permission of Oxford University Press from their publication entitled *Ethnicity, Islam, and Nationalism: Muslim Politics in the North-West Frontier Province 1937-47* by Sayed Wiqar Ali Shah, 1999, p. 144.

39. On 27 May 1944, cited in Wali Khan, *Facts are Sacred*, Peshawar: Jaun Publishers, 1991, p. 92.

40. Tendulkar, p. 361.

41. Sharma, *OHT*, pp. 18-19.

42. Tendulkar, p. 366.

43. Ibid., p. 367.

44. *Khyber Mail*, 30 November 1945, cited in Wiqar Shah, p. 163.

45. Wiqar Shah, p. 166, citing the governor's assessment, dated 17 March 1946, in India Office Library, London.

46. Ibid., p. 166.

47. Ibid., p. 148.

48. Letter to Wavell, 27 February 1946, from *The Transfer of Power*, Vol. VI, pp. 1085-86, cited in Wiqar Shah, p. 166.

49. Quoted in Wiqar Shah, p. 155.

Chapter Five

1. The book was dedicated to Dr Khan Sahib. See Erland Jansson, *India, Pakistan or Pakhtunistan?: The Nationalist Movements in the NWFP, 1937–47*, Uppsala, Sweden: University of Uppsala, 1981, p. 161 fn.

2. Penderel Moon (ed.), *Wavell: The Viceroy's Journal*, London:

Oxford University Press, 1973, pp. 232-33.

3. D.G. Tendulkar, *Abdul Ghaffar Khan: Faith is a Battle*, Bombay: Popular Prakashan, 1967, pp. 367-68.

4. Moon (ed.), *Wavell*, pp. 258-59.

5. Tendulkar, p. 371.

6. Ibid., pp. 370-71.

7. Ibid., p. 373.

8. From *Pakhtun*, 17 July 1946, in Sayed Wiqar Ali Shah, *Ethnicity, Islam and Nationalism: Muslim Politics in the North-West Frontier Province 1937–1947*, Karachi: Oxford University Press, 1999, p. 173.

9. Quoted from Stephen Alan Rittenberg, *The Independence Movement in India's North-West Frontier Province*, New York: Columbia University Press, 1977 (microfilm), p. 337, reproduced in Wiqar Ali Shah, p. 187.

10. For details of these negotiations, see Rajmohan Gandhi, *Patel*, Ahmedabad: Navajivan, 1990, pp. 365-67.

11. Tendulkar, pp. 380-81.

12. Ibid., pp. 380-81.

13. Ibid., p. 380.

14. Ibid., p. 381.

15. Ibid., p. 382.

16. Ibid., p. 382.

17. Abdul Wali Khan, *Facts are Sacred*, Peshawar: Jaun Publishers, 1991, p. 88.

18. Linlithgow's letter of 14 July 1938, cited in Wali Khan, *Facts are Sacred*, p. 88.

19. Cunningham's Papers are cited in Wali Khan, *Facts are Sacred*, pp. 77-83.

20. See Wiqar Ali Shah, p. 177.

21. Tendulkar, pp. 383-84.

22. Jansson, *India, Pakistan or Pakhtunistan?*, p. 182.

23. Tendulkar, p. 384.

24. Ibid., pp. 384-86.

25. Ibid., pp. 386-87.

26. See Jansson, *India, Pakistan or Pakhtunistan?*, p. 183.

27. Tendulkar, pp. 388-89.

28. Ibid., pp. 392-93.

29. See ibid., pp. 384-94.

30. See Wiqar Ali Shah, p. 181, citing Ian Stephens in *Statesman*, New Delhi, of 2 January 1947.

31. The Mallam Papers are cited in Wiqar Ali Shah, p. 181.

32. Letter of 25 October 1946, quoted in Wiqar Ali Shah, p.182.

33. On p. 190 of his study, Wiqar Ali Shah names the places he visited and the people he interviewed.

34. Jansson, *India, Pakistan or Pakhtunistan?*, pp. 185-86.

35. See Wali Khan, *Facts are Sacred*, pp. 195-96.

36. Tendulkar, p. 397.

37. Ibid., pp. 406-07.

38. Ibid., pp. 397-98.

39. Wiqar Ali Shah, p. 195.

40. Ibid., pp. 203-04.

41. Ibid., pp. 209-10.

42. See letter of 17 January 1947, in Gandhi, *Patel*, p. 405.

43. Unable to win a majority, the Khan of Mamdot soon resigned, and the Punjab was placed under governor's rule.

44. See Gandhi, *Patel*, p. 390.

45. Tendulkar, p. 404.

46. See Nicholas Mansergh (ed.), *The Transfer of Power 1942–47*, Vol. 10, London: H.M.S.O., 1970–1983, p. 86.

47. See Gandhi, *Patel*, pp. 392-93.
48. In Pyarelal, *The Last Phase*, Vol. 2, Ahmedabad: Navajivan, pp. 84-85.
49. Quoted by B.R. Nanda in C.H. Phillips and M.D. Wainwright (eds.), *The Partition of India*, London: Allen & Unwin, 1970, p. 185.
50. Tendulkar, p. 427.
51. See Pyarelal, *The Last Phase*, Vol. 2, p. 257.
52. Tendulkar, p. 447.
53. Ibid., p. 413.
54. Ibid., p. 418.
55. Jansson, pp. 208-09.
56. Tendulkar, p. 420.
57. In Abdullah Hussain and M. Aslam (eds.), *Badshah Khan*, Delhi: Janchetna, 2000 (Hindi tr. of Lahore publication).
58. Tendulkar, pp. 419-21.
59. Ram Manohar Lohia, *Guilty Men of India's Partition*, Allahabad: Kitabistan, 1960, p. 21.
60. See H.V. Hodson, *The Great Divide: Britain–India–Pakistan*, London: Hutchinson, 1969, pp. 284-85; S. Gopal, *Nehru*, New Delhi: Oxford University Press, Vol. 1, p. 352; Pyarelal, *The Last Phase*, Vol. 2, p. 270.
61. Tendulkar, p. 430.
62. Ibid., p. 432.
63. 'My! My!' or 'Shame! Shame!' or 'My God! My God!'
64. Tendulkar, pp. 416-17.
65. Ibid., p. 417.
66. Ibid., p. 422.
67. Ibid., p. 424.
68. Ibid., pp. 424-25. We may never know for certain whether Ghani reported Gandhi accurately, or whether

he heard what he wanted to hear. His father certainly
believed Ghani's account and repeated it.

69. Haridev Sharma, Interview with Badshah Khan in Kabul,
    July 10, 1968, Oral History Transcript, NMML, New
    Delhi, p. 4.
70. Ibid., p. 12.
71. Ibid., p. 19.
72. Tendulkar, p. 447.
73. Ibid., p. 428.
74. Ibid., p. 429.
75. Ibid., pp. 432-33.
76. Ibid., p. 433.
77. Letter of 11 June 1947 from Ghaffar Khan to Gandhi,
    in Tendulkar, p. 434.
78. Ibid., pp. 436-37.
79. Ibid., p. 437.
80. Ibid., pp. 437-38.
81. Ibid., p. 439.
82. Ibid., p. 443.
83. It is not clear whether Gandhi is referring to the Nehru-
    led interim government or Dr Khan Sahib's ministry in
    the Frontier.
84. Tendulkar, pp. 443-44.
85. Ibid., p. 439.
86. Ibid., pp. 440-41.
87. Ibid., p. 441.
88. Ibid., p. 441.
89. Ibid., pp. 442-43.
90. Ibid., pp. 445-46.
91. Ibid., p. 448. The Gandhi–Ghaffar Khan conversations
    are mentioned in *Hindustan Times*, 28 July, 29 July, and 31

July 1947, and in Brij Krishna Chandiwala, *Gandhiji Ki Dilli Dairi*, Delhi: Gyan Deep, 1970, Vol. 3, pp. 240-41.

Chapter Six

1. Quoted in Hector Bolitho, *Jinnah: Creator of Pakistan*, Westport, CT: Greenwood Press, 1981, p. 197, and elsewhere.

2. D.G. Tendulkar, *Abdul Ghaffar Khan: Faith is a Battle*, Bombay: Popular Prakashan, 1967, pp. 450-51.

3. Sohan Mathur and Ramjanma Chaturvedi (eds.), *Gandhi Ke Hamrahi: Seemaant Gandhi*, Jaipur: Rekha, 1970, pp. 160-63, and Tendulkar, pp. 448-49.

4. Wali Khan, *Facts are Sacred*, tr. from Pakhto into Urdu by Naseem Wali Khan, and from Urdu into English by Aziz Siddiqui, Peshawar: Jaun Publishers, 1991, p. 184.

5. Sayed Wiqar Ali Shah, *Ethnicity, Islam and Nationalism: Muslim Politics in the North-West Frontier Province, 1937–47*, Karachi: Oxford University Press, 1999, p. xxxvi.

6. Quoted in H.V. Hodson, *The Great Divide: Britain–India–Pakistan*, London: Hutchinson, 1969, p. 447.

7. Press statement by Ghaffar Khan in February 1954, recalling the offer, cited in Tendulkar, p. 476.

8. See Tendulkar, pp. 453-58.

9. Ibid., p. 462.

10. Ibid., p. 498.

11. Ibid., p. 464.

12. Ibid., p. 465.

13. Ibid., p. 470.

14. Ibid., p. 477.

15. Erland Jansson, *India, Pakistan or Pakhtunistan?: The Nationalist Movements in the North-West Frontier Province,*

1937–1947, Uppsala, Sweden: University of Uppsala, 1991, p. 230.

16. Tendulkar, p. 479.

17. Ibid., p. 476.

18. Ibid., pp. 498-99.

19. Ibid., p. 476.

20. To the author in May 2003 in Peshawar.

21. Jansson, *India, Pakistan or Pakhtunistan?*, p. 49.

22. Ahmad Salim, *Iskander Mirza: Rise and Fall of a President*, Lahore: Gora Publishers, 1997, p.195.

23. Tendulkar, p. 501.

24. Hiro Shroff, *Down Memory Lane*, Mumbai: Eeshwar, 1998, p. 35.

25. Tendulkar, p. 481.

26. Ibid., pp. 477-78.

27. Ibid., pp. 479-80.

28. Hamida Khuhro, *Mohammed Ayub Khuhro: A Life of Courage in Politics*, Karachi: Ferozsons, 1998, p. 418.

29. Ghani Khan in Omar Khan interview.

30. Tendulkar, p. 487.

31. Ibid., p. 488.

32. Salim, *Iskander Mirza*, pp. 210-11.

33. Tendulkar, p. 490.

34. Speech cited in Salim, *Iskander Mirza*, pp. 418-19.

35. Mirza quoted in ibid., p. 241.

36. Suhrawardy quoted in ibid., p. 242.

37. Tendulkar, p. 503.

38. Ibid., p. 506.

39. Ibid., p. 516.

40. As quoted in Charles Miller, *Khyber: British India's North-West Frontier: The Story of an Imperial Migraine*, New York:

Macmillan, 1977, p. 370.

41. Tendulkar, p. 517.

42. Ibid., p. 518.

43. Ibid., p. 520.

44. Ibid., p. 520.

45. Ibid., p. 520.

46. Ibid., p. 527.

47. Ghaffar Khan, *My Life and Struggle: Autobiography of Badshah Khan*, as narrated to K.B. Narang, Delhi: Hind Pocket Books, 1969, p. 199.

48. Tendulkar, p. 520.

49. Ibid., p. 521.

50. Letter of 5 April 1965, in Tendulkar, pp. 521-22.

51. Tendulkar, pp. 522-23.

52. Pyarelal, *Thrown to the Wolves: Abdul Ghaffar*, Calcutta: Eastlight Book House, 1966, p. 113.

53. Ibid., pp. 118-19.

54. Nehru quoted in P.S. Ramu, *Badshah Khan*, Delhi: S.S. Publishers, 1991, pp. 98-99.

55. Haribhau Joshi, *Badshah Khan,* Varanasi: Nagari Pracharini Sabha, 1970 (tr. from Marathi).

56. Omar Khan interview.

57. Ghaffar Khan, *My Life and Struggle*, p. 237.

58. Ibid., p. 225.

59. Ibid., p. 218.

60. Ibid., p. 220.

61. On 31 August 1966, ibid., pp. 230-31.

62. Ibid., p. 235.

63. On 31 August 1967, ibid., p. 244.

64. Sher Zaman Taizi, *Bacha Khan in Afghanistan: A Memoir, June 2002*, in www.asianreflection.com edited by Damon

Lynch, August 2002.

65. On 31 August 1967, Ghaffar Khan, *My Life and Struggle*, pp. 243-44.

66. Mohammed Talukdar (ed.), *Memoirs of H.S. Suhrawardy*, Dhaka: University Press, 1987, p. 99.

67. Pyarelal, *Thrown to the Wolves*, p. 127.

68. Ibid., p. 128.

69. Ibid., p. 130.

70. Ibid., pp. 111-12.

71. Ibid., p. 118.

72. Sher Zaman Taizi, *Bacha Khan in Afghanistan*.

73. Rajendra Mathur, in Sohan Mathur and Ramjanma Chaturvedi (eds.), *Gandhi Ke Hamrahi: Seemaant Gandhi*, Jaipur: Rekha, 1970, p. 165.

74. Haribhau Joshi, *Badshah Khan*, p. 3.

75. Quoted in Ramu, *Badshah Khan*, p. 94.

76. 'Address to Muslims', Delhi, 10 October 1969, in ibid., p. 93.

77. According to S.K. Singh, Indian ambassador to Afghanistan, 1977-79, Badshah Khan recalled this conversation to Singh in the late 1970s in Jalalabad. Singh to author, New Delhi, January 2003.

78. Singh to author, January 2003.

79. Quoted in Ramu, *Badshah Khan*, p. 103.

80. Sher Zaman Taizi, *Bacha Khan in Afghanistan*.

81. S.K. Singh, Indian ambassador to Kabul, who often visited Badshah Khan in this house, to author, New Delhi, January 2003.

82. Quoted in N. Radhakrishnan, *Khan Abdul Ghaffar Khan*, New Delhi: Gandhi Smriti and Darshan Samiti, 1998, p. 43.

83. Sher Zaman Taizi, *Bacha Khan in Afghanistan*.

84. Op. cit.

85. Op. cit.

86. J.N. Dixit, ambassador to Afghanistan, to author, Delhi, December 2002.

87. Singh to author, Delhi, January 2003.

88. To author, Delhi, January 2003.

89. Remark to Dixit, related by Dixit to author, Delhi, December 2002.

90. J.N. Dixit, *An Afghan Diary: Zahir Shah to Taliban*, New Delhi: Konark, 2000, p. 66.

91. Bansi Lal to author, New Delhi, 19 July 2002.

92. Dixit, *An Afghan Diary*, p. 30.

93. Ibid., p. 31.

94. Ibid., p. 76.

95. Ibid., p. 93.

96. Ibid., p. 93.

97. Ibid., p. 62.

98. Ibid., p. 66.

99. Ibid., p. 71.

100. Ibid., p. 71.

101. Ibid., pp. 62-63.

102. Ibid., p. 68.

103. Dixit to author, Delhi, December 2002.

104. Dixit, *An Afghan Diary*, p. 66.

105. Dixit to author, Delhi, December 2002.

106. G.L. Puri, *Khan Abdul Ghaffar Khan*, New Delhi: Congress Centenary Committee, 1985, p. xxxi.

107. Dixit, *An Afghan Diary*, p. 322.

108. M.S. Korejo, *The Frontier Gandhi: His Place in History*, Karachi: Oxford University Press, 1993, p. 232.

Chapter Seven

1. Erland Jansson, *India, Pakistan or Pakhtunistan?: The Nationalist Movements in the North-West Frontier Province, 1937–47*, Uppsala, Sweden: University of Uppsala, 1981, p. 49.

2. Sher Zaman Taizi, *Bacha Khan in Afghanistan: A Memoir, June 2002*, in www.asianreflection.com edited by Damon Lynch, August 2002.

3. Sher Zaman Taizi, *Bacha Khan in Afghanistan*.

4. Sir Reginald Coupland in *The Indian Problem*, London: Oxford University Press, 1944, Part II, p. 22.

5. Halide Edib, *Inside India*, London: Allen & Unwin, 1937, p. 336, as quoted in Joan V. Bondurant, *Conquest of Violence: The Gandhian Philosophy of Conflict*, Princeton, NJ: Princeton University Press, 1988, p. 140.

6. Jansson, *India, Pakistan or Pakhtunistan?*, p. 243.

7. Ibid., p. 49.

8. Ahmad Sha Mohabbat, *Pakhtun National Self-determination*, University of St. Louis, 1979 (microfilm), quoted in Baren Ray, *Khan Abdul Ghaffar Khan: A Centennial Tribute*, New Delhi: Har-Anand Publications with NMML, 1995, p. 75.

9. Statement made in the summer of 1931. See Chapter Three in the foregoing.

10. Quoted by Amitabh Pal, 'A pacifist uncovered (Abdul Ghaffar Khan, Pakistani pacifist)', *Progressive*, February 2002.

11. Harold A. Gould, 'Radical Islam in need for a radical rethink', *Indian Express*, 20 June 2003.

12. See Chapter Five in the foregoing.

Bibliography

Mohammed Ali, *Afghanistan: The Mohammedzai Period: A political history of the country since the beginning of the nineteenth century with emphasis on its foreign relations* (Kabul: Khan Mohammed Ali Khan, 1959)

Mohamed Amin, Duncan Willetts and Graham Hancock, *Journey through Pakistan* (Nairobi: Camerapix, 1982)

Badshah Khan Visits India: A brief report of his visit and tours, with a statement of accounts of purse fund (New Delhi: Gaffarkhan-Sarhad Gandhi Salgirah Samiti, 1970)

Mukulika Banerjee, *The Pathan Unarmed: Opposition and Memory in the North-West Frontier* (New Delhi: Oxford University Press, 2001)

Fredrik Barth (ed.), *Ethnic Groups and Boundaries: The social organization of culture difference* (Results of a symposium held at the University of Bergen, 23rd to 26th February 1967) Bergen, Universitetsforlaget (London: Allen & Unwin, 1969)

Joan V. Bondurant, *Conquest of Violence: The Gandhian Philosophy of Conflict* (Princeton, NJ: Princeton University Press, 1958)

Olaf Caroe, *The Pathans: 550 B.C.–A.D. 1957* (Karachi: Oxford University Press, 1976. First published London: Macmillan, 1958)

——, *Wells of Power: The Oilfields of South-western Asia: A regional and global study* (London: Macmillan, 1951)

Mahadev Desai, *Two Servants of God* (New Delhi: Hindustan Times Press, 1935)

J.N. Dixit, *An Afghan Diary: Zahir Shah to Taliban* (New Delhi: Konark Publishers, 2000)

Louis Dupree, *Afghanistan* (Princeton, NJ: Princeton University Press, 1973)

Eknath Easwaran, *Badshah Khan: A Man to Match his Mountains* (New Delhi: Penguin Books India, 2001)

M.K. Gandhi, *Collected Works* (Publications Division, Ministry of Information and Broadcasting, Government of India, New Delhi, 1958–94)

Rajmohan Gandhi, *Patel: A Life* (Ahmedabad: Navajivan Publishing House, 1990)

Michael Griffin, *Reaping the Whirlwind: The Taliban Movement in Afghanistan* (London: Pluto Press, 2001)

Abdullah Hussain and M. Aslam (eds.), *Badshah Khan* (Delhi: Janchetna, 2000) (Hindi tr. of Lahore publication)

Erland Jansson, *India, Pakistan or Pakhtunistan?: The Nationalist Movements in the North-West Frontier Province, 1937–47* (Uppsala, Sweden: University of Uppsala, 1981)

Haribhau Joshi, *Badshah Khan* (Kashi: Nagari Pracharini Sabha, 1970) (Hindi)

Abdul Ghaffar Khan, *My Life and Struggle: Autobiography of Badshah Khan*, as narrated to K.B. Narang (Delhi: Hind Pocket Books, 1969)

Abdul Ghani Khan, *The Pathans: A Sketch* (Islamabad: Pushto Adabi Society, 1990 edition) (First edition, Bombay: National Information and Publications, 1947)

Omar Khan, *Interview, May 19, 1990, with Ghani Khan*, www.harappa.com

Wali Khan, *Facts are Facts: The Untold Story of India's Partition*, rendered into English by Syeda Hameed from the Urdu translation by Naseem Wali Khan (New Delhi: Vikas, 1987)

Wali Khan, *Facts are Sacred*, translated from Pakhto into Urdu by Naseem Wali Khan, and from Urdu into English by Aziz Siddiqui (Peshawar: Jaun Publishers, 1991)

Hamida Khuhro, *Mohammed Ayub Khuhro: A Life of Courage in Politics* (Karachi: Ferozsons, 1998)

M.S. Korejo, *The Frontier Gandhi: His Place in History* (Karachi: Oxford

University Press, 1993)

Ravinder Kumar (ed.), *Khan Abdul Ghaffar Khan: A Centennial Tribute* (New Delhi: Har-Anand Publications, with Nehru Museum and Memorial Library, 1995)

Dr Fazal-ur-Rahim Marwat, *Ghani Khan: The Renaissance Man*, www.geocities.com/khyber007/ghani2.html

Humayun Mirza, *From Plassey to Pakistan: The family history of Iskander Mirza, the first president of Pakistan* (Lanham, MD: University Press of America Inc., 1999)

Ahmad Sha Mohabbat, *Pakhtun National Self-determination: The Partition of India and Relations with Pakistan* (St. Louis University, 1979, microfilm)

Penderel Moon (ed.), *Wavell: The Viceroy's Journal* (London: Oxford University Press, 1973)

Geoffrey Moorhouse, *To the Frontier: A Journey to the Khyber Pass* (London: Phoenix, 1998)

Sayed Askar Mousavi, *The Hazaras of Afghanistan: An Historical, Cultural, Economic and Political Study* (Richmond, Surrey: Curzon, 1998)

Rafiq Mukhlis, *Badshah Khan* (Delhi: Maktaba Jamia, 1952)

G.L. Puri, *Khan Abdul Ghaffar Khan: A True Servant of Humanity* (New Delhi: Congress Centenary Celebrations Committee, 1985)

Pyarelal, *Pilgrimage for Peace: Gandhi and Frontier Gandhi Among N.W.F. Pathans* (Ahmedabad: Navajivan Publishing House, 1950)

———, *Thrown to the Wolves: Abdul Ghaffar* (Calcutta: Eastlight Book House, 1966)

N. Radhakrishnan, *Khan Abdul Ghaffar Khan* (New Delhi: Gandhi Smriti and Darshan Samiti, 1998)

P.S. Ramu, *Badshah Khan: Indo-Pakistan Relations* (Delhi: S.S. Publishers, 1991)

Stephen Alan Rittenburg, *The Independence Movement in India's North-West Frontier Province* (New York: Columbia University Press, 1977, microfilm)

Ahmad Salim, *Iskander Mirza: Rise and Fall of a President* (Lahore: Gora Publishers, 1997)

Ahmad Salim (compiled and edited by), *Iskander Mirza Speaks: Speeches, statements and private papers* (Lahore: Gora Publishers, 1997)

Sayed Wiqar Ali Shah, *Ethnicity, Islam, and Nationalism: Muslim Politics in the*

North-West Frontier Province, 1937–47 (Karachi: Oxford University Press, 1999)

Haridev Sharma, Interview with Badshah Khan in Kabul, July 10, 1968 (Oral History Transcript, Nehru Museum and Memorial Library, New Delhi)

Ganda Singh, *Ahmad Shah Durrani: Father of Modern Afghanistan* (Bombay: Asia Publishing House, 1959)

Sher Zaman Taizi, *Bacha Khan in Afghanistan: A Memoir, June 2002*, in www.asianreflection.com. Edited by Damon Lynch, August 2002. http://www.asianreflection.com/khanafghanistan.shtml

Ian Talbot, *Khizr Tiwana: The Punjab Unionist Party and the Partition of India* (Surrey, UK: Curzon, 1996)

Mohammed Talukdar (ed.), *Memoirs of H.S. Suhrawardy* (Dhaka: University Press, 1987)

G.P. Tate, *The Kingdom of Afghanistan: A Historical Sketch* (1910)

D.G. Tendulkar, *Abdul Ghaffar Khan: Faith is a Battle* (Bombay: Popular Prakashan, 1967)

Lowell Thomas, *Beyond Khyber Pass* (London: Hutchinson, 1923)

Mohammad Yunus, *Frontier Pathans and freedom struggle*; foreword by Jawahar Lal Nehru, preface by Khan Abdul Ghaffar Khan (Delhi: Anmol Publications, 1985)

Mohammad Yunus, *Frontier Speaks* (Bombay: Hind Kitabs, 1947)

G.L. Zutshi, *Frontier Gandhi: The fighter, the politician, the saint* (Delhi: National Publishing House, 1970)